DRIVING ON
By MG Carroll D. Childers (Ret)

DRIVING ON

This personal account of RANGER School was first written in 1981, shortly after I graduated with RANGER Class 6-81. The concept of writing it came to me as I was organizing a pre-RANGER course for members of my Army National Guard Infantry Battalion. It was to be a handout for the students, which would give them a vivid account of exactly what the course was all about. The real truth. It would save me having to spend a lot of time trying to get across the simple essence of RANGER School; that though the course is extremely difficult both mentally and physically, the real key is whether or not the student has the will to persist in the face of difficult and sometimes seemingly impossible situations. This writing could be taken home by the student and shared with his family and supporters so that they too could understand and empathize with their soldier as he trained for and attempted this most difficult challenge. It was written before time blurred what really happened; before repetitive telling resulted in distorted embellishment of the truth.

Since its initial informal publication of about 100 (Xerox) copies and a second informal publication of about 100 copies some 6 years later, a lot of people have read it and enjoyed it. Many have encouraged me to seek publication. For most, it helped them to understand what a RANGER really is. Desert One, Grenada, Panama, Desert Storm, and Mogadishu all could take on a different meaning now with an understanding of what the heroes of these operations actually had to accomplish to become part of the elite RANGERs who played such an important part in those operations. And of course, for those who remember or have read history, many RANGER operations in WWII, Korea, and Vietnam have preceded these more recent operations and continued the strong traditions established by Rodger's RANGERs and Morgan RANGERs of centuries gone by. When 4 RANGER students died of exposure in the swamps of Florida in 1995[1], some sense of what RANGER students endure perhaps took on a new meaning. RANGER School is not for the faint-hearted nor prima donna nor badge finder. It is tough, demanding, and occasionally dangerous. America has no sense of what her sons go through to be able to proudly wear the RANGER Tab.

Not much has really changed about RANGER School since I first wrote this. The course went through a period wherein a Desert Phase was introduced to support mission profiles that included Southwest Asia and the Middle East. That too has gone full circle and the course is currently back to only three phases, Benning, Mountain, and Florida. Food has changed considerably, not only in its form but also in quantity and caloric value. Environmental sensors have been installed at the Florida

---

[1] Appendix C provides and account of this tragic event

training site to assist the school in risk assessment during swamp operations there as a result of the accidental deaths in the 1995 tragedy. But aside from these minor perturbations, RANGER School is still very much the same as it has always been.

It is unquestionably the best leadership school the Army has to offer, and arguably the best that any service anywhere in the world has to offer; it is a very tough course with an abnormally high attrition rate; it maintains tough rigid standards of participation and performance; it gives no quarter. The Coveted Black and Gold Tab is still earned the hard way by every soldier who has the military ability and will power to see it through. The school still turns out a soldier whose tab gives him instant credibility with peers and unquestioned confidence by juniors. The RANGER Tab still carries with it the price of performance to a standard that few are willing to pay. It still carries with it the commitment to earn it every day by displaying the full array of qualities that one expects of a RANGER. It still means what it has always meant; that here is a soldier who can be relied upon to find a way to complete the mission; to adhere to the RANGER Creed; to embrace Rodgers' original 19 standing orders; to return victorious or upon his shield.

Now, 18 years after the event and some encouragement from many who have read it, I have decided to expand upon the basic story and update it in terms of things that have occurred since. For me personally, the lessons learned, the confidence gained, and the simple credibility of the Tab have arguably helped me to advance from Major to Major General. I can say without a moments hesitation and absolute zero doubt that the basic lessons and principles from RANGER School have been completely applicable at all levels of responsibility that I have been given over the years. From the simple rules such as the 5-point contingency plan given when a leader leaves his group to the more far reaching and intangible concepts of discipline and self-discipline which sustains one through difficult times both physically, mentally, and emotionally; all are important if properly accepted and nurtured; all are equal in that each contributes to the whole; all are timeless and echelon-less in applicability; all are given to those who will accept.

Now, 18 years (referencing 1999) after the event, RANGER School remains my benchmark. Whenever I consider a condition such as being cold, hot, tired, hungry, wet, dirty, sleepy; or being harassed, losing patience, or feeling some form of discrimination; or simply feeling stressed, discouraged by events of the day, or wondering if I can respond to the boss's demands........my stake is in the ground at Ft Benning and Dahlonega and Eglin. My benchmark is RANGER School. When I ask myself the question, "Is it tougher than RANGER School?". The answer has always been a solid "No."

DEDICATION
There was never a doubt; not a moments hesitation in my consideration of who I should dedicate this work to.

*To my wife, H. Dayle Childers for her unerring faith,
Her endless patience, he galactic depth of understanding,
Her compassion towards my second love – The National Guard-
and, her willingness to my undertaking such a mission in our later
years. Certainly it was one that I did not have to undertake, nor one
which she had to stand behind with full support.*

MG Carroll D. Childers (Ret)

* A special note of thanks to Jim Bartlett for taking the time to get this into printed form utilizing his skills with the Internet. Let it be known to all that he was the one who single handedly infiltrated through the wire of the brigade TOC all those years ago and left the chal ked caricature of a Viet Cong Sapper on the door of my command Blazer, among other things. Lots of folks tried to take credit for that, but it was Jim. Not a bad little raid for a PFC from my 229th Engineers. Jim's situation is an all so common one in the Guard where one cannot necessarily equate total skill to acquired rank. So it has been his skill and willingness to collaborate which has brought this work from the archaic Xerox form to the internet published form so that it can be easily accessed and procured.

The US Army Ranger Association will be the beneficiary of the profit from this work. It was never, nor is it now, my intent to profit from the honor to serve. The honor to serve has cost many Rangers severe injury or death. Nothing can repay that but the Ranger Association has numerous programs and activities aimed at providing that level of support that can be mustered. The hope is that the reading of this account of a rigorous training program will cause the reader to recommend it to others, that the proceeds might be a blessing.

FORWARD

RANGER School is the most demanding and also the most fulfilling, rewarding experience that a soldier can experience and yet no one has ever, to my knowledge, written an adequate description of it. It needs to be described! The American public has read accounts of guys who scale tall buildings; of self-made millionaires; of radio and TV talk show stars; of Olympic Gold Medal winners; of rodeo heroes, movie stars, great ball players, and guitar pluckers; of military heroes of all services, ranks, gender, races, religions, countries, and eras from the beginning of time. But few people are knowledgeable of the cyclic trauma that has been occurring 14 times a year at Fort Benning, Georgia since 1968.

It's not done for fame or fortune but for a real and often forgotten virtue - the development of leadership which can defend America so that the others can enjoy the fruits of freedom, for that well worn saying that "freedom is not free" rings as true today as it did the first time whoever said it. The fanfare of television cameras and press conferences are absent at Todd Field on graduation day. The simple patrol uniform worn belies the exuberant feeling of the RANGER inside it as he waits to receive his dues for surviving. Graduates go not to their manager's office to strike a bargain for a publicity tour but to their next assignment and put to use what they have learned during eight weeks of what can only be described as hardship. These are the unsung hero's; America's silent majority; shadow people whose only reward is the distinct privilege of wearing the simple but coveted black and gold RANGER Tab that sets him apart from other soldiers.

I think that RANGERS deserve to be illuminated so that they can receive the recognition and respect that they have earned; so that when you, the reader, see the RANGER tab on a soldier's sleeve you will know that here is a special soldier; one that has marched to a different drum; one that has accepted the RANGER CREED. And yes, a lot of things have happened since I attended which have made the general public take notice of RANGERs. The loss of 18 warriors in Mogidishu focused the world on RANGERs. The loss of 4 RANGERs in a training accident in Florida made the headlines and caused national attention for a period. Finally, the Spielberg movie "Saving Private Ryan" gave a historical snapshot of the Second RANGER Battalion. That horizontally elongated diamond on the left shoulder of Captain Miller and his men, bearing the word RANGER; the shoulder patch of the 2nd Ranger Battalion. More recently, in 2005 the popular movie "The Great Raid" in which a RANGER unit conducted a daring and dangerous mission to rescue over 500 allied soldiers imprisoned by the Japanese in the Phillipines.

Hopefully, DRIVING ON will adequately describe the course and encourage or inspire the men who are inclined toward such adventure and dedication to apply for entrance. At the same time, it should bring reality to the weak hearted and make more room for those who are soldiers with uncommon will. It may serve as a tribute to determination and self-confidence; as encouragement for those who have lost their self-confidence to compete because of their age or other imagined disadvantages; as proof that one should not be reluctant to try difficult tasks against great odds.

"The leader can secure obedience from his men because he can convince them that he knows best, precisely as a good doctor makes his patients obey him. Also he must be ready to suffer more hardships than he asks of his soldiers, more fatigue, greater extremes of heat and cold."
Xenopon, 430-350 B.C.

I have made no attempt herein to maintain chronological order, rather, I have recalled events as they naturally occurred to me. I surrounded these events with the details necessary to illuminate the event without being accused of trying to impose alignment on the tangled, sometimes confusing web of personal history that occurred under circumstances not conducive to orderly memory.

What my parents used to call "foul language" is a normal part of RANGER School. Such is in fact the "norm" for any male-dominated group whether it is RANGERS, Marines, the locker room of a ball club, a hunt club, or the crap game in the back room of the service station. When men are thrown together, they curse, a lot. I will not try to justify it or excuse it; it is simply a fact of life. We know that colors stimulate certain things; maybe camouflage stimulates machismo and cursing.

"When I want my men to remember something important, to really make it stick, I give it to them double dirty. It may not sound nice to some bunch of little old ladies at an afternoon tea party, but it helps my soldiers to remember. You can't run an army without profanity; and it has to be eloquent profanity. An army without profanity couldn't fight it's way out of a piss-soaked paper bag."

"As for the types of comments I make," he continued with a wry smile, *"sometimes I just, By God, get carried away with my own eloquence."* ....From an interview with General George Smith Patton, charismatic commanding general of the Third US Army, World War II.

Because one of my objectives in writing this book was to inform a potential RANGER Student's family and friends, I felt that the complete verbal account would be unacceptably crude and certainly not necessary to paint the desired picture. I want it to be readable by anyone who has the inclination so I have replaced phrases and words that might be objectionable to many people and replaced them with a string of meaningless icons (!@#$%^&*). For those readers who will enjoy it more in the raw form, you may insert your own favorite words, phrases, and strings of words at will. Whatever you substitute will probably not be far off base.

The original text contained the actual names of people in this adventure. I have decided to give some of those people a fictitious name to avoid the obvious difficulties that could result from such use of names. To locate them and get their permission to use their names would be just too large of an investment of energy for the return it would provide. But they were in fact a very colorful cast of characters, particularly the RANGER Instructors (RI's)...... the dreaded RIs.

But of all of the people who played a part in this story, Sergeant Rock was the RI who made the course for Class 6-81[2]. A master of profanity, eloquent by Patton's description, a senior NCO of incredible interactive skills, and a soldier who through personal experience knew how far a soldier or a unit could be pushed both mentally and physically. He proudly wore the Tab on the left shoulder above his airborne and division patch. The Combat Infantry Badge above the Pathfinder and Airborne wings of his pocket flap were only capstones to the RANGER Battalion scroll on his right shoulder signifying combat service in Viet Nam in a RANGER Unit.

Class 6-81 simply could not ask for finer credentials than those worn by our Tactical Non-Commissioned Officer (TAC NCO). We didn't know until much later how highly we would come to regard, even revere, this soldier; but never openly to him. Rock was the single most unifying force that kept us striving for success; for the coveted black and gold tab that represents a human quality that few people ever gain a true measure of -- their own will.

---

[2] The designation 6-81 indicates serial Class number 6 (of 11 per year) in the Fiscal Year 1981

LIST OF APPENDICES

MOVE OUT

So how do you start a book like this? Perhaps with a few words to outline what the course entails and some basic ground rules that the students must perform to. Soldiers have some vague idea about what RANGER School is, but unless they have spent a lot of time talking in detail to a RANGER, their idea is indeed vague. The Military Channel on TV has done an excellent job of covering an annual event known as the Best RANGER Competition. This gives some insight into what RANGERS are expected to do but still does not reveal what a soldier must endure to be able to enter that contest. Non-soldiers and even military people serving in other services likely do not know a RANGER from a SEAL (Navy Special Forces) or a Green Beret (Army Special Forces) or a Force Recon Marine.

There are probably at least 3 kinds of RANGER graduates. First, there are those who go on to serve in a RANGER Battalion. There they continue to train in the specialized missions for which RANGERS are really organized. They are basically Light Infantry who have been augmented with special weapons and equipment, supported by specialized units, and provided with some unique mobility and entry assets. RANGER Battalions have a proud history with commanders like Darby, Rudder, and Merrill who became household words during WWII. They are the icons that we probably all wish we could become but circumstances and opportunity will be our nemesis to that aspiration.

With America's entry into the Second World War, RANGERS came forth to add to the pages of history as they had since the first RANGERS were organized by Maj. Robert Rogers in 1756 (Rogers' RANGERs). They were further developed during the Revolutionary War by Colonel Daniel Morgan and Francis Marion (The Swamp Fox). And the Civil War had such masters as John S. Mosby who, though known for his Cavalry exploits, was nonetheless a RANGER in the highest order.

Maj. William O. Darby organized and activated the 1ST RANGER Battalion on 19 June 1942 at Carrickfergus, North Ireland. I think it is interesting to note that Darby was stationed in the United Kingdom training for entry into the European theater with the 34TH Infantry Division; a National Guard Division activated for WWII. The 1ST RANGER Battalion was formed entirely from volunteers, 80% of whom were 34TH Division members. The members were hand picked volunteers, 50 of whom participated in the gallant Dieppe raid on the northern coast of France with British and Canadian commandos.

The 1ST, 3RD, and 4TH RANGER Battalions participated, with distinction, in the North African, Sicilian, and Italian campaigns. Darby's RANGER Battalion's spearheaded the Seventh Army landing at Gela and

Licata during the Sicilian invasion and played a key role in the subsequent campaign, which culminated in the capture of Messina. They infiltrated German lines and mounted an attack against Cisterna, where they virtually annihilated an entire German parachute regiment during close in, night, bayonet and hand-to-hand fighting.

The 2ND and 5TH RANGER Battalions participated in the D-Day landings at Omaha Beach, Normandy. When you see the highly acclaimed movie, "Saving Private Ryan," you will note two things with a tie to this work; the 29TH Infantry Division was the first assault wave on Omaha Beach and was the subject of the first thirty minutes of that film and second, the team searching for Private Ryan was from the 2ND RANGER Battalion.

It was during the bitter fighting along the beach that the RANGERs gained their official motto. As the situation became critical on Omaha Beach, the division commander of the 29TH Infantry Division (a National Guard division from Virginia and Maryland) stated that the entire force must clear the beach and advance inland. He then turned to Lieutenant Colonel Max Schneider, commanding the 5TH RANGER Battalion, and said. "RANGERs, lead the way." This has of course become the motto of the RANGERs. So I consider it a great though coincidental honor to have commanded the 29th Division that was the origin for the motto of the RANGERs. The 5TH RANGER Battalion spearheaded the entire breakthrough and thus enabled the Allies to drive inland away from the invasion beach. (I had the great fortune and honor to command the 29th Infantry Division from July 1996 - August 1999.)

The 6TH RANGER Battalion, operating in the Pacific, conducted RANGER type missions behind enemy lines, which involved reconnaissance and hard-hitting long-range raids. They were the first American contingent to return to the Philippines, destroying key coastal installations prior to the invasion. A reinforced company from the 6TH RANGER Battalion formed the entire rescue force, which liberated American and Allied prisoners of war from the Japanese prison camp at Cabanatuan. In 2005, a popular movie of this rescue was released, entitled "The Great Raid".

Another RANGER Type unit was the 5307TH Composite Unit (Provisional), organized and trained as a long-range penetration unit for employment behind enemy lines in Japanese occupied Burma. The official unit designation was later changed to 75TH Infantry. (This designation is carried today by the only active duty RANGER Regiment in the force structure.) Commanded by Brigadier General (later Major General) Frank D. Merrill, its 2997 officers and men became popularly known as Merrill's Marauders. Certainly this is a much more imposing and impressive name than something that sounds more like a street address than a military unit.

The men composing Merrill's Marauders were volunteers from the 33RD Infantry Regiment, the 14TH Infantry Regiment, the 5TH Regiment, and from Infantry regiments engaged in combat in the southwest and South Pacific. These men responded to a call from then Chief of Staff, General George C. Marshall, for volunteers for a hazardous mission. These volunteers were to be of a high state of physical ruggedness and stamina, and they were to come from jungle-trained and jungle-tested units.

Prior to their entry into the Northern Burma Campaign, Merrill's Marauders trained in India under the overall supervision of Major General Orde C. Wingate, British Army. There they were trained from February to June 1943, in long-range penetration tactics and techniques of the type developed and first employed by General Wingate in the operations of the 77Th Indian Infantry Brigade from Burma.

From February to May 1944, the operations of the Marauders were closely coordinated with those of the Chinese 22ND and 38Th Divisions in a drive to recover northern Burma and clear the way for the construction of the Ledo Road, which was to link the Indian Railhead at Ledo with the old Burma Road to China. The Marauders marched and fought through jungle and over mountains from the Hukawng Valley in northwestern Burma to Myitkyina on the Irrawaddy River. In five major and 30 minor engagements, they met and defeated the veteran soldiers of the Japanese 18TH Division. Operating in the rear of the main forces of the Japanese, they prepared the way for the southward advance of the Chinese by disorganizing supply lines and communications. The climax of the Marauder's operations was the capture of the Myitkyina Airfield, the only all weather strip in northern Burma. This was the final victory of "Merrill's Marauders" which was disbanded in August 1944.

With the outbreak of hostilities in Korea in June 1950, the need arose once again for RANGERs. Fourteen Airborne-RANGER companies were formed and trained between September 1950 and September 1951, at the RANGER Training Command, Fort Benning, Georgia. In October 1951, the Army Chief of Staff, General J. Lawton Collins, directed that "RANGER training be extended to all combat units in the Army." The Commandant of the Infantry School was directed to establish a RANGER Department for the purpose of conducting a RANGER course of instruction. The overall objective of RANGER training was to raise the standard of training in all combat units. This program was built upon what had been learned from the RANGER Battalions of World War II and the Airborne-RANGER companies of the Korean conflict.

Fourteen RANGER companies consisting of highly motivated volunteers, served with distinction in Vietnam from the Mekong Delta to the DMZ. Assigned to independent Brigade, Division and Field Force units they conducted long range reconnaissance and exploitation operations into enemy held and denied areas providing valuable combat intelligence, thus, the origin of the term LRRP (Long Range Reconnaissance Patrol). LRRPs are legendary in the aftermath of the Vietnam era.

Recognizing the necessity of having a responsive quick reaction force, the Army Chief of Staff in 1974 directed the activation of the 1ST Battalion (RANGER), 75TH Infantry, Fort Stewart, Georgia and the 2ND Battalion (RANGER), 75TH Infantry, Fort Lewis, Washington.

The 75TH RANGER Regiment was organized in 1984. Elements of the Regiment have been employed in specialized missions including the rescue attempt of the Iranian Hostages (Desert One), Grenada, Panama, Operation Desert Storm, and Mogadishu. (More detail on the history of RANGERs is presented in **Appendix A.**)

So it took a little longer for me to describe the first type of RANGER, the RANGER Battalion RANGER, than I had anticipated. But they are, after all, the "real" RANGERs. The rest of us are graduates of the school; soul RANGERs; want-to-be's. But that is life. Just as everyone cannot make it into and through the school, everyone who earns the honor to wear the Tab cannot go on to make a career in a RANGER Battalion.

That leaves us with the other two types of RANGER graduates. One is the soldier who makes it though, wears the Tab for the rest of his career, but otherwise never exhibits the attributes of a RANGER, never exhibits the RANGER Creed, never teaches soldiering in RANGER fashion, and generally abhors the environment that real RANGERs feel natural in; cold, wet, hungry, tired, muddy, sleepy; but always ready and willing to "drive on."

But then, secondly, there is the type RANGER that, though he does not draw a career as a RANGER Battalion soldier, emulates and lives the RANGER Creed throughout his career. He measured the depth and breadth of his will during those 54 days of rigorous discovery. He learned how far he can personally go. He learned to recognize how far others can be pushed and the signals that precede the breaking point. He learned valuable lessons through doing and observing that serve him throughout his career, no matter what level of leadership he climbs to. He learns to accept a level of pain, hunger, discomfort, uncertainty, thirst, heat and cold, fatigue, and fear that he can otherwise only get probably in extended combat or POW status. Out of this experience comes a level of self-confidence that is unlikely to be acquired during any other 54-day experience that one can point to. Out of this experience comes our very best leaders and our very best followers. Out of this experience comes a brotherhood without peer.

Just as there are three types of RANGERS who graduate, there are four levels of status for those soldiers who survive the 54-day course. First, there are those few who did indeed survive to the end, but did not have sufficient total score to be awarded the Tab. Usually these are given the opportunity to make another attempt. Second, there is that large portion of each class that does make the required total score to be awarded the Tab. Third, is a small percentage that may make scores high enough to be recognized as honor graduates - and there are NCO honor grads and Officer honor grads. Sometimes a class may not have any honor grads. Finally, there may be the single soldier who makes a total score that earns him the designation of Distinguished Honor Graduate (DHG). Often, a class will not produce a DHG.

OLD PEOPLE LEAD THE WAY

As I stood on Todd Field looking beyond the color guard at 102 classmates, fragments of the previous 54 days flashed through my mind in an attempt to assemble a catchy impromptu speech that Colonel Cameron had just announced that I would make. News to me; but hey, nothing is impossible for a RANGER; and I am about to be tabbed as one. The occasion was the graduation of Class 6-81, US Army RANGER School. A "young man's" course. It seems that most of the events that my mind reviewed concerned age differential, precipitated I am sure by the words of Colonel Cameron echoing in the background.......".....in my 27 years with the RANGER Department, I can only recall two or maybe three people who were so outstanding that I would categorize them as special, and RANGER Childers is one of those individuals."

He went on talking about my "advanced" age relative to the age of my classmates and the stress and strain we had been through. Then suddenly I realized that he was calling me to the podium; time to choke out a few words to the assembled masses. In front of me on the field were 102 tired soldiers waiting on their tab; most of them about the same age as my own son. In fact, I had collected some statistics the morning before in the mess hall because I happened to be designated as the head-counter for the meal. The class average age was 22 years, including the statistical addition that my age of 42 and that of a 33 year old Marine named Bryant added to the total.

To the flanks, the smiling faces of the RANGER Instructors and staff. To the rear, a bleacher full of family members of the class, curiosity seekers, well-wishers, RANGER Association members, and my wife. A lot of people to consider in what I may say and I didn't really know how long the Colonel intended for me to keep the microphone. Maybe it was my final test before he would release me from the course with the honors that he had just bestowed on me.

But it was only really then, that moment that I stepped up to the mike and adjusted it slightly for my height, that it dawned on me that this was indeed a special moment. The mind is a wonderful creation. It can cover so much time and so many events in such a short period at times. And things were going through my mind at warp-7. I had told my wife before I left home that I was "going to keep a low profile, try to avoid injury, and just graduate."

"I'll take it easy and let the young guys lead the charge and go for the glory" I assured her.

"Yeah, sure, I'm holding my breath. You be careful now, don't get carried away," she charged.

So here I am, 3 months shy of being 43 years old; the oldest RANGER to ever graduate as the Distinguished Honor Graduate. That record still stands in 2005, and my wife is sitting in the bleachers waiting for me to explain myself to the waiting crowd. What can I say? She knew all along!!

"It's been a great experience for me and I have a lot of people to thank for being here today. First is my wife who has been understanding and patient enough with me to endure my goal to do this very difficult thing at this time of my life." I am sure that she and I were the only two people who really thought I could even get through the course. And she knew, more than I, that my nature would simply drive me to the head of the column in spite of my own proclamations that I simply intended to graduate in silent gratitude.

"Next is Sergeant Rock, our TAC NCO. He didn't have any faith in me at first, but later on he was making bets with other RANGER Instructors on my behalf. But he did more than I can describe here for our entire class. He is a tribute to the NCO Corps and especially to RANGERs everywhere. And finally, my classmates; a great bunch of soldiers who learned to function as a team to accomplish a lot of tough training missions to simulate combat. No one can get through RANGER School alone and I certainly could not have even survived this last 54 days without their support and cooperation. I am truly honored and humbled to have met the standards established for Distinguished Honor Graduate. Good fortune, a few more years of experience than my classmates had, and their cooperation all combined to yield the score. Thank you all for being here today. It means a lot to Class 6-81."

I must tell you that before I attended RANGER School I did not know that there was any such category as Distinguished Honor Graduate. Yeah, somewhere in the in-briefing to the school when they were telling us about the merit and demerit system, they very well could have described the method of selecting honor graduates (NCO and Officer) and a Distinguished Honor Graduate. The "friendly" staff of RANGER Instructors (RIs) have a capacity for creating enough distractions and confusion in the class that it is easy to imagine that minor details about graduation day would be totally lost to even the most sensitive and observant student.

So quite frankly, I was not cognizant of the levels of performance to which one might aspire, given that one had the inclination at the time, with all that is going on. There was some discussion among my fellow RANGERS and an occasional comment on the subject by some of the RI's from time to time, but I did not know with certainty that I had met the standard until graduation morning on Todd Field. I think also that I didn't really care too much one way or the other at the time; I was simply glad it was all over and I had at least succeeded in making it to Todd Field.

My nature is that I don't set myself up for disappointment by specifying goals to myself. It follows that I would not share such a goal with others even if it were somewhere in my subconscious. But I am also privately very competitive and if I decide to beat an opponent, I will do everything in my power to do so. If I lose, I can lose gracefully and accept that someone legitimately outdid me.

In this case, I loved what we were doing. Every day and every moment was a great challenge both individually and as part of a team of special people. But still, at the end of the course, I was certainly glad it was over. There was a sense of invincibility and great risk. Or as some famous person once said, "A soldier is just as proud of hardships overcome as of dangers faced." We had overcome a lot of hardship. We were very proud. And as I became the "pappy" and "Gramps" to the younger soldiers, I felt a little extra responsibility to work even harder, risk more, and set the example for them by "driving on" even beyond the extreme limits that RANGER students are normally driven to by the hype and euphoria of the environment.

Theodore Roosevelt's quote came to me somewhere along the way. "Far better it is to dare mighty things, to win glorious triumphs, even though checkered by failure, than to take rank with those poor spirits who neither enjoy much nor suffer much, because they live in the gray twilight than knows neither victory nor defeat." I felt this day glorious triumph. I felt that I had dared a mighty thing and had beat failure.

So I made it!! Me, a nearly 43 year old Major, Army National Guardsman from Virginia, not only survived the course with only a minor long term damage to my body from which I would probably never recover, but met the standard for award of the Distinguished Honor Graduate status and established a new notch on the high-jump pole of Army accomplishment.

It is informative to note that all classes may not have either Honor Graduates or a Distinguished Honor Graduate. I have tried, since I graduated, to attend the graduation of every Virginia Guardsman who makes it through the RANGER course. The most recent was the graduation of Class 1-97 because a young Lieutenant from my Engineer Battalion was graduating. We remarked on the way to the graduation what a chance we were taking going to the graduation of a Lt. named Murphy on the 13TH of the month.

They had only two Honor Grads, and no Distinguished Honor Graduate. These require thresholds of cumulative scores and evaluations and often a class simply will not have someone who breaks the threshold for some or all of these honors. And that is the beauty of this system. Everything is measured against a rigid standard. Everything is objective, not subjective. Everything is hard. RANGER School has always been hard. But as Clausewitz observed:

War is the domain of physical exertion and suffering. If one is not to be overcome by them , he must possess a certain bodily and spiritual strength, native or acquired, which makes him indifferent to them.

The RANGER Department has taken this observation to heart and have created a domain of physical exertion and suffering. And if you don't have native bodily and spiritual strength, they offer the opportunity for you to acquire it. Clausewitz also observed that :

Physical exertions must be practiced, not so much to train the body but to train the mind. In war, the recruit is often inclined to consider unusual exertions to be the result of gross errors by the commander, and hence to be unduly influenced by them.

Again, the RANGER Department is in sync with Clausewitz because much of what they do is actually a mind game. It is boot camp without restrictions. It is Officer Candidate School Tactical Officers without visible constraint.

At the heart of all sound teaching through the centuries, whether within military institutions or without, has dwelt the simple idea that every vigorous man needs some kind of contest, some realization of resistance overcome, before he can feel that he is making the best use of his faculties.

RANGER School is most definitely for the vigorous man. Contests abound. Those that are real and those that are imagined by each student as he perceives things unfold around himself. There are physical contests between the student and other students, between students and the staff, and between the student and the environment. The contest to "drive on" when every bone and sinew, molecule and electron, and all of the gray matter you can stir is telling you no no. Enough is enough. Stop. Rest. Recover. There are mental contests, mostly between the student and the staff or between the student's left and right brain; between will power and conscious, common sense. There is plenty of resistance to be overcome. And though it is physically demanding because of the synergistic effects of lack of sleep, limited diet, pressures of all sorts, long hard hours, and fear............in the end it is the fight in the man, not the man in the fight that counts; it is will power, whatever that really is; it is what you have determined that you will do; it is in the end, mental; mind over matter.

Fear you query?? You thought RANGERs were fearless!! What fear??

I'll tell you what fear is. The fear of failure. It is always present. The RIs tell you constantly, up close and personal, in your face, loudly and crudely that you are going to fail; that you have already failed; that you have been a failure all your life and RANGER School is just going to be one more event in your sorry life. You would like to wipe the spittle off your face, but don't dare. Sometimes I thought they may have rinsed their mouth with something foul just to test how much up-close and personal in your face could be tolerated. Failure is a very emotional experience. Fear is an emotion. I doubt if there is any stronger human response than the combination of these factors; fear of failure. One needs to be aware of this ahead of time so that he can control fear.

Wellington would have approved of RANGER School. In his General Order of 15 May 1811, he stated,

"That quality which I wish to see the officers possess, who are at the end of the troops, is a cool, discriminating judgment when in action, which will enable them to decide with promptitude how far they can go and ought to go, with propriety; and to convey their orders, and act with such vigor and decision, that the soldiers will look up to them with confidence in the moment of action, and obey them with alacrity."

These are exactly the qualities and characteristics and experiences that RANGER School strives to develop and provide to those who survive; coolness in chaos, decisiveness, credibility among soldiers, confidence, and of great importance, to know the extent to which soldiers can be driven or led or inspired. There may be limits to which you can go that you are not taken to in RANGER School; but you don't want to know about it. Perhaps you don't even want to think about it.

To prepare one's self to meet the challenge of RANGER School through knowledge of what it is, and what it is not, is one of the primary aims of this work.

"So what is RANGER School" some of my non-military oriented friends have asked. For that matter, what is a RANGER?? In the words of one RANGER Instructor, a RANGER is a "fine tuned, well oiled, motivated fighting machine." Another said "hard as woodpecker lips, tough as a beaver tail, trained to lead, and conditioned to conquer." The definitions of a RANGER are as varied and as colorful as are the personalities of those men who wear the coveted RANGER Tab, but perhaps the best description of a RANGER is contained in the RANGER CREED:

THE RANGER CREED

R--ecognizing that I volunteered as a RANGER, fully knowing the hazards of my chosen profession, I will always endeavor to uphold the prestige, honor and high "Esprit de Corps" of my RANGER Battalion.

A--cknowledging the fact that a RANGER is more elite soldier who arrives at the cutting edge of battle by land, sea, or air. I accept the fact that, as a RANGER, my country expects me to move further, faster, and fight harder than any other soldier.

N--ever shall I fail my comrades. I will always keep myself mentally alert, physically strong and morally straight and I will shoulder more than my share of the task whatever it may be. One hundred percent and then some.

G--allantly will I show the world that I am a specially selected and well trained soldier. My courtesy to superior officers, my neatness of dress and care of equipment shall set the example for others to follow.

E--nergetically will I meet the enemies of my country. I shall defeat them on the field of battle for I am better trained and will fight with all my might. Surrender is not a RANGER word nor will I leave a fallen comrade to fall into the hands of the enemy and under no circumstances will I ever embarrass my country.

R--eadily will I display the intestinal fortitude and desire to fight on to the RANGER objective and complete the mission, though I be the lone survivor.

There are many misconceptions of what a RANGER is and thus misconceptions about RANGER School. A RANGER is first and foremost a human. Next, he is a man. There are no female RANGERS. I did not make that rule, I'm just stating it. Like any man, RANGERS have faults and, as we would find out several times a day, RANGER students have even more faults.

A RANGER is not faster than a speeding bullet and he cannot leap tall buildings in a single bound. Forgiving those two shortcomings, however, he is the next thing to Superman. Through 54 days (that was the length of the course in 1981. It is a few days longer now) of exposure to physical, mental, and emotional abuse he has proven to himself that he can function reliably, confidently, and reasonably. These 54 days have been designed to simulate the stress conditions encountered in combat. He functions on an extremely low caloric intake (a condition that changed with the death of 4 students in 1995), almost no rest, one or two hours of sleep in 36, shoulders a very heavy load during most of the day, and is subjected to continuous harassment by the ever present RANGER Instructor (RI).

A typical 3-day patrol cycle for a RANGER element begins at first call usually around 0300 in the morning after having gone to bed the night before about 2300-2400. By 0400 he has squared away his Spartan quarters, completed his final packing for the upcoming field problem, taken care of his more pressing personal physiological needs and is standing in line for breakfast--his first hot meal for several days. 0500 (5 AM) finds him unpacking everything he has packed the night before for a full layout inspection by the RI. A full layout inspection means that the RANGER element, (Squad, Section, or Platoon) assumes a military formation appropriate to the size of the element. Once aligned, each member positions his poncho and precisely aligns each item of equipment on the poncho according to the layout design prescribed by the RANGER Department..........or the whim of the RI, whichever happens to satisfy the fancy of the RI at the time. The object of the inspection is meaningful.

Each RANGER carries the same identical equipment and in approximately the same location upon the load bearing equipment or within the rucksack. Rucksack is the military name for a backpack. The primary difference between a backpack and a rucksack is that the military had never been, up to most recently, quite as smart as the civilian sector in the practical design of the device.

The military concept of this inspection is to ensure uniformity among soldiers and to ensure that the absolute necessities are always carried and that the nice to have things are not taken so as to prevent the soldier from wearing himself out carrying things that have no absolute value. As you will see later, this theory does not hold up very well. You will see that RANGERS carry a lot of stuff for the sole purpose of making a load.

But back to the theory of packing the Ruck (short for Rucksack); if you are forced to abandon your equipment or you lose it in some event, you could be re-supplied by air drop, for example, and you would receive exactly what you needed. Another theory is that if you are forced to use a fallen comrade's equipment, you would find essentially everything you needed to continue your mission.

The inspection may be very thorough or it may be quite cursory depending upon the individual RI, his mood of the day, circumstances he has observed prior to the inspection, the apparent readiness of the RANGERS, or the reputation and performance history of the particular group of RANGERS. If your group has been doing real good, you'll probably get a sharp stick in the eye kind of an inspection. If your group has been doing badly, you'll probably get a real sharp stick in the eye kind of an inspection. There is simply no way that a Squad of RANGER students, let alone a Platoon, can get 25 or so items arranged similarly enough on a poncho to satisfy the discerning eye of the RI. Something is going to be wrong; and if there is not something wrong, then obviously you spent too much time arranging it. Trying to impress the RI in the hope of getting something in return.

Actually there are three inspections prior to each patrol during the early phases of RANGER School. There is the initial inspection, followed by the full layout inspection of equipment, and the final inspection which concentrates on the individual and his knowledge and individual preparedness for the mission. The initial inspection is conducted by the RANGER leaders of each echelon, i.e. fire team, squad, and platoon. For instance, Platoon Leaders inspect Squad leaders; Squad leaders inspect Fire Team Leaders; Fire Team leaders inspect individuals. This is a detailed head-to-toe inspection.

Does the individual have:

Full Canteens of water; full magazines, properly loaded and inserted in the pouches; dog tags, Identification (ID) cards, proper uniform; proper camouflage; full knowledge of his task, responsibilities and mission; compromising data on his body such as marked maps, codes, or letters from home; anything that rattles, shakes, or breaks; compass, RANGER Handbook, pace cord; unauthorized luxuries such as gum, candy, tobacco products, C-Rations, or "poggie bait" (a soldier's term for junk food such as sardines, Vienna sausage, etc.).

Leaders take notes on deficiencies during the initial inspection so that during the final inspection the emphasis is on whether or not the deficiency has been corrected and this is closely monitored by the RI. Both parties (the inspector and the inspected) can get negative spot reports during this process. It is a matter of integrity as well as attention to detail

The full layout inspection was not the highlight of the day. Not too surprisingly, it was often revealed that some RANGERS tried to get by with packing "light," that is, they would not take everything on the packing list. This really got under my skin because I had accepted the RANGER CREED fully and seriously and thought everyone else had or should; packing light is a form of lying to your fellow RANGERS. In a patrol rucksack, every ounce of weight is noticeable, particularly in the mountain phase of RANGER School. Then there were two or three guys who always smuggled extra food. That to me was a double crime because invariably they would pack light on the packing list equipment and smuggle food with the weigh savings. The Marines seemed to be the most frequent violators of the food code; or at least they got caught more often. Once a Marine got caught with 13 Granola bars over the limit. I would say that the RANGER Battalion (commonly called RANGER Bats) students knew the most tricks and methods of deception with regard to getting away with things for which they would be punished if they were caught by the RIs. This is because probably more RANGER Battalion students pass through the course than any other single organization. The RANGER Bats conduct a very thorough pre-RANGER training course and there are a lot of graduates for a prospective student to get smart from before he attends. The rumor was that RANGER Bat students could not go back to the Battalion if they failed RANGER School, so that was an added incentive for them to hang in there and pass at all costs. Students like me had only talked to a few graduates before attending and typically they had attended 10-15 years earlier and probably were not current on the course and its many facets

Food was a precious thing in RANGER School. I can say that with special sensitivities and feeling because before RANGER School, food was essentially unimportant to me. I had always been an advocate of the "food pill". Not because I don't like to eat (there was always a few things that I was especially fond of) but because of the time involved in eating. It just seems like the complete cycle caused by eating has never been addressed systematically.

Eating consumes easily 30 percent of a persons time if you consider the total cycle that is affected by eating; acquiring food, preparation for eating, waiting for food to be served or cooled, cleaning up after eating, relaxing to digest, excrement processes, and talking about food. One thing about food and time, though, in RANGER School, you do not spend much time in the mess hall. Class 6-81 was at one point 128 men. We could cycle through the mess hall in 35 minutes flat. Most of us are used to a company- sized unit being pushed for time to cycle through in an hour. Actually the 35 minute cycle is easy. All you have to do is turn the people into animals, threaten them with unmentionable bodily harm and punishment, or both..........and presto, the company zips through the mess hall like a well oiled machine. We were issued one large spoon to eat with; no fork, no knife; just one large spoon.

The chow hall is a place to eat. It is not a place for talking," said Sgt. Rock.

"You can't talk with your mouth full so I'm giving you studs this large spoon to keep your mouth stuffed with. With your right hand, you will shovel your food from the plate to the mouth and with the left hand you will operate your glass or cup, stuff bread into your mouth, or pick up your meat to bite on since it would be bad manners to try to cut your meat with your spoon."

He would pace back and forth very deliberately; hands behind the back carefully watching the placement of each foot as if he might step off the edge of the earth if he didn't. He'd pause at the end of his directional pace, look up at us out from under his Beret then pivot sharply and pace the other direction.

"You got that?"
"Yes Sergeanttttttt," we would yell back at the top of our lungs.

"Well move out!!!! What the *#@!++$#% are you waiting for? You people are wasting my time and I got plenty of important things to do and places to go before this day is over. MOVE! MOVE! MOVE like you got a purpose!!!!"

Entry into the mess hall was closely controlled. In the beginning, we lined up outside in two files at parade rest and would enter by two's and report to the TAC NOC, Sergeant Rock. The RANGER Patrol Cap

(PC) was held in a closely prescribed and inspected manner in the left hand. No one could hold it correctly. Like arranging things on a poncho for inspection. Can't be done. It had to be held tenderly because it was a symbol of something. Couldn't be clutched.

The RANGER Eyes that had been carefully sewed on to demanding standards must be positioned forward. RANGER Eyes are the strips of luminous tape on the back of the PC. One half inch wide and exactly one inch long, the normal arrangement was to affix two pieces vertically on the back of the PC, spaced exactly one inch apart. Each strip was affixed by 12 precisely spaced and arranged loops of white thread. Each loop had to be tied firmly with a perfect square knot and the ends trimmed just so. It takes hours to affix the RANGER Eyes on, and you are given only minutes at a time.

RANGER Eyes serve a very useful purpose, two in fact. First, they act as a range finder. When the patrol is moving cross- country at night, if you are too far behind the RANGER in front of you, the two strips will merge into a single glowing spot. If you are just about the right range from the RANGER in front of you, you will see the two separate strips.

The second function they serve is as an indicator of swimming ability. Weak swimmers or no swimmers have a different arrangement of the luminous strips, in fact they have three strips arranged in accordance with the swimming ability of the RANGER wearing the PC. The theory is that if you see the RANGER Eyes disappear under the water as you are crossing a body of water, you will know whether or not to be concerned about that RANGER surfacing.

"When you report I want them RANGER Eyes looking square into mine," insisted Sergeant Rock.

First the RANGER on the left would report and sound off as loud as he could.

"Sergeant!! RANGER Childers, 3rd Squad, 3rd Platoon, Company B, Roster # 10 reports for breakfast."

Then one might be required to give a little speech or come up with a reason why he was even there besides just reporting for breakfast. One could not be there simply because he was hungry. RANGERs don't get cold or wet or tired or miserable or hungry.

"I am not really hungry this morning because of last evenings fine menu. The food here is so good and enjoyable and it is such a pleasure to dine in this fine facility. I am really here because I cannot allow my RANGER Buddy to go places alone, nor be alone myself. But since I am here for those reasons, I will consent to honor the mess team by consuming their fine preparations."

"That is soooo good RANGER Childers. That is really #%$@&** GOOD. I hope your buddy can come up with an equally good bunch of pure unadulterated crap so I can throw up on the two of you!!!!"

Then the other RANGER would report and after a general tongue-lashing for not being born of the right parents or some other totally unrealistic thing, we would be told to "Drive on RANGERs" or "Get out of here" or "Go to the back of the line". We would then do an about face, tuck the PC into the waist band in the small of the back and scurry off to wherever he told us to go...... screaming as loud as we could of course; and what else would we be saying but "RANGERS LEAD THE WAY SERGEANT."

"Take all you want but eat all you take" was the rule. Better not even attempt to throw something away at the utensil turn-in window. If you did you might just end up eating out of the garbage can for several minutes to ensure that all that you tried to throw away was consumed. I could never figure out how food accumulated in the garbage can if no one was allowed to attempt to throw something in there without retrieving and eating more than he supposedly threw in there??????? Was it a way of giving students a outlet to eat a little extra??? It was very easy to take too much because about 5 minutes of sit-down time is all that was allowed. Then the mess officer, a TAC, or an RI would be "on your case" to get you up and out.

There was no winning in the mess hall game. You've got to have the food because of all the energy you are burning up all day. The problem is getting it from the plate into the stomach in only about 5 minutes. The mathematics of chewing simply make it impossible. Think about how many bites are on a plate and how long it takes to comfortably chew a bite and prepare it for swallowing. Basically this meant only half chewing at best. Shoveling, swallowing, and washing it down with liquid at cyclic rate is the only known method of clearing the plate in the time allowed and still consume enough to maintain the pace required. No food could be taken out of the mess hall, either in your hands, pockets, or in your mouth. You could continue to stuff food down your mouth in the line to the utensil turn-in window. What a shock to the system. Not only do you eat much more in RANGER School mess halls than you did back home, but you stuff it down partially chewed causing your digestive system to work two or three times as hard. My system rebelled and refused to function for 5 days. My own system had always been extremely reliable and predictable. I would eat three light meals a day plus the normal red-blooded American between meals snacks and eliminate waste products like clockwork once a day. After 5 days in RANGER School, I was bowel dysfunctional and resorted to healthy doses of Maalox. Slowly, almost cautiously, my system restored itself in another week.

The system experiences several harsh extremes during the course of 54 days that can be directly related to diet changes and to no small degree, stress. As I've indicated, we got all we could eat in five minutes, three times a day during the Benning Phase, but that's not exactly true because the Benning Phase is divided into two distinct sub-phases. The first 9 days are fondly referred to as the "City Phase" because it was conducted on the main post in an area known as Harmony Church area. During the city phase we got three squares a day but during the 10 following days at Camp Darby, called the "Darby Phase", we usually got only two meals a day. Of these two meals, one would usually be a "C" ration.

One of the first shocking realizations that I got during RANGER School was when I discovered that we were only getting two meals a day. Somehow that had not soaked through to me until the final moment. We had returned from a patrol shortly after dawn and went to the planning hut for a debrief. I kept thinking, "I wish they would hurry up so we could have breakfast." Not that breakfast, particularly in the field, were particularly appetizing. It was usually lukewarm at best, dark so you couldn't really see what you are eating, and rushed so that enjoyment is not an apt description in any case. But eggs is eggs and one can conjure up a fairly nice vision of what cold eggs hastily eaten can be if he really is hungry and tries halfway. We had gotten up about 0300 the morning before and had a rather skimpy "A" ration. This was not unusual----rations were always skimpy at Camp Darby. Rations were cooked at Harmony Church and brought to the field in Mermite cans (an insulated container which the army uses to transport food in to maintain it either cold or hot) which, as every soldier knows, is not the state-of-the-art in food preservation.

Anyway, we ate the early morning breakfast, drew one "C" ration, and went through the preparation for our first patrol. Along about 1200 or 1300 hours that day, nine hours or so and several "clicks" (that's kilometers in army speak) of rucksack movement, we sat and consumed our "C" Rat. We knew there would be no supper meal-----no illusions of that. We just ate the only food we had and we knew an all night patrol was in store for us. I considered eating only a portion of the meal and saving the rest for the evening, but then I figured I probably wouldn't have another opportunity to sit and eat in the evening. Besides, what do I save and what do I eat? Then too, I figured I could miss supper "knowing" that a good, hopefully hot, breakfast awaited me.

All day and night we "humped" (trudged along under load of the Ruck and the harassment of the RI) up and down the rolling terrain of Darby. By midnight my stomach begins to tell me little secrets. By dawn

I'm telling my stomach "hold on, breakfast is only a moment away." I was impatient to get through the after action debrief, clean weapons, and turn in equipment so as to get on to the real "gut issue," which was to fill my gut. Breakfast!!! I'm still not sure how many other RANGERS thought we would get breakfast, but like me were reluctant to ask. But I don't think anyone really made the connection. Finally about 0800, I made some casual off-hand remark to the Assistant Patrol Leader (APL). He didn't have a good answer right off but after some discussion with the patrol, we collectively concluded that our next meal would be noon. This was our first taste of going 24 hours without food; also our first time to go 40 hours without sleep----0300 of a morning, thorough dawn the following day and on until 2200 at night. When that first cycle of no food/no sleep/no rest was over, I lay down that night a very tired puppy and reflected upon what we had done.

Then I began to recall some of the discussions that I had earlier with RANGERS who had gone through the course in years gone by. Things they said then had little real meaning until experienced first hand. I took it all very lightly; very remotely; very unrealistically. Now it was real. I was tired, hungry, sleepy, cold, wet, and a little torqued off. The stories of five and twelve day patrols in the mountains and Florida on short rations and hard times began to take on a new dimension in my view of my recently acquired yardstick of 42 hours of what can largely be described and clearly classified as misery. Could anyone in their right mind really enjoy that? Why would anyone do this to themselves??

And I said out loud to myself, "Self! Why are you doing this?"

"Because I love it," I answered myself.

"Who the heck are you talking to Pappy,'" my RANGER Buddy asked rolling over and looking quizzical.

"Just giving myself a pep talk," I answered; "Go to sleep."

Camp Darby was our first exposure to the field environment - to being cold, wet, hungry, tired, sleepy, harassed, frustrated, and discouraged; all at once. This state of physical and emotional stress brings out the worst - or the best - in a man. And of course that is the basic objective of the RANGER course; to bring out the best and the worst side of a man, evaluate those characteristics as they relate to the RANGER concept of operations, and decide if that man deserves the honor of being awarded the RANGER tab. As one particular RI expressed it, "the coveted Black and Gold." Every one that stands on Todd Field on graduation day feels like he is on hallowed ground and that God Himself is going to pin on the tab. The tab is what many people are there for. They become obsessed with getting the tab. They are not driven by the desire to experience, to learn & teach, to share, nor by a spirit of comradeship; nor by duty/ honor/country. The goal is the tab; to punch the ticket. As one RI put it, "some of you people are just going to be tab-wearers.... not RANGERS!" I didn't think he was being fair at the time he said that but looking back now from a different vantage point, I see the wisdom of his remark.

We called him SGT Brunswick and we thought he was a real anus. He was the instructor in Escape and Evasion (E&E) and was one of the few instructors in the entire school that went all out to try to impress us with how great he was. He had been to some school in Brunswick, Maine, where they subject students to some controlled level of physical torture and to a high degree of mental anguish. They simulate the rigors of a classical POW camp that disregards basic human rights. I certainly admire the courage, or whatever, that it must take to admit yourself to treatment such as he described and demonstrated by the use of a TV tape. But he came across like no matter if you go to RANGER School, Airborne, whatever, if you haven't been to Brunswick; if you haven't been to SERE School, "you ain't nothing." So out of contempt and general disrespect we referred to him (privately) as SGT Brunswick. To be perfectly fair to him, however, he was really quite a reasonable person in a one-on-one encounter. But in front of the class he wanted everyone to know that he was the model, the man in charge, the greatest. He was as good as the best in creating, a situation where the worst side of a person came out.

He was a "walker" on an all day patrol, which eventually led to a night raid which we all thought was executed in an outstanding manner but which he berated as a total and miserable failure. Somehow, during the movement to the raid site the RTO (Radio Telephone Operator) lost his CEOI. The CEOI is a mission essential equipment. Lost mission essential equipment normally rates a major minus spot report. The entire platoon spent about an hour in a fruitless search in the darkness for the CEOI with Sgt. Brunswick mercilessly berating us for incompetence. Finally, it was obvious that we would not find the CEOI. This, together with our "miserable failure" in the raid, was sufficient grounds to put the class through a little exercise of remembrance.

The night was uncommonly dark as we started off at a fast pace across sparsely vegetated flat land. A heavy covering of course grass about knee high covered the ground giving a deceptively smooth appearance to the area. But the actual surface was extremely uneven. Each step was a potential sprained ankle, and the tough grass clung to your legs and tried to anchor each step. It was like trying to walk through a field littered with baseballs. It was particularly harrowing for me as I was walking with a "half sprained" ankle and carrying my normal rucksack plus an M-60 Machine Gun. The thought of ruining an ankle at this point in the school and having to drop out was a vivid illusion. It weighted me down like carrying another M-60. I stumbled on for what seemed like an eternity, occasionally falling behind further than SOP allowed, then double timing to close the gap. Double timing made it worse, I know, but I couldn't seem to balance all of the problems. I silently cursed the platoon leader for not considering those of us who were carrying extra weight like machine guns and radios. It seemed that every time I opened a gap, SGT Brunswick was right there to wonder why. "Old man, if you can't keep up, just fall out to one side and we'll send the Girl Scouts to police you up." There is no such thing in RANGER School as an excuse so I didn't bother to give him one, I just gritted my teeth, closed the gap, and hoped I didn't break an ankle.

I had never been so glad to get back into the "jungle." The jungle, at least, meant we would be moving slower. Here I could at least feel the ground with my feet and avoid my greatest fear, spraining an ankle. After about a half hour of "gouging" through the woods, we came out on an old firebreak which had evolved into a heavily rutted jeep trail. I focused on the luminous hands of my watch just as SGT Brunswick announced that we were behind schedule. It was 0200.

"You should be in your patrol base sleeping by now. If you hadn't wasted so much time on that raid; if you hadn't lost that CEOI and wasted time looking for it; if you hadn't wasted so much time gouging through that little old piece of woods back there; you'd be in your patrol base now. You are the only patrol I have ever walked on this problem that was not in their patrol base by now. Don't you people even want to rest?"

We are still standing under our loads, wishing he would shut up. A large crash in the brush signaled that one of our patrol had gone to sleep on his feet and fell on his back like a large turtle - not an uncommon occurrence in RANGER School. Almost everyone experiences going to sleep while standing and some actually discover that they can sleep while walking; or is it walk while sleeping? It's actually sort of funny to see someone go to sleep standing and fall. There you stand with some 100lbs cantilevered off your back some 10-12 inches from your center of gravity. There seems to be a direct circuit between the sleep switch in your brain and the static knee joints. The moment you go to sleep, the knees buckle forward slightly thus increasing the imbalance in overturning moment between the body center of gravity and the rucksack center of gravity. The result is an irreversible, exponentially increasing overturning moment that converts a RANGER into a turtle. Normally you land square on your rucksack with both feet and both hands flailing in the air trying to grasp something. A surprising way to awake. You immediately go into denial.

"Go to sleep did ya RANGER?"

"No, I was not sleeping Sergeant, just lost my balance there for some reason."

We recovered the bewildered RANGER from the brush. It was 0230 and time to move.

"Follow me and keep it tight" snarled SGT Brunswick; and off down the jeep trail he went at a fast jog. Thirty-six cold, tired, sleepy, hungry RANGERS fell in behind him in a RANGER file and stumbled through the darkness after him. How far we went I don't know; nor how long. All of my concentration and energy was going to carrying that M-60 and keeping up - keeping one foot in front of the other. The pace carrying that M-60 was nearly unbearable. Occasionally, he would stop running and walk for 100 yards or so, then start running again. This was not a jog or an airborne shuffle. It was a run.

I kept thinking that a fellow RANGER would offer to carry the M-60 some as I had done for many of them during long moves. Nobody did. That began to work on my mind. Why didn't someone offer to help? Why didn't the stupid PL call for equipment rotation? The more I thought about it the madder I got. I began breathing hard; supercharging my lungs with air in cadence with the run and growing more determined with each step. My mood was suddenly interrupted by the sound of flesh crashing into the ground and the clatter of stamped metal pieces, punctuated hastily by meaningless curse words. It was me, taking and unscheduled rest stop. It was only a small limb in the trail, but perfectly positioned to cause me to go head over heels in the dark and get run over by two RANGER buddies before the remainder of the column could react. Naturally SGT Brunswick was right there.

"What are you doing Old Man, taking a break? If you get tired carrying that M-60 it's perfectly all right to get the assistant gunner to carry it part time." He left me scrambling in the dark to get up.

We are up moving again at a fast walk "Driving On" as they say. That suggestion of getting someone else to carry the M-60 sure sounded good. I began to estimate my condition. I couldn't focus on my watch while moving so I don't know how long we had been moving or how far we had come or had yet to go. I did know that we were moving back to the swamp and that a water obstacle crossing was part of the night's entertainment. We break into a jog and I discover that the fall knocked my rucksack out of adjustment and the hip rest is digging into the small of my back. Pain! Excruciating pain. God! Isn't someone going to take this load off me, I thought. Am I a Wimp? Is it a sign of weakness to ask for help? I still don't know how to answer that question and looking back now

I wish that I had not asked for help. It is clearly obvious now that I did not really need help but at the time, things really felt desperate and in a moment of weakness and maybe bad judgment, I turned in the run and asked the RANGER behind me if he would swap loads with me for awhile. I hated myself immediately and wished I hadn't said that, but no sweat; he couldn't do it but he was very helpful. He passed the buck down the line, trying to find me a relief.

We are back to a fast walk now and I am seething with rage inside. Maybe I'm feeling sorry for myself, I don't know, but I remember thinking, it's a hell of a case when an "Old Man" has to carry the load of an M-60 while a bunch of young studs trot along with M-16's. My response to myself was swift. The school did not discriminate against me because of my age - they let me enter the young man's course - so I should get no slack because of my age. We were running again when a fellow RANGER shuffled up beside me from the rear and offered to swap loads for awhile. He already had his M-16 untied from his LBE so I knew he was sincere in the offer. By now I was determined to carry the damned thing but at the same time I didn't want to reject his offer, so I asked him to just take the M-60 for a few minutes so I could have both hands free to adjust my rucksack and end the pain it was causing me. We jogged on as I made some adjustments to the shoulder straps. God! What sweet relief! I took the M-60 back just as we slowed to a fast walk.

THE COURSE

Not counting processing in, processing out, graduation day, and short breaks between the phases, RANGER School can be described in three phases totaling 54[3] days of rigorous training designed to physically and mentally harden the student. These phases are comprised of the Benning Phase (19 days), the Mountain Phase (18 days), and the Florida Phase (17 days.)

The Benning Phase can be subdivided into two phases of 9 days at the Harmony Church area and 10 days at Camp Darby, Fort Benning. After a few days at Harmony Church, SGT Rock called me aside for counseling. I took a liking to Rock from the beginning, and as I told him on graduation day, he was a "Classic NCO." Anyway, he questioned me about how I was getting along against the young "studs" as he called us.

"No sweat" I replied. "I am enjoying it."

He encouraged me to "drive on Old Man. If you can make it through the first nine days, you've got it licked."

Not many words were exchanged between us but I got the feeling that he had some special confidence in me and I felt a strange obligation to not disappoint him.

"Sgt. Rock, if I don't break something or get sick I will be on Todd Field for graduation."

The secret of the nine-day threshold is fairly simple to explain when you look back on the whole experience. The first nine days are dominated by the Morgan Team - an absolutely sinister group whose sole purpose in life seems to be to make you quit RANGER School. They are the people who greet you very early each morning, lead you in PT, accompany you on the RANGER Runs, harass you through the dreaded "worm pit," and reward you on your return from Camp Darby with a ticket to the Victory Pond Confidence Course.

Recognizing what the Morgan Team is for, I think, is a great aid in surviving the nine days with them. They are your standard OCS TAC multiplied by a factor of somewhere between 10 and 50. An OCS TAC harasses you to find out where you are weak. Then he counsels you to try to help you overcome that weakness. The Morgan Team does not

---

[3] Note: Class 6-81 was the last class before a Desert phase was inserted which caused the course to increase to 64 days. Later, the Desert phase was dropped but the course did not revert back to 54 days.

counsel - they cancel. If you can't take the heat, you do the "duffel bag drag" on back to where you came from and they could care less. A "quitter" is never referenced; never talked about. Nobody says good-bye, it's been great knowing you, sorry you couldn't make it or NOTHING. A quitter just disappears. Like a large ax falling on your hand; clunk! clean and swift, you're gone.

The Morgan Team is made up of a variety of personalities. Some you like immediately; some you despise immediately; and some you change your mind about as time goes on. SGT Ponder was one of those that I changed my mind about. He probably didn't weigh 120 pounds soaking wet and half of that, it seemed was mouth. He reminded me of a little Bantam rooster as he strutted around the demonstration circle in the hand-to-hand combat pit. He was the ideal bad guy for a good guy/bad guy psycho team.

"Wimps! That's what you are. Give me three laps around the pit and the last one through is in deep trouble."

His favorite punishment was to put us in the front leaning -rest position for push-ups. 1-2-3-4-1-2-3-4-1-1-1; and he would leave us down in the one position for I don't know how long, but well beyond the onset of pain. Your shoulders would begin to burn. And you were never in the correct position; too low, too high, back not straight - - - "Wimps! 2-3-4. His favorite reason (as if he really needed one) for punishment was "I can't hear you RANGERS!" After three days in RANGER School almost everyone has some degradation of the voice; many have laryngitis so bad they can hardly speak much less yell. But everything you do must be done in cadence, in unison, and at the top of your lungs.

One morning as I am dying in the one count position it occurred to me that we could sound louder simply if everyone would turn their voice towards the center of the ring rather than yelling at the ground or up or out towards the tree line. The next time we went to the arena, we (the class) tried it. We were willing to try anything! I don't know if it worked or if the RI was just tired of the game of punishment. I later came to like SGT Ponder, but for the time I would have liked to have his scrawny neck in my hands. I'm sure I was not alone in that desire and of course that is the kind of reaction that the school is trying to illicit from the students. One of the secrets to graduation is to recognize that they are playing games with your mind and emotions. To win the game you swallow your pride; you hide your contempt; you absorb the harassment like a sponge. Your reward is that you always get the last word with an RI: "Yes, Sergeant!" SGT Ponder did his part well.

During the summer of 1997 while attending the annual Infantry Conference at Ft Benning, I had one of those once in a lifetime encounters with two of my RI's from 16 years earlier in my life. Ponder had advanced to the position of CSM for the JRTC Ft Polk and SSGT England, to be mentioned later, had advanced to the position of CSM of the 82ND Airborne Division. My advancement to Major General was probably far more of a shock to them than their advancements to CSM was to me. I felt a certain sense of pride in having known them as young NCOs and was elated that they had both done so well. CSM England presented me with one of his CSM coins, saying "You did good sir; better than any other student that I have taught so far. We instructors usually don't survive long enough to see a student become a General." A very pleasant encounter I thought after so many years.

Within a few months, as if that were not enough coincidences for a lifetime, I met another fellow RANGER. I was in an auditorium in the Headquarters of the Marine Corps Combat Developments Command, Quantico, Virginia for a conference. After an hour or so of presentations, the order was given to take a 15 minute break. As the attendees were filing out, much like departing a theatre, an officer in Canadian battle dress was passing along the aisle as I melded into the line from my row of seats. He had an American RANGER Tab on his sleeve so I inquired as to when he had gone to the course. He looked at me in surprise, did a slight step backwards as if in disbelief, and blurted out "RANGER Childers; I went with you!!" Then I looked at his nametag and recognized a name that was familiar: McAdams. He was probably a 22 year old lieutenant when we went to school and now he was approaching 40. I would never have recognized him cold but as I talked to him, the familiarity returned. I guess I pretty much look the same. He returned after the lunch break to tell me that he had related the "It's a small world story" to his wife and her response to him was "How could you possibly remember someone from RANGER School 16 years ago when you can't remember what you did yesterday?"

"Well," he told her, "there are some things you just don't ever forget; especially in RANGER School."

The other extreme of Morgan personalities is well represented by SGT Swakhammer. I don't know which came first, the name or the man, but the two were a perfect match. Swakhammer was just about exactly two of SGT Ponder and I don't think he had any flab on him. He had the kind of face you would expect to see on a recruiting poster for Mercenary Inc. - handsome but mean as a proverbial junk-yard dog. I think his eyes were green but whatever the color, they looked straight through you like two cold laser beams. My first impression of him was, "I want him on my side in a brawl" the kind of a guy that you would be reluctant to hit from behind with a ball bat. I never saw him smile and he didn't harass; he just spoke and you KNEW to do whatever it was he said. You did NOT want to be the one to find out that Swakhammer was not his real name, but one awarded to him for doing well whatever one would do to earn such a name. Swakhammer was the MC of our first session in hand-to-hand combat. We were paired off with a buddy for this event, and basically we beat the hay out of each other for two hours at a time. As I recall, the schedule for the first nine days at Harmony Church alternated between PT followed by hand-to-hand, and a run followed by the Worm Pit.

So every other day we engaged each other in the art of hand-to-hand combat for two hours at a crack expect for the last period which was to be the King Of The Pit madness.

Appendix B is the training schedule that Class 6-81 followed, as reconstructed from my Benning Phase notes. There is no "lights out" time given in the schedule because one could never tell if or when that event would occur.

DIARY

From the beginning, I tried to keep a rough diary but as time passed, it became more and more difficult, and finally impossible to do so. My notes on the Harmony Church portion of the Benning Phase are accurate because much of it was a classroom/barracks environment and thus conducive to diary keeping during the day because we were constantly taking notes on training, missions, and other things all day long anyway. As we moved to Camp Darby, most of the day time routine was filled with patrolling exercises and note taking became very sketchy except for the basic schedule. I figured that if I could record the schedule accurately, I could use that as a key to reconstructing events. By the end of the Benning Phase, I had filled one pocket notebook with a combination of class notes and diary type notes.

Upon moving into the Mountain Phase, I decided to maintain class notes and diary type notes in separate books. There were several reasons for this but primarily because the "pre-combat" inspections precluded taking that type of information on the patrol; just like in the movies, no letters from home, no diaries. Only your name, rank, SSAN, and date of birth forward of the friendly lines. Besides, it was easy for me to imagine what an RI would do if he confiscated such data; particularly if unsavory mention was made of him or one of his RI contemporaries. And I'll admit that I did make some unsavory remarks about people and events at the time. But as the cliché goes, 'time heals all 'and one finds more complimentary and less vindictive ways of describing events in retrospect.

For me to make a condemnation of the RANGER School would be to demean the very honor they bestowed upon me. And certainly, no one in the school really deserves serious criticism. After all, they are paid to do a particular job and we students all volunteered to be their subjects and take whatever they dished out in stride. This does not mean that I am covering up or misrepresenting the facts; but that all things must be placed in their proper perspective.

One must hearken back to the definition and purpose of the RANGER course - to develop mentally and physically hardened leadership. The only way to do this short of throwing us into a battle line in Ethiopia is to create artificial combat stress through cold and hunger, lack of sleep and rest, mental and emotional stress through the constant threat of failure, and being bone tired from what appears, at the time, to be totally pointless or even dangerous harassment.

"War is the realm of physical exertion and suffering. These will destroy us unless we can make ourselves indifferent to them and for this, birth or training, must provide us with a certain strength of body and soul."
Clausewitz

In retrospect I can accurately report that we did a lot of things that were, in fact, dangerous! But war by definition is dangerous and war, like a sport, must be practiced to develop a winning team. As General Patton stated, "Practice those things in peacetime that you intend to do in war." No one should complain about the dangers of RANGER School. All students are volunteers and they should realize that some events in the program are dangerous - but well supervised.

RI's, though they appear to be cold, callous, and uncaring, are constantly alert for safety infractions. Headcount during patrols are so often that the students sometimes reach the point where they consider it a source of harassment. A break in contact on patrol is punishable by a major minus spot report for those involved. There have been a few deaths in RANGER school. The most recent and most highly publicized was the accidental death of 4 RANGER Students in 1995 during the Florida Phase. A series of events, lack of ability to predict water conditions, and some delays in equipment availability contributed to eventual hypothermia related death. (**Appendix C** gives an account of this incident.)

The second volume of my diary would have been the most important because it detailed the Mountain Phase much more clearly than I can recall it without notes. So it would have been with the Florida Phase, which was to have been in the same notebook. That notebook lies somewhere in the Yellow River swamp- lost during the slimmest river crossing in RANGER History, or so it seemed at the time.

SAFETY

As a student in RANGER School, you may often doubt the sanity of the RI's as well as the safety consciousness of the RANGER Department. But the illusion that all RI's were former henchmen of Adolph Hitler and that your personal health and safety is entirely in the hands of the BIG RANGER IN THE SKY is just that - an illusion. Students are subtlety monitored continuously by RI's, your TAC Officer and NCO, and the medics. Even more subtle, in a surreptitious manner, is the department instituted buddy system. Many students perhaps never realize the real purpose and value for the buddy system.

Most students find that the buddy system is too inconvenient to adequately describe in words. Each student is "issued" a buddy about the second day of the course. The instructions for using your buddy are very simple -"don't do nothing without your RANGER buddy." Now that is an all-encompassing requirement!

"If I catch you without your RANGER buddy, I'm gonna tie you together with a RANGER assist cord (dummy cord) until you are trained," threatened SGT Rock.

It was not an idle threat. You go to chow with your RANGER Buddy (RB); you clean your rifle, you study, you, go on work detail, you wash your clothes, and you do corrective exercise (variously known as concentrated horizontal hip dips or push ups) with your buddy. And yes, you "go to the bathroom" with your RB. This is a no win situation; if you don't go with him you get accused of not liking him and if you do go you get accused of maybe liking him too much. I don't know how to describe it except to say that it is certainly a new experience.

So what else can you do - you both dig the cat hole and discuss the adequacy of its dimensions and position relative to thorns, sticks, and possible habitat for lurking reptiles. That agreed to, one then assumes the duty of local security while the other fills the hole then covers and camouflages the area. The possibility of some future RANGER digging a fighting position in the same location is usually broached with some humor. More often than not though the call of nature will come while you are in a patrol base. In this case a patrol slit trench must be dug within the perimeter and you can go without your RB standing by your side. Privacy is one of the things you give up in RANGER School. Most people find that there is such a little bit of food and a correspondingly small amount of solid waste generated that you can delay this duty on a three-day patrol and enjoy the sanctuary of the three-holer or the ceramic throne back in base camp.

As you might surmise by now, the buddy system is extremely inefficient from a manpower utilization viewpoint. It always takes a minimum of two people to do a one man job. It tests your level of frustration and causes you to become extremely tolerant of others under difficult conditions. You learn to monitor your buddy's status as well as that of other RANGERS. I had an almost continual problem with my feet from the Mountain Phase through Florida, as did my RANGER buddy. Sometimes it is almost impossible to take your assigned RB with you so you got to know other RANGERS with similar problems and you would "swap" RB's to visit the medic for a foot check in the middle of the night. I was never criticized by an RI for having the "wrong" RB - so long as I knew where my real one was.

My first impression of the buddy system was "this is a humorous form of making things difficult." That impression quickly changed to one of "this is a pain in the posterior." Then I came to the conclusion that it was a very serious safety measure for the benefit of the student. Buddies get each other through RANGER School. You keep watch on each other's equipment, uniform and appearance; you share food and water; you keep each other awake on ambush; you "cover" for each other; you develop mutual respect and confidence in your assigned buddy and the natural evolution is that you do these things not just for your own buddy but for the rest of your squad and then for your whole platoon. By the end of the course you no longer resent someone kicking you in the rib cage at 0300 hours to keep you awake on the ambush site. You know it's one of 33 RANGER buddies getting to you before an RI does. A RANGER buddy only kicks you in the ribs; the RI gives you a major minus spot report, and that's a kick in the head.

Perhaps one of the greatest hazards in RANGER School is a malady referred to a "Zombieing Out." Everyone knows what a zombie is - that's a being arisen from the dead and condemned to wander pale and ashen with out stretched arms and sightless eyes; driven by some compelling force from Point A to Point B. That also is a RANGER at the end of the Florida Phase: pale and ashen (beneath the camouflage paint) from being overworked and underfed; arms outstretched to fend off the brush as he gouges through the undergrowth; sightless eyes because when the moon goes down on the swamps of Florida "you don't see nothing;" and the compelling force that drives him is the fear of being recycled.

The first signs of zombieing out is when you begin to go to sleep while standing. Some people fall when they go to sleep while others rock gently to and fro. It's a frightening experience to fall because you almost invariably fall on your back, pulled down by your rucksack. To say the least, it is a rude awakening and baffling because you can't immediately ascertain how you got from where you were to where you are. Ever see a cat fall to sleep and slide off of whatever it is sleeping on (like a TV or night stand)? They immediately jump up and scan around to see who is looking at them. So it is with RANGERs; thrashing and groping and trying to recover dignity or deny the event. "Who, me? No SGT, I didn't go to sleep; I'm trying to adjust my rucksack." "Well, when you get it adjusted just go to the nearest tree and elevate your feet for one-zero."

Elevate your feet is RANGER Instructorese for doing pushups with your feet up on a tree. With a -rucksack that is a real trick. Every time you go down the pack slips forward and bangs you in the back of the head, and by the end of 10 repetitions, the Ruck has lodged itself squarely on your head and is breaking your neck. If you happen to be near a stream you don't have to put your feet on a tree. They let you put your feet on the bank and do pushups in the stream, weapon and all. The logic of it all escaped me. If you did pushups on dry land you always had to position your M-16 on the back of your hands so you didn't get it dirty. If you did pushups in the water, the M-16 still had to be placed on the back of your hands. By the end of our penance, your hands are elbow deep in the rotten creek bottom and your M-16, securely tied to your body by the dummy cord and likely laying in the mud on the bottom, is literally pumped full of slime. Actually, that was not a common occurrence in my platoon. We all learned well in three lessons.

Once I went to sleep standing up while receiving the OPORD from an RI. For one reason or another "they" had decided that I should be the company commander for our first company level operation. Up until this point we had functioned only to the platoon level of organization. I was ordered to meet Sgt. Parker at a time and place along with my First Sergeant/Executive Officer who also functioned as my RANGER buddy. I had one foot propped up on his jeep bumper, using the hood as a desk. It was about 10 o'clock in the morning and the sun reflecting off the hood felt so good. I don't remember how long it had been since I had slept but I know it was not the preceding night nor the day before that because I had been in a squad leader position then and squad leaders don't get much sleep. I was looking forward to this tour as company commander because I thought it would be the easiest command tour I would have. Anyway, I was busily taking notes as the RI rapidly "laid the FRAG Order on me." As I wrote I began making an estimate of the situation and to formulate fragments of a plan off in one corner of my mind. The mind is a wonderful thing. It can make a moment last for hours or it can play an entire battle scene in a matter of seconds and not miss a single detail. The plan in the corner of my mind must have expanded into the execution phase because suddenly I was a casualty, lying on the ground with a medic tearing at my shirt sleeve to get at the wound. But I wasn't on the ground; I was still standing by the jeep; and it wasn't a medic tearing at my sleeve - it was the RI jabbing my arm.

"You haven't gone to sleep on me have you RANGER Childers? You better wake up Old Man. Read me back what you have written down so far." Sgt. Parker was trying to force back a grin of amusement as he agitated me back to full consciousness. I glanced at the page quickly. Everything beyond paragraph 2 was pure gibberish.

"I guess I drifted off in paragraph 3, Sergeant," I admitted.

That's one time I would have been happy to do pushups in a river and there we stood not 10 steps from a cool clear running stream. I guess he must have felt sorry for me. I'm sure I looked more like a zombie than anyone else. About 42 hours later I would be back in the cantonment area standing before a bathroom mirror washing the green and black camo-paint from my face - dog tired but elated. It was over. We had done our last patrol. As the paint dissolved, the drawn face appeared. There was no fat to fill the skin and places that were once smooth were now lined by loose skin. I could see virtually every rib in my torso; the blood vessels along the front of my biceps stood out plainly; something I had wanted as a young man because I thought it was a sign of strength. The first real look I had taken at myself in 8 weeks.

"You OK Old Man?" It was SGT Rock with his head hooked around the entrance to the lavatory room.

"Yes, SGT Rock, I'm fine - just tired."

"Don't crap out on me now God Damit! I got money riding on your old funky hide" he said hopefully. "You know, they didn't think you would make it; ya fooled em old man, but not me. I knew you was gonna make it."

"Thanks Sgt. Rock," I said, " That makes it all worth it."

"Aw B@#$)~!$## old man; Drive on RANGER!" And he was gone; screaming obscenities at other RANGER Students.

One form of zombieism manifested itself in hallucinating, and in this form one might go wandering off into the swamp in search of whatever zombies search for, never to be seen again. This is a job for RANGER buddy - to grab you by the stacking swivel and jerk you back to reality. It is said that some people actually put quarters into holes in trees thinking it is a soft drink machine. I don't know if I believe that or not, but I don't disbelieve it. I conjured up a giant stop sign one night. There it was as plain as the Harold's in Reno sign - STOP; the size of a Volkswagen; standing just beyond reach and pulsing slowly from a soft glow to brilliance. Just about that time the patrol came to a halt and the signal was passed to "Take a knee." I took a knee then I took a canteen and poured water in my patrol cap and put it back on my head. If done properly with the right fit of the cap, the water will trickle out slowly down over your sagging eyelids and down the back of your neck in cold rivulets.

"How's it going Pappy?" came a whispered voice to my rear.

"I think I I'm going zombie" I said, "I just saw a stop sign back there."

"Yeah, me too. Which side of the path was yours on?" Once again the buddy system proves its close ties. You even go "nutso" together.

People go to RANGER School for a variety of reasons. One of my reasons was to learn techniques that I could use in training. I was particularly interested in control techniques and so I was alert for how the RI's were able to follow lost RANGERS all over the swamps of Florida and yet not be lost themselves. Also, what was the contingency for getting aid to injured RANGERS. As I said earlier, on the surface it appears that our fate was entirely in the hands of the Big RANGER in the Sky. To the casual observer it would appear that a RANGER patrol was all alone but several incidents make me believe that there is someone only a few minutes away much of the time.

These incidents occurred during the Florida Phase which, for the Class 6-81 cycle, was by far the phase most susceptible to something going wrong. It started with a waterborne movement down an inland waterway, i.e., a float trip in a rubber boat down the Yellow River. Done by the RANGER method, a rubber boat will glide along with surprising efficiency. After about a six click move down river, we landed and began a cross country move, after dark, of course. Because of less than flawless river navigation by our navigator, who incidentally went to sleep and lost his place on the river chart, we apparently put ashore in the wrong place. After gouging through some pretty bad stuff for an hour or so, it finally got to be even too much for our RI. You see, in Florida, if you choose the wrong azimuth for a cross country move, or if you start in the wrong place, you may have to cross the same river 5 times in a kilometer.

The RI didn't know exactly where we were but he knew we weren't' where he wanted us to be so he more or less took charge of the move, and we gouged along behind his crooked trail for another hour. I would never accuse an RI of being lost, but ours that night was certainly frustrated. Now it was not time for Clark Kent to slip into the phone booth; it was time for the RI to call a halt and wander off out of earshot to make a radio call for a spotting round. What he didn't know was that our RANGER file had just made a follow your own tracks move and when he moved out from the head of the file to get some radio privacy, he walked up to within earshot of me on the tail of the file. I could hear a two-way conversation going by PRC 88 but could not make out precisely what was said. Presently in the distance, I heard the faint thud of probably an artillery simulator going off. There was a brief flurry of map and compass work with a red filtered flashlight, some more PRC 88 traffic, and then he moved off the way he had come, apparently back to the head of our file because within a few minutes we were moving again.

After about 15 minutes of hard gouging toward the sound of the simulator, we "took a knee" for five minutes. Taking a knee in a swamp is a real joke. Within a minute of our halt, a star cluster went skyward a few hundred meters ahead. Another locator aid I suspect; no one ever explained or commented on two star clusters in the middle of nowhere. When we started moving again I filed past both RI's standing to the side so apparently they were happy with our current location and had turned the patrol back to the RANGERS. Ummm. VELLY INTERESTING!

On another boating occasion, we had loaded our gear in the LRB (Little Rubber Boats) and were preparing to begin a 5-6 km move down river when water began to fill the boat. We were only ten feet from shore when someone said, "Hey, I think the boat's leaking!" It didn't have to be discussed. We all looked down almost simultaneously, it seemed, to see the water rising around the rucksacks.

"Paddle to the rear!" And we all stroked furiously, unbelievably in almost perfect cadence, and we got it beached.

"Someone doesn't want to go on this trip, right! So he poked a hole in my boat" accused the RI. He spoke into his PRC-88 as he waded out onto the sandy bank and before we could get our rucksacks untied, a flat bottom johnboat powered by a large Mercury outboard appeared in the cove towing a replacement LRB. Again, just out of sight and sound additional support people were waiting to provide emergency assistance. The new boat was dropped and the leaky one was taken in tow and off he went, probably to post himself somewhere along our night's route.

It was our last daylight patrol of the Florida Phase. We slipped out of the patrol base at about 1000 hours and movement was smooth as silk as we glided almost silently through scattered palmetto. In RANGER School a silent patrol is not your most frequently occurring phenomenon, so I knew right away that something had to go wrong soon. I was the platoon Sergeant for this problem, which was another surprise for me. I had led 5 patrols already and carried a very enviable total of "5 and O" on all of them. In RANGER jargonese, this is called being "Tabbed Out". What's more, people were saying that I would be the officer distinguished honor grad even if I broke a leg because all of the other contenders had "fallen out of the finals," so to speak, back during the Mountain Phase - a lifetime ago. I wasn't too sure what a Distinguished Honor Graduate was nor did I have the time nor energy to give it much thought. But when my name was called out this morning to get a leadership role in the chain of command, you could have bought me for a plug of tobacco. I moved my rucksack to the center of the patrol base, gave up the M-60 I was manning and retrieved my M-16. I turned to doing my PLT SGT things; readjusting the perimeter, getting a detailed status of water, food, ammo, and personnel; ensuring that a reconnaissance beyond the perimeter was done and the other two dozen things that a PLT SGT does while the PLT LDR worries with the next mission.

The next mission - the last one - promised to be a long arduous one. A move across country to raid and free "American POWs" followed by a river crossing, then on to a link up with the other platoons to form a company sized raid across the Santa Rosa Sound in the Gulf of Mexico. The status sheet showed less than one C--RAT per man and we hadn't eaten since late afternoon the day before. I personally had one tin of tuna, one tin of crackers and candy, two packs of cocoa powder and four packs (four teaspoons) of sugar. A quiet but efficient trade fair started around the perimeter.

"Who wants to trade a tin of jam for cheddar cheese?"
"Two John Wayne bars for applesauce."
"What are you, nuts?"

I mused at the things people would trade for. Sometimes a trade would be made just to take part in the action, and the prize would be quickly re-traded for something else. Finally, and most important, a water re-supply party was organized. A map study indicated that the nearest potential water was 800 meters away. We had long since learned that it was better to leave a patrol base with a good water supply rather than depend on re-supply enroute. We sometimes were able to supplement our supply enroute by removing the canteen lids and allow them to fill up while wading a stream.

Everything was going really smooth and I needed that after experiencing my darkest day of the whole school the very day before. The RI's were apparently happy with what they saw. No hassle, no raving and ranting. The senior RI was a fairly young E-8 Henderson; a super RI, as were his two assistants. I chatted casually with them as I moved about my duties in the patrol base. It was the first time I had met this crew and they were obviously curious or fascinated or enthralled or flabbergasted or whatever by my being in the program. A National Guardsman!!?? A Major #*@&*##!? 42 YEARS OLD! I think they simplified the descriptive adjectives - you've got to be plain crazy! "Has your mother ever admitted that she dropped you on your head?"

By the time the watering party returned the frag order had been briefed by the P.L. The watering party was briefed in position and the signal was given to move out. The perimeter rose by squad, almost like a ballet, and moved to the pass-out point behind the compass man. I counted every man out, took a last look for patrol base sterility, and passed up the headcount. Within minutes the count came back. Perfect! RANGER School cannot be like this. Any moment now the Big RANGER in the Sky is gonna urinate on us or something. Oh, Holy Crap! That quarter ton that the recon party reported is not the RI's vehicle; it's an ambush party vehicle. I grabbed the handset of the 77 to advise the P.L. and half way through the call sign I heard the shrill whistle of the first artillery simulator. The point had just run out of smooth sailing.

The ambush was sprung just as the point encountered the worst tanglefoot of the entire 8 weeks training. Contact was broken in about 5 minutes of often-practiced fire and maneuver with no assessed casualties. The patrol continued with the real problem - the terrain. We were in what appeared to be a "clear cut" area complicated by thick undergrowth that had sprung up in the absence of a canopy that would normally control such undergrowth by restricting sunlight.

Adding to this problem was 6 or 8 inches of gummy muck that clung to the boots making each foot weigh 20 pounds. Clear cutting is where every tree over about 6 inches in diameter is felled. The trunks are removed and the tops are left where they fall. Recall the pictures of the tree blow down around the Mount Saint Helen's eruption; add to that undergrowth or grass, cane, thorn brush, and random second growth trees and you have what we had to travel through for about a kilometer. About every other step was up and over a rotten limb obstacle from knee to crotch high. I had no way of knowing the temperature, but I am sure it must have been the hottest day of the course. With little foliage to block the sun and the effort that it took to climb the dead fall with weighted boots, we were completely beat. We came to a large open area that had obviously been the log-marshaling yard. We just stumbled across it without precaution. The RI's were just shaking their heads and making notes but they didn't rake us over the coals. We were glad to reach the sanctuary of the standard jungle once again. I drank two quarts of water during the move, which for me was more than a click, because I doubled the formation several times supervising the move, correcting headcount, and making sure that heavy loads were redistributed. In this kind of terrain and weather we swapped off M-60's and PRC 77's every 400-500 meters.

The remainder of the move to the Objective Rally Point (ORP) was uneventful drudgery. We made the ORP about 1400 hours; a large mud flat on the bank of a river, shaded nicely by large oak and cypress very tastefully done up in Spanish moss - and occupied by the biggest baddest water moccasin in the state of Florida. He had absolutely no respect for RANGERS! Maybe he had heard that RANGERS eat snakes. I was born and raised in the swamps of southern Arkansas and thought I had seen some big Moccasins in the Ouachita and Saline River bottoms - wrong. This sucker was full 5 feet long and unlike the dark brown/black cottonmouths I knew as a boy, this monster was multicolored. By the time I had moved into the site, the RI had already captured him (or it). Held out at arms length, the tail almost touched the ground. Here again, I saw an instance to verify my belief that there is always someone lurking just minutes away. The RI put the snake into a clear plastic bag and stood by the river as we went through the ORP security routine. Before I even had the perimeter adjusted, I heard the sound of a powerboat coming down river. It was a Boston Whaler that our RI called in with his 88 to pick up the snake. They took the snake and roared off down river; and we - kept our eyes open for relatives. I didn't have any trouble with people wanting to sleep in that ORP.

During the Florida and Mountain Phases, dawn would always find us either in a patrol base or trying to find one - more often than not, the latter. Try as we might, we could not make a patrol base by 0200 and rest till dawn as the RI's proclaimed was done by "every class but this one. They had me believing that for awhile, until I began to analyze and question the kinds of circumstances that kept us walking all night. I am convinced that we were not that different than other classes, that nobody could make the patrol base and rest unless the RI wanted you to. Oh they were good - at making us think it was our own ineptness that prevented us from getting rest, but in fact, lack of rest is part of the program and the RI's have a number of subtle methods to generate lost time. Long and frequent lectures in the middle of the night was the most common method. Causing the patrol to take a difficult route or delaying the arrival of the target on an ambush mission were other commonly used tricks. Equipment inventory sometimes hourly, depending on what the activity was. And, of course being in charge, they could "frag" you out of a patrol base into a new one or modify your route outright so that the task always matched the available time. The magic time was 0700 - time to get a new set of RI's or "walkers." Sometimes they might be a little late but always before 0800. When the new crew arrived we were expected to be ready to receive the new mission, which meant everyone was shaved, fed, and freshly camouflaged. All equipment had to be cleaned, inventoried, and laid out for inspection and reissue by the new chain of command; and of course the patrol base itself had to be well organized and secure.

With rare exception, all of the RI's were outstanding instructors. Their personality range covered the spectrum from comical to downright grouchy. The first thing they always did was to introduce themselves and establish their tone. They may as well have clawed the trees like a bear marking territory or pawed the ground. But they all had some sort of little routine that said "There is a new guy in charge of your destiny now and there is only three things you need to know; I am the boss, what will make me happy, and just do it."

"RANGERS, I'm SGT no-nonsense and this is my assistant, SGT Regulation. We will be your instructors for the next 24 hours and by God we are going to do our level best to either kill or cripple you, and by God if we don't do that I'll guarantee-DAMN-tee-you that you'll quit before dawn!"

A slow survey of the class for reaction would follow then a classic, practiced expulsion of tobacco juice; Phatooey! A full six-footer. A shift of the tobacco from one side of the jaw to the other.

"Any questions?"
"NO SERGEANT!!"
"All right RANGERS, grab yourself a piece of real estate, we're gonna have ourselves a safety brief - AND BY GOD NOBODY BETTER GO TO SLEEP".

And a long discourse would follow on why we should not be sleepy, how unworthy we were of his time, etc., etc. The safety brief was always the same. How many times we heard it, I cannot begin to guess. RANGER School is accepted as potentially dangerous and safety is not taken lightly by the Department. There were times when I thought the SGT Hard Cores were taking the rules into their own hands, but in hindsight there were probably factors which I was unaware of, which, if I had known about, would have given me a different impression - I keep telling myself that, and I can conjure up factors for every incident but one.

The Mountain instructors came in with blood in one eye and you-know what in the other one. Our patrol had made a less than favorable impression on the chief instructor the day before and our 15th day of the Mountain Phase found us squarely behind the proverbial eight ball as far as our new RI's were concerned. I had been determined that our patrol would not leave another bad impression so from "stand-to" until the relief RI's came on, I was overstepping the bounds of my authority pushing and prodding everybody. I was thoroughly beat but I could see things that were wrong all around me and I attacked the problems with all the energy that I could call on. I encouraged, cajoled, cursed - whatever it took; and it takes different things for different people; but mostly, I DID. And for most people, even beat people, DOING and SAYING "follow me" through action is enough.

"Calm down, Gramps," advised my RANGER buddy.

"Calm down hell, we're too beat to take another day like yesterday. We've got to get off on the right foot today!" Looking back, it's a wonder some young stud didn't crack my bald skull because I wasn't even in the chain of command in that patrol. But I took charge for about 2 hours.

By the time the new RI's arrived we were standing tall! Every piece of equipment was clean as a whistle and neatly laid out on ponchos not even a stray pine needle was on the poncho. We were formed in perfect formation, freshly shaved, camouflaged to regulation, and looking lively. We had eaten, policed the patrol base, packed our rucksacks - we were ready! A rousing, RANGER School "GOOD MORNING, SERGEANT" that literally shook pinecones out of the trees did not visibly impress them. It was a coincidence, I know, but a cluster of 3 pine cones did fall in perfect unison with our greeting - right past the bill of the assistant RI's patrol cap and landed square between his feet. He stood there for a moment staring at it in disbelief. His gaze moved slowly up to engage us. Hands on hips, his eyes moved left then right down our front rank, then he tried to turn before the smile broke. He took a few steps away shaking his head slowly as he aimlessly kicked at pinecones. Meanwhile, the chief RI unaware of the humor to his rear is wanting to know,

"What the ---- do you think this is? This is supposed to be a patrol base in a combat zone and here you stand like you're on a parade ground." He raved on as we all went into the "pass thru" mode (in one ear and out the other). This is not an indictment or criticism of the School, rather, a warning that many incidents in RANGER School are no-win situations by definition. Normally the changeover of RI's in the morning was done in an "admin" atmosphere. Perhaps we went one step too far. I thought it was a beautiful touch of inconsistency, which the RI's were perplexed to reconcile. They had obviously been prepared by the outgoing RI's to expect to walk in and find a bunch of beat, disorganized gypsies; "wimps" and quitters. What they found was a platoon of standing tall driving-on RANGERS.

My RANGER buddy was the lucky guy of the day; he became platoon leader for the planning phase and I became a squad leader. After an orderly inventory and redistribution of equipment, we made the shortest move in our experience into a new patrol base - only a couple hundred yards.

Well, maybe the RI's didn't have blood in one eye after all. Encouraged by this the platoon "turned too", everyone doing his job and by 1000 all the priorities of work had been accomplished, and we were ready for priority 5 - rest. The patrol leader had organized his team to write the patrol order well. From 1000 until 1230 there were only three activities going on in the patrol base: writing inputs to the order, security, and organized sleep. This was a first for our platoon actually getting sleep in a daytime patrol base.

At 1300 hours, RANGER Campana gave what I thought was the best field order that I had heard although the RI's would later tell him otherwise and give him a "No Go" for it. The mission looked like a piece of cake: a helo insertion followed by an 8-click move to an ambush site with a hit time of 2100 hours. As soon as the patrol order had been given a new chain of command was named.

By 1430 the transition of the mission to the new chain of command was complete. We "rucked up" for the move, which by map recon promised to be an easy move as mountain movement goes. I felt real good about it all; the patrol base occupation, the patrol order, the transition of chain of command, everything. The RI's had hardly said a word all day but for the first arrival speech. The whole platoon was exchanging whispered expectations about a neat clean ambush; we were in high spirits looking forward to arrival in a patrol base maybe by midnight. As a word of explanation, our exchanges were whispered because when "in the bush," normal conversations are a lost art. Everything is hand and arm signals and whispering.

The first part of the move was to be by helicopter, which for us was provided by the US Marine Corps flying the CH-46. Air movement was very predictable. One could always count on three things: ambush in the Pickup Zone (PZ); ambush in the Landing Zone (LZ); and the pilot getting lost in between. As was usual in an air movement, all three platoons would be moved together so that we would all link up at a given LZ and be "chalked out" by the aircraft rather than by squad or even platoon. The first platoon to reach the PZ was supposed to secure it. Somehow this never did work because we always got "fired up" by aggressors. I had learned the difference between secure and unsecured PZ's/LZ's in Vietnam 13 years before and I knew we weren't doing it like I would do it for real. We would have all been dead every time. There is nothing that we could do in our circumstance; PZ's and LZ's were simply a no-win situation. Another given in air movement with those Marines was that if you thought you could be a ground controller in a LZ and "bring the ship in" - wrong! You better get the heck out of the way unless you could hold a CH-46 on your head. They could be depended upon to arrive as soon as they could find the LZ and make a controlled crash landing square in the middle. Perhaps their technique is a result of landing on heaving decks of ships at sea.

Anyway, you better get your scrawny bones into a seat quick because he won't sit there very long before he's pulling pitch out of the PZ to make room for the next one. They were quite impressive in getting 4 or 5 ships in and out of a one-ship zone in minutes.

I was on the last ship to be inserted and as expected, the lead squads in were engaged in a terrific firefight. Our pilot unzipped his jacket to expose the big S on his chest and flew straight into the fracas. The ramp was down by the time he dropped the front wheels to the grass and we went charging out screaming and yelling, loading our weapons, and looking for the nearest cover. We dropped into a creek bed to G-2 the situation. Most of the action was across the clearing some 300 yards away. We linked up with the rest of our patrol, and began to work our way around the area to pick up our route or fight, whichever came first. What we fought was not the enemy but a woods fire. We had moved perhaps 500 yards around the clearing when we saw that the aggressors had caused a small forest fire with their pyrotechnics. We dropped our rucksacks, stacked arms, and fought the fire for about 40 minutes before bringing it under control. By the time we recovered our gear and our breath a full hour of unplanned time came right off the top of our schedule. In addition, we consumed enough water that it was obvious that a stop to re-supply at the first suitable creek would be necessary.

We moved about 4 clicks before coming to a fast running stream that looked good enough to drink. We were spoiled by clear mountain streams, a habit soon to be broken. In Florida we would strain stump water through our spare socks, add a few P-tabs (Water Purification Tablets) and drink it like it was cold beer. A secure water re-supply in the mountains is a time consuming process, unlike Florida where often you can fill up in the natural process of crossing a stream. Mountain streams were not deep within arms reach of the bank, in fact, most of the time spent in filling a canteen was because it was rare to find a hole deep enough to submerge your canteen in deep enough to get head enough to displace the air. Of course, if you wanted to wade in and get wet, you could find deep water easy enough, but March in the Mountains is not a wise time to get wet unless you have to.

By the time we established security, organized the watering teams, collected, filled and distributed filled canteens, 45 minutes or more had passed. Storm clouds begin to form as we began to move again - that meant it would get dark earlier. Adding it all up, I began to get worried so I dropped out of the formation to wait for the platoon Sergeant to come by. As he came along, I got up and tracked along with him and shared my fears with him. "You're right, Pappy. We have lost a lot of time." He hustled off to double the column and advise the PL. Within a few minutes we took a knee for a short halt probably the conference between the PL and the platoon Sergeant - then we moved out briskly. We moved briskly for a little over an hour the ORP had been reached we thought. I took out my map and compass to make a terrain check. Yep, we should be near the ORP. Daytime navigation in the mountains was as easy as following street signs in a checkerboard city; not to be confused with night navigation which is perhaps to most difficult. I figured we had less than an hour of light left - it was gonna be tight getting in a good daylight recon of the ambush site and without that, organizing the assault line and coordinating the support element would be more difficult and more time consuming; a commodity suddenly in short supply.

The ORP was reconned rapidly; a sense of urgency accompanied the occupation phase because we all realized now that the piece of cake had molded. Everyone held their breath as the chain of command was relieved. The movement phase was over. Whoever had to carry the ball now would have his hands full and I guess no one wanted the job.

The new PL selected me to go with the Leaders Recon party. The PL decided to modify the normal leaders recon procedure due to the time factor; we would take our rucksacks along, do a quick recon, and call the main body in by radio. The main body would be met at a prearranged release point and brought to the ambush site for positioning. Clinging to a small tree to hold my position on the steep slope, I advised the PL "We ought to set it right here; good fields of fire down on the convoy. Don't assault across because that means going downhill which means a climb back up in the dark; and if the target gets relief, we don't want to have to climb back to the assault line under pressure." The RI with the recon party had other ideas. "Follow me, there must be a better place." Yeah, SGT, there is a better place but it ain't that direction! I didn't tell him that but I wanted to. If he hadn't said follow me we would have just had time to locate a place for the support element and post a guide before dark.

" Follow me. I am the Infantry-Queen of Battle. For two centuries I have kept our Nation safe, purchasing freedom with my blood. To tyrants, I am the day of reckoning; to the suppressed, the hope of the future. Where the fighting is thick, there I am - I am the Infantry! Follow me."

An infantryman cannot ignore the command "Follow me" particularly when given by an RI. The map contour intervals indicated, to me, no better place and sure enough, as we gouged in the waning light, my left foot kept getting lower and lower and much lower than my right foot. I was walking on the sides of my boots. I could imagine the medic asking "and how did you get blisters on your right ankle bone, RANGER?" The term "driving on" came to me. It means, in RANGER jargonese, continuing in the face of adversity, carrying the baton to the finish line, even when the race is over, or following your plan through to the end - right or wrong. Whichever case he fit, the RI was driving on that night. When he halted us it was so dark I could not see the ground, but I estimated the slope we were on to be about 185%. A 100% slope is 45 degrees. "Leave the recon here and you come with me. There is one more place I want to check out," said the RI, and off he stumbled with the PL struggling behind. We sat in the dark and whispered about the "tentative" places we had looked at since those immortal words, "Follow Me". Looked at! No, that is not the exact picture. Maybe estimated the relative slope of is more like it.

A noise to our rear brought us to the alert. Pssssttt! Pssssttt!
"Halt, who goes there?"
"The PL"
"Advance and be recognized."
"HALT. "
"SEVEN."
"Six.
"Come on in."
"God, I thought I'd never find you guys!"
"What are you doing coming from that direction . . .
"Never mind, it's a long story. Look, the RI fell plumb down to the roadway, and........
"Is he hurt?"

"No, but he is p -----   He wants us to radio the main body and place the ambush back at that last spot we looked at. We will meet him there. He is going to walk back down the road and stand there with his red filter so we can reference it as we move back parallel to the road. Let's go."

The point of the main body arrived almost simultaneously with the sound of gunfire and exploding simulators off to our West. That meant our target would be passing our site within minutes. Our mission was a back up mission to the patrol to our West. They were to conduct the major ambush and our job was to prevent escape or reinforcement. The "flash to bang time" of their ordnance told me they were about 3 kilometers down the valley. I knew this location was wrong! Verified! Not that we had navigated wrong, our ORP was where the OPORD put it, but the grid coordinates were obviously in error by one or two grid squares; obvious because we were supposed to be closer to the other patrol than we were and obvious because RI's are seldom wrong and ours kept looking for the place that wasn't.

"Light em up if you've got em."...... an age-old expression in the military referring to permission by the leader for the followers to smoke cigarettes. We clustered on the dark slope for the after action critique by the RI. He was standing on a stump beating the toe of his boot with a walking stick silhouetted by the headlights of jeeps and burning flares in the ambush site below.

"You panicked didn't you? When that ambush went off to the west and you weren't in position, you panicked, RANGERS! RANGERS don't panic! RANGERS use their head and drive on!"

A matter of opinion; point of view; semantics. It is not always easy to use your head in a clear objective, logical manner. RANGER students have a lot on their minds. They are almost always tired, sleepy, cold or hot, hungry, thirsty, harried, scared, suspicious, cautious, mad at someone or something, anxious, or otherwise distracted by any one of a thousand things including insects, wait-a-minute vines, mud, water up to your neck, sore muscles, a rucksack strap eating into your shoulder blade, or blisters. We did a lot of scurrying around trying to set the ambush but we got it set. As support element leader I located the M-60's by giving them an azimuth and distance the best I could do under the circumstances. No time to check their field of fire; no time to make final coordination on signals; whatever happened now would depend on experience and how well information was disseminated after RANGER Campana's original patrol order of some hours ago.

"The volume of fire was unsat! You call that an ambush? RANGERS, that was not an ambush!" His silhouette flickered on and off as the rising wind obscured the dying flares with smoke from the kill zone. If RANGERS were allowed to explain situations ("whimpering and making excuses" in RI terminology), I could have told him that our M-60's were all almost out of ammo due to the firefights in the PZ and LZ; and that half of our M-16's were in the choppers that landed first in the LZ and they also used a lot of ammo. After redistribution, there just wasn't much. But excuses are not allowed in RANGER School; the rules of the game; if you don't like it, don't go. "You are all volunteers" they used to say; "If you can't take the heat just let me know and I'll have you back to Benning in a $#@&^%* minute RANGERS" was SGT Rock's favorite by-line.

The sky flashed timidly with lightening in the distance as the RI's continued the tirade, which substituted as a critique. They had gone full circle - from coming in mad - through a very silent period most of the day - to mad again after the ambush. It must have been his fall down the ravine or perhaps the fact that the ambush site was not topographically suited to what he had been expecting; whatever, we would soon receive his wrath.

"RUCKUP! RANGER file, 1st squad leading. Compass man, move out on an azimuth of 192 mils." The RI was yelling orders.

It was not the azimuth of the original order! The wind was gusting now and thunder could be heard with the lightening; a slow ominous rumble far to the West. In a few minutes it would be tomorrow, the beginning of our 16th day in the mountains. Maybe there was a bad storm coming in; maybe they had given us a new azimuth to get us out of the storm. We clawed our way up the incline, laurel bush by laurel bush. When we reached the top, my back with the radio on it said stop, but we didn't stop. The pace picked up to a level that approached urgency; moisture could be 'felt' in the air and we knew the clouds were about to dump on us. The uncluttered level ground of the ridge gave way to undergrowth and dead fall as be began to descend via a ravine or draw. I don't know why we didn't move left or right and go down a finger. Because it would have been easier I guess. I cursed the ice age for creating this mess!

Down we went, clinging to vines, stumbling and falling over roots and deadfall. Now I knew why they made us go through that Darby Queen obstacle made up of a series of logs mounted horizontal off of the ground about 2 1/2 feet; to give us practice for negotiating deadfall. Ahead of me I could see a long line of luminous dots; the RANGER's compass' fixed to the back of rucksacks so that the man behind could maintain contact in the darkness. Down and down we went; would we never reach bottom? I thought. I always meant to look back at the map and try to see just what kind of terrain we went through, how far we walked, how high we climbed, etc., but I never did.

Finally we came out on a gravel road; it was beginning to sprinkle lightly. Down the road we went in an airborne shuffle, still on a downhill grade. I was convinced now that we were enroute to a place where trucks awaited to give us a ride back to semi-civilization. Just as in civilian life where the end of a long drive one tends to drive faster in anticipation of ending the trip; in RANGER School, that anticipation tends to make the rucksack get heavier. Mine weighed a ton! I could taste that mess hall chow now.

A large bridge loomed in the curve of the road ahead, I could see the point leading off to the left and off of the road as though to cross the river the hard way, but no, we were to follow a jeep trail upstream paralleling the river. A vast area to our left appeared, from what little I could see once as the clouds broke around the moon, to be sparsely dotted with very large trees. I imagined that it would be a beautiful place to camp - large spacious trees beside a roaring stream. The moon disappeared again, this time for good, and the occasional drop of rain turned into a light rain. By the time I was soaked to the skin, my illusions of linking up with a truck had faded completely. The night was unbelievably dark as we continued a steady climb, picking our way among rock outcroppings, dead fall, and brush.

We had hardly arrived at what I sensed as a small meadow when the real rain stated. We heard it coming across the forest canopy even above the roar of the river some yards to our right. The word came back to put on our rain parkas, and rubber over boots. What a Joke! The rain came down in sheets, driven by the wind, as we opened our rucksacks to remove parka and boots.

"They must be absolutely crazy, we're already soaked to the bone."

"No hoods, RANGERS! I said to put on your parkas, but I did not say to pull the hoods up. It is not wet enough or cold enough for hoods. Your patrol cap is all you need and do not let me catch anyone with his earflaps down. Is that clear?"

"CLEAR SERGEANT!!" I would call someone a liar if he tried to tell me it could possibly rain like it did for an hour, but it did. Monsoon in the winter!

No "Hawk Gear." A common warning in RANGER School. I did not know what it was. Never heard of it before but the folklore of the name was soon explained to me by one of the RANGER Battalion guys. High in the mountains, when the wind blows hard and cold through trees and cliffs it sometimes makes a shrill whistle that sounds a lot like that made by a soaring Hawk. So when it is really cold and miserable, RANGERs usually say the "Hawk is out today." And you can almost hear the squeal of a Hawk or the whistle of cold high velocity wind blowing across frozen precipice. Hawk Gear is anything that will give you some comfort against the wind; earflaps on the patrol cap, gloves, rubber overshoes, a field jacket, a wool scarf, or more than one set of long underwear.

We were no longer a patrol. We were 33 chunks of meat stumbling along behind two RI's. Just keeping in sight of the luminous dot ahead became an almost impossible task. At times the dot would appear to be getting too far ahead, and I would go shuffling ahead to close the gap and run square into the guy ahead. It was so dark that I had the feeling that the darkness had form or substance; that I could stick out my hand and part it like a curtain; that I could mold it or shape it; cut it with my machete or stack it up like cordwood; get bogged down in it. I could not focus on anything nor perceive depth nor maintain my balance well.

My feet were extremely heavy and I visualized that each foot was as big as a pumpkin. The heavy rain had made a muck of the ground. I had resorted to unloading my M-16 and using it as a walking stick to feel the path ahead and simply helping me maintain a reference point for balance.

To our right was what I perceived to be the only outright dangerous thing that we did during the entire course; the only thing for which I have never been able to find a safety valve. The sound was deafening. I imagined we were walking a narrow path along the rim of a canyon into which this river was cascading. The darkness contributed to this vision and amplified the sound of water probably much higher than it likely really was. But stress and anxiety does amplify things. To me, there was a raging river surging madly over strewn boulders and jagged outcroppings. Several times I stopped and strained my eyes down into the void but could see absolutely nothing. It shouldn't have been a surprise, I couldn't even see my feet but I knew they were there; they were wet, they hurt, and they were heavy. But I kept looking I think because I couldn't believe we were doing this. We trekked in this shadow of imagined danger for about two or three hundred yards, it seemed, then the roar slowly faded away. I had the feeling that if someone had slipped to the right side of the path that he would have fallen into a deep rocky ravine alive with water beat to a froth by the jagged features of the river. Was there a safety valve here? RANGERS don't ask. They just DRIVE ON!

How long we had been walking, or how far, I do not know. My watch crystal was clouded with water so that I could not tell the time. This was my first hint that my eyesight was succumbing to the over-40 failing and before the course was over I would realize that I could hardly read the brown contour lines on the map at night. I was plodding along, abusing my M-16, using it as a probe when I lost my footing, slipped down a small incline and bottomed out in a small pool of water. I got up on one knee and looked around for the nearest luminous dot. The strange feeling came over me that I was enclosed in something; an almost ominous feeling. My outstretched hand felt mud, limbs (or roots). I slung my rifle and began to grope with both hands. My best guess is that a large tree had blown over pulling its roots and a large chunk of earth with it and I had slid down into the cavity. I groped for a way out, frantically for a second because every attempt seemed to be blocked by the tangle of roots, like bars on a cell. Then as suddenly as I fell in, I was out; but I was disoriented…lost. Probably the entire episode only lasted a minute or perhaps a little more, but I had completely lost my sense of direction. Everything around me looked the same - dark. Everything sounded the same; quiet. I listened; rain falling lightly; my heart beating; nothing. The lost RANGER policy came to mind; I should load my rifle and fire two spaced rounds. I was considering doing that when I heard a groan, the rustle of nylon rucksack, and the clank of an M-16 butt stock on rock; the unmistakable sound of a RANGER patrol getting up from a halt. They must have paused for a map check or something about the same instant that I slipped. I fell back into the file between two luminous dots having never been missed. Plodding through the sheets of cold rain. I visualized myself as a miner's burro; beast of burden.

Only once more did we stop. There was a break in contact, i.e., someone did not keep up with the man to his front resulting in the formation of two groups. Fortunately, the break was discovered soon after it happened and the lead group halted. The RI ordered them to turn on their white lights so that we in the rear group could locate the lead group better. Our reconsolidation was the occasion for a tongue lashing by the RI.

"A break in contact is a safety violation," he said, "the two people at the break point get a major minus spot report!"

I couldn't believe what I was hearing! The most dangerous thing in the whole school was following the RI's along that riverbank in total darkness during a rainstorm, or at least that's the way I saw it at that moment. But RI's have already gotten their grades and RANGERS don't complain; they just DRIVE ON.

The night was not over yet! We left the lecture stop practically holding on to the rucksack ahead like a bunch of circus elephants. At one point the order was passed back for everyone to use his white light to negotiate a ravine and streambed. Check one for the RI's good sense. Finally just before dawn, we moved up a hillside, which was almost barren except for a few scrub bushes. The slope was over 100% for sure.

"All right RANGERS," drawled the RI, "this is your patrol base. Squads secure your sectors and begin priorities of work."

We sat with our heels dug into the mud hillside or hooked on a shrub and shivered in the cold. Rain was falling again and now that we had stopped moving the temperature was beginning to take control of my body. I was shaking uncontrollably.

"You cold Gramps?" asked Campana.

"If SGT. Rock were here he would say that I am not cold yet, but I assure you, I am cold and I'm going to do something about it right now and I don't give a #@^&!# who knows it."

I dug into my rucksack pocket for my poncho, which I stretched out over two pieces of deadfall. Crawling under this out of the rain, I took off my parka, shirt, and undershirt and put on a dry wool OG shirt from a plastic bag within my rucksack; then back on with the rain parka. I dug out my wool scarf, wool watch cap, and a pair of dry glove inserts. Having put all this on, I made one final act of defiance I guess--I pulled up my hood and drew the closure string tightly about my face; this all in the dark of course. Then I kept a sharper alert for the RI than I did the "enemy" because that would probably have been a minus spot. Call it a calculated risk. Call it survival. Call it what you will, but it put me back in control. My body temperature came back into sector. I could feel all my toes. I felt GOOD!!

Out of the darkness came the voice of an RI "All-right, RANGERS, you can put on your rain trousers now." I was just one step ahead of him!

The shivering subsided within a few minutes, my upper body warmed by the dry wool. God, I'd like to have some dry socks on, but taking one's boots off was a dangerous thing to do. We were subject to move on 60 seconds notice. I was still under my poncho shelter watching my section of the perimeter when I heard a noise that sounded like something tumbling past me. Campana had been called off by the RI to get his grade for the morning patrol base. I threw my poncho aside just as Campana's rucksack tumbled away downhill in the early morning light. I yelled a warning "Falling Rock" across the perimeter and someone attempted to catch it as it bounced by - no luck. Well, what's a buddy for?; I slid down the hill after it. It was fully light by the time I retrieved the runaway ruck and dragged it and myself back up the slick slope. The rain had stopped and it promised to be a beautiful day if some RI didn't screw it up.

Breakfast consisted of the other half of an LRRP ration that I opened at noon the day before - Chili ConCarne. You have to be hungry to eat LRRP Chili ConCarne dry! We went "admin" then to get a critique on every-thing since the ambush but since all that we did since the ambush was hump, gouge, get wet and cold, the critique was not too exciting. "Get all of that 'HAWK GEAR' off, we still have a long walk to the truck pickup point. We move in 5 minutes." I took off my 10-Buckle overshoes first; no need to wear them. My feet were as wet as they could get and the overshoes were heavy on the feet. We moved out down the hill in squad wedges feeling pretty good knowing we were going to the trucks, then back to Camp Merrill.

At the base of the hill was a small creek, which we had to cross to reach a firebreak, which would, eventually, lead to the trucks. The RI's began to look for a suitable crossing site, for what I don't know. I just waded on across and some began to follow. "You trying to get pneumonia so you can get out of this course, Old Man?"

"No SGT, just changing the water in my socks."

We never got back to Camp Merrill that morning and I don't know exactly where it was that we did get to. After a rough ride packed in the back of a 6x6, the driver crashed to a stop and someone was screaming to get out. We must have been a sorry looking bunch as we piled out into the red mud. I did not recognize where we were but I did recognize who was unhappy with us - it was SGT MAJ Monroe. He was your classic country boy who I imagined might have run away from home at 15 to join the Army and made good. I don't mean to say that he did, but that's my visualization of him. The cud of tobacco, the slow deliberate drawl, and the cold distant stare might make him a native of Tennessee or maybe, Carolina. I say that because he reminded me of Gary Cooper in the role of Alvin York. SGM Monroe was a soldier; a no nonsense soldier who expected a lot out of his RANGERS. He was about to prove this!

"All right, RANGERS, I want you to ground them Rucks, leave a guard, and load back up on them there trucks. You lost a piece of Guv-a-mint' property and you are going to find it if you have to retrace every step you have taken. You are going to learn the value of equipment and the responsibility of keeping up with it. That battery case cost the guv-a-mint thirteen dollars and nita-five cents." After a long lecture on the virtues of supply economy, and the sins of carelessness; "Now git on them G -- ---- trucks and be quick about it." Another wild ride and we were returned to where he picked us up on the morning of 30 March, two days before. We spread out to search every patrol base, every security halt area, every ORP, and every ambush or enemy action site that he had walked us through. We spread out 4 deep and wide enough to cover a squad wedge front and walked the entire route between sequential sites. I guessed the outcome before we ever started. ZIP! We were looking for the battery cage from a PRC 88 transmitter. Imagine a wire cage with 111 mesh, large enough to hold 2 packs of cigarettes, O.D. in color and dropped in the leaves somewhere on patrol. The odds of finding it was somewhere in the order of millions to one. Ironically, the RANGER who actually lost it went on sick call and was not on the search. The search was finally called off and we returned to Camp Merrill about noon. My platoon never lost another piece of "Guv-a-mint' equipment!"

FOOD IS A LUXURY, NOT A NECESSITY

Returning to base camp really meant returning to the mess hall. The mess hall was heaven. It was warm, dry, friendly, and filled with stuff that made you feel good and rejuvenated you in a most delicious way. In Camp Darby that was like returning to nothing, but the mountains and Florida were different. Each of them had their good points and I would be unfair to say that one was better than the other. As I recall, we never had more than two or three noon meals in the mess hall in the mountains and we, for sure, never had an evening meal in the mess hall in Florida. Breakfast in the Mountain Mess Hall was always at 0400 when we were not on patrol; eggs to order, French toast and syrup, grits, creamed beef on toast, sausage, bacon, cereal, juice, fruit, milk, and coffee. The rule was 'no seconds,' but you could take all you could eat the first trip through. We were allowed knife, fork and spoon and about 50 minutes to eat it - a touch of civilization. A two, three or five day patrol was normally started immediately after breakfast (0400) with Long Range Recon Patrol (LRRP) rations until we returned. The evening meal in the Mountain Mess Hall was like dying and going to heaven. The food was as fine as any to be found in any restaurant; it looked good, tasted fabulous, and the quantity - absolutely more than the average RANGER could eat, and we were a hungry bunch. There was good reason for such a fine array of food though; the Mountain Phase was by far the most demanding of all phases.

Words like demanding, taxing, exhausting, debilitating, and challenging are inadequate to describe the experience. It was during this phase that I sustained the greatest weight loss, going to under 160 pounds with boots and fatigues on. That also included about 3 pounds of blisters and calluses on my feet! The evening meal in the Mountain Mess Hall is the one I remember most fondly. First of all, it was the most leisurely meal of the entire course. I was the RANGER Company Commander for the entire Mountain Phase, which gave me the responsibility, or duty, to eat last. It was a pleasure to eat last as it gave me a rare opportunity to do the nearest thing to relaxing that there was to be had in RANGER School. My First Sergeant and I always ate last together and took advantage of the time to discuss all manner of RANGER company business between bites. Talking with your mouth full is part of RANGER etiquette. Before RANGER School, First Sergeant Ivory was a Staff Sergeant in the 10th Special Forces, a veteran of Viet Nam, and one of the older ones of the class. He was 31, but like most black men, did not show the years in terms of wrinkles, etc. He could have been 21, all except his eyes, which seemed to change age with his mood. We got on like lifelong buddies and ran a good company. He and I always ate in 10 minutes from the time our tray hit the table until we rose to leave - no more. Leisure is a relative term and we still had schedules to maintain. We set a rule that when he and I left the mess hall that everyone except the people on serving detail would also be gone. God, how I wanted to just sit 5 more minutes and have another cup of coffee or eat slower and enjoy that beautiful food! There was always a choice of 3-5 meat items, a large variety of vegetables, salad bar, and a variety of drinks and deserts. I always got 8 or 10 pads of butter and several glasses of milk to help me through the next patrol. "Have we got to get up Pappy," he would ask good-naturedly. "Yep" I'd say; "If we make the rules we've got to follow them .....it goes with the job."

In Florida it was the breakfast meal that everyone seemed to enjoy most and I think there were several reasons for that. The main reason is that breakfast was always the first decent meal we would have had in several days. We usually returned to the Florida RANGER camp about 0300 in the morning or later. Whatever time it was, there always seemed to be just enough time to clean equipment, shower, and pack for the next mission before breakfast, but never enough time to get any sleep, so breakfast always tasted extremely good. I never realized how many people liked peanut butter and jelly, but we would eat a large serving pan full of each on these occasions. By large, I mean about two gallons. Milk was another item that we consumed large quantities of, so much in fact that the mess steward made some discouraging remark about it which infuriated SGT Rock. "Studs, " he said, "I want you to drink all the G-- D--- milk you want. Matter of fact, I want you to drain that --- ---machine every#*9@# time you get the chance." It was always a great pleasure to have SGT Rock to say anything to us that remotely resembled praise or support or positive encouragement.

Another unique thing about the Florida Mess Hall was the evening meal. We never had a sit down meal there that I recall, but whenever we were in camp in the evening, they would provide us with sack lunches, which included a soda and a large candy bar. That was like Christmas to us, and of course, there was a lot of trading going on; a Three-Musketeers for a Baby Ruth or a Pepsi for a Crass. Candy and cokes was something that was carefully rationed.

Except for the sack lunches, we had to "earn" the luxury of treats.

"RANGERS, your morale is dragging in the dirt behind you! I've never seen a sorrier bunch in my life than you and I've seen a lot of sorry #*@# *&#@@# in my life. Now you're gonna have to pull yourselves together; you're gonna have to get your head out of your third point of contact or you ain't gonna graduate!" It was SGT Rock going into one of his tongue-lashings. He was an absolute classic

Airborne RANGER Platoon Sergeant, and a credit to his profession. I suppose that the school had others like him, as TAC'S, but I personally am glad that our class had him. Rock is the most colorful soldier I have ever known, both in his language and his off-duty life, which he often referred to as he addressed us. His mastery of profanity was absolutely fascinating, the way he could flow a string of 8 to 10 socially unacceptable words together and make it sound like poetry. He called us "studs" when he was getting serious, and in his southern drawl, it took him about 3 seconds to say "stuuuddds," and he always had a slight pause at the end of it in which he seemed to look at all 103 of us. We all thought at the time that he was calling us that out of some macho regard for us; but over the years I have decided that Stud was simply short for Students.

"Now stuuuddds . . . if you don't want me standing on Todd Field all by myself on 23 April, you better get your -----together! I didn't invite you here and I'm not asking you to stay. I'll hum you a tune while you do the duffel bag drag." And he would pace back and forth between phrases and one-liners to emphasize the seriousness of what he was telling us. He would stop and face us squarely, hands on hips or occasionally, pointing or gesturing, head cocked slightly, eyes slightly squinted, jaw set; thinking; measuring the tension he was creating with a performance that would make George C. Scott cry with envy. All of the staff wore the black beret of the RANGERs. And each had some hard to describe personal touch to how they fitted their beret to their head. They all looked pretty much at home in their beret, but Sgt. Rock seemed to have yet another level of connectivity with his beret. If anyone was ever made for the beret, it was Rock. "Stuudds? If I hear one more report that your morale has fallen down around your ankles, I'm gonna kick your #!*#@@# up a-round your earlobes! IS THAT CLEAR?"

"CLEAR SGT ROCK," we would scream in unison at the top of our lungs.

"I was thinking about letting you go to the PX and get one pack of lifesavers - but not now! Not #@!%ing now!!" He shook his finger, snarled, and furrowed his brow up so tight that it's a wonder his black beret didn't simply pop off his head.

"You gotta show me something now or you ain't never going again."

"YES SERGEANT," we screamed in unison.

No threat had greater effect than to threaten our lifesavers! We would walk an extra 10 clicks for a lifesaver. My fondest memory of

Rock's mass corrective counseling sessions are the ones we got in the mountains. We got more in the mountains than any other phase. He would call a formation in front of the houches at most any time of the day or night. If he was mad, he would call us studs; if not he would address us as RANGERS. There was a large above-ground propane tank about 20 feet long parallel to and in front of the houches and he would mount the tank and pace back and forth from one end to the other. If he was proud of us for something, and there were several occasions when he was, he would step off the tank, hold outstretched arms like a shepherd calling his flock and we would eagerly gather around in a tight horseshoe formation to receive the word. At times like this you could feel the bond between the class and Rock. At other times he would curse us for scumbags, even bust people out for recycle, but the bond was still there. Of course, this had not always been the case. It takes time for a relationship to develop between the class and the TAC.

I remember the first time SGT Rock addressed the class. It was in a large classroom painted with black and gold, the color of the RANGER Tab.

"RANGERS, I'm SGT Rock, the best #@**#!ing TAC in this #@*&#@ing School. Anything you do will be cleared through me. For the next eight weeks, or however long you last, I will be your Mother, Father, Doctor and Priest. You won't need anybody else but me. You do what I tell you and do it well and you'll be on Todd Field on 23 April; if you don't you're gonna pack your #@&**#! and get out! From this moment on, you are all RANGERS until you prove yourself unworthy."

There were 128 freshly shaven heads in the classroom but suddenly he stopped dead in his tracks and pointed to me. "You there! Stand the #@&%**!# up when I *#@*##ing point to you. AND SOUND OFF, RANGER!"

"YES, SERGEANT!" I screamed in my best voice, and since I had not been smart enough to include screaming in my train-up routine, I felt the first crack in my throat.

He put his hands on his hips, contorted his face slightly and sort of looked at me sideways;

"How old are you, RANGER?"

"42 and climbing, Sergeant," I replied.

He dropped his hands to his side briskly, opened his eyes widely and said

"Well, don't climb too high Old Man, your bones are brittle you know."

He took a few quick steps then turned quickly, bending at the hips, "FOURTEY-TWOOO? -----#*@##@*//!! What the #@%^*%*#! are you doing here?"

That was my first recall of Rock and to him., I was the "Old Man" from then on.

He would use me to goad the rest of the class with. I didn't mind, matter of fact I sort of enjoyed it. I remember the first time he did it was after we took the PT test. SGT England had us in formation when SGT Rock came stroking up. He had this devilish kind of a "gottcha" smile on.

"Where's my Old Man? RANGER Childers, get your #*@!%$ing hindquarters out here!" I gave out with a loud AHHHH as I double-timed out front. We always had to sound off at the top of our lungs when "posted" from the time we started moving until we stopped. Then he also posted RANGER Bryant, a Marine, who was the second oldest in the class. I thought he was 34 at the time, but later I got a copy of part of our class records on which he was indicated as 31. We had both made 290 on the PT test, out of 300. I am sure that we would have both made 300 on the test if given anywhere but RANGER School. They simply don't count all repetitions. "I just want you young studs to see who made the highest scores on the PT test," mocked Rock. "The two oldest #@*%@@# in the #@%^%*#! class made the highest scores; if I was you, I'd feel like #@%^%*#! !"

"Maybe this is the new math Sgt. Rock, posed Sgt. England, "highest age equals highest score; lowest age equals lowest score."

"New math my aching ###! Bunch of Wimps." Retorted Sgt. Rock.

SGT Rock always looked exactly the same. He must have had a score of helpers hidden away somewhere to polish boots and iron uniforms, because no matter what time of the day or night he might appear, his personal appearance was impeccable. You could shave with the creases in his uniform and use the toe of his boots for a mirror. Whether it was the heat of Florida or the cold of the mountains, Rock didn't seem to be effected by the weather. He didn't sweat., he didn't shiver, and he didn't wear any cold weather gear. "HAWK" gear it was called. "You are NOT COLD RANGERS - not yet! I'll let you know when you can be cold. You think you are cold but you don't know what cold is - yet. You are not authorized to be tired, or cold, or hungry, or sleepy, or to bleed excessively! Is that clear?"

"YES, SERGEANT!"

SGT Rock was a professor of psychology - or he could have been because he could manipulate us like puppets on a string. It's hard to believe that 100+ grown men could be manipulated for something as simple as a bar of candy or a pack of lifesavers. It was Rock who planted the seed in our minds and the seed grew to a candy tree. We had been at the Harmony Church about a week being ridden hard and 'put away wet, so to speak, with no privileges whatsoever. "I might let you go down to the PX tonight if everything goes well today and buy one candy bar - ONE If I catch anyone buying more than one - I got something for him!!" He would do a pivot and a couple of short steps reminiscent of the German goose step, then turn and face us, feet spread, hands clasped behind the back; held thrust out his chin and sort of bare his bottom teeth as he squinted subtlety; "I mean I got something for you RANGERS!" And held pause again to be sure that it sunk in. I don't think anyone had even thought about a candy bar until then, certainly I had not, but now that he suggested it, the candy bar became a goal. We became hooked m the idea of going to the PX and buying candy. It was a very subtle lever for Rock and he used it again and again to make the class perform. Then he expanded upon the trick and turned it into a traumatic decision process.

"All right RANGERS, when you go to Camp Darby you can take 10 PX items to the field with you. TEN!" He held up 10 fingers to emphasize the importance of the number.

"You can take lifesavers; chewing gum; cigarettes; hot chocolate; packages of Campbell's Soup; - any combination, but only 10!" He counted these off carefully on his fingers.

"Now the first thing that's gonna happen when you get off of those buses at Darby is a shakedown. DO NOT try to smuggle in anything extra. Those people out there at Darby have all been in the business long enough to know all of the hiding places. ALL OF 'EM, RANGERS! There is no place that you can hide even one M&M that they can't find. Understand me RANGERS?"

"Yes Sergeant Rock" we screamed.

"Less you stuff em up your rear end; nobody gonna be looking there." And as the days turned into long nights, a simple lifesaver became a treat equivalent to a filet mignon back in the civilian world.

BURY THE DEAD

Realism in RANGER School is stressed at all times. You must always be in a "ready position." Carry your M-16 at high port, finger on the trigger, thumb on the selector, eyes scanning continuously. Reaction to ambush or artillery fire must be swift, violent, controlled. Target sites were always manned by well-rehearsed aggressors who would be there and ready to resist attack no matter what time of the day or night we might finally arrive. The sites also always had some replica of Soviet block equipment which we would simulate destroying. There were always documents on POW's as well as replica weapons to be identified and counted. And of course, the stress of combat was simulated with a great flair of realism. The threat of recycle was real, but I think the touch of realism that I shall always rate the highest occurred during the Florida Phase.

We were on a cross-country move as part of a coordinated move, that is, we knew other patrols were in the area and that our paths might cross somewhere. I was the RTO for the platoon leader. As we moved along I began to pick up radio traffic from another patrol who was "in contact" with the enemy. I advised the PL of this and we continued to move. Soon we began to hear a firefight in the distance and it appeared to be on our azimuth. The radio traffic was reporting "casualties." We were getting closer and closer to the fighting and the PL seemed to be oblivious to the whole affair; completely wrapped up in controlling the movement of his patrol. I was reluctant to say much more to him because the RI was staying near to the PL, and I did not want to appear like a spotlighter.

Finally, I decided I had to do something as we were about to get involved in the fight ahead. "Do you want me to contact the CO and ask if he wants us to relieve pressure on him, or otherwise do a bypass around the area?" I suggested. We went into a security halt while the PL talked to the CO by radio. By the time the conversation was over, the firing ahead had stopped. The CO did not need us to assist the patrol in contact, so after a few more minutes, we continued the march on the same azimuth. I had a bad feeling about the whole affair and within 10 minutes we were engaged in a well laid ambush. We were assessed several casualties immediately. Within a few minutes we gained firepower superiority and we were driving the enemy off with great vigor. I am not sure we were too tactical, but we put them on the run. There were several RI's doubling as aggressors and our guys were trying hard to capture them. We had groups of two or three going every-which-way, but the RI's were just as determined not to get caught. We were pretty well scattered by the time we decided that we could not catch an RI/Aggressor. Our own RI's were having a field day with the whole affair - small groups dispersed all over, casualties laying all about.

"All right PL, what are you going to do about these casualties" quizzed the RI. Recalling the patrol order, the PL replied, "Bury the dead and dust-off the wounded."

"I've already radioed for the dust-off" I added, "But it's about 200 yards to the nearest LZ."

"Forget the LZ, they can drop a hook right through the treetops" said the RI.

With our position reconsolidated, casualties gathered in the middle, status taken and reported, I figured our casualties would be "reincarnated" and we would continue the problem. Nothing could have been further from the truth. The Medivac chopper came up on our frequency and asked for a marker. Rather than waste smoke, I vectored him in by listening to his rotor. When he spotted us through the trees he hovered and lowered the jungle penetrator through the overhead. We placed our sucking chest wound casualty on the seat that is built into the penetrator, and he disappeared up through the trees. We did not hear from or see him again for the remainder of that mission.

The next surprise was the "dead" casualties.

"Your patrol order says bury the dead," asked the RI?

"Yes, Sergeant," replied the PL.

"Well, dig a #@%*!#@ hole and bury his smelly #@#@!!!"

We dug a hole, wrapped the casualty in a poncho and put him in the shallow grave 2ft by 6ft by 2ft. His M-16 was taken apart and the muzzle placed inside the poncho at the head with the chamber end sticking up in the air to provide a .223 caliber breathing hole - and we buried him for real! We then had about a 10 minute critique of the action by the RI, . . . maybe 15 minutes. Seemed like forever.

"OK, go dig up that RANGER and put him back in his squad" said the RI. That RANGER was glad to be unearthed! That was what I call realism. "You can bet your sweet --- that I ain't gonna be "killed" again" said the unearthed RANGER! "That is a strange feeling, being buried!"

HOW THE RANGERS ARE EVALUATED

Evaluation of the RANGERS begins from the moment they report in to the School. Most people don't know exactly how the evaluation system works, in fact, most arrive at the School armed with a lot of rumors, stories passed on third or fourth hand, and outright un-truths. Students are given an overall briefing on the phase scenarios and the grading scheme but little of this information is really taken on board and retained by more than a small percentage of the class. It did not take hold in my brain housing group. But with some advance information which can be studied in a relaxed atmosphere, one can arrive at RANGER School better prepared to meet the challenge. For instance, a RANGER is given a specific time limit in which to take charge of a patrol in the field. Many students will fail that task one time or more before they figure it out for themselves or are told. Then there are other tasks that vary with the phase, e.g., 15 minutes in Benning, 20 minutes in the mountains, and 30 minutes in Florida.

The details of grading leader-ship positions are given in what is referred to as an Observation Report (OR). This document is identified by the US Government Printing Office as 1981-740-000/187. It is 50 pages printed front and back, and is approximately 3-1/2 in. by 4-1/2 inches by 1/4 in. thick and fits nicely in a fatigue (now Battle Dress Uniform) shirt pocket. It is really a score book which the RI fills out on each RANGER in a leadership position. Leadership positions which are graded are the Patrol Leader/Platoon Leader, Assistant Patrol Leader/Platoon Sergeant, and Squad Leaders/Team Leaders/Element Leaders.

Each RANGER is issued an OR along with his RANGER Handbook and is allowed to keep it until he moves to Camp Darby. Frankly, I never realized how important the OR was while I had it and I did little more than read it rapidly a time or two. After the first patrol at Darby, I realized how critical the data in the OR was and I managed to get another one for a short period and re-read and absorb it. I passed this on to other members in my patrol and to the other platoons/patrols of the company whenever I had the opportunity, or when the occasion dictated. Then, during the Florida Phase, we were given a few copies for each platoon which we got to keep for a few days before turning them back in. In all cases when we had possession of the OR, we were under the threat of a Major Minus Spot Report if we lost one. At the time I assumed that the OR's were not available to anyone but the RANGER Department, and they were trying to control general distribution. As I was out-processing after graduation, I went by a building on Main Post which distributed printed materials (FM's, Circulars, etc.) to "shop" for the latest in published doctrine and there in one of the bins was a stack of OR's. I asked the man in charge if there was any restrictions on who could have copies of it, and he said there was no restriction; "Take all you need" he said. So I did, and I have included the OR as **Appendix D**. Those who are going to RANGER School should study the actions and standards of each task in the OR remembering that some of the tasks are considered "critical' tasks. RANGERS are graded either <u>GO</u> or NO-GO on each task and <u>GO</u> or NO-GO on the patrol as a whole. Get a current copy, learn it prior.

Each RANGER will be placed in a graded leadership a minimum of four times and he must receive a GO in at least 50% of his patrols no matter how many he is assigned. He must pass at least one in both Florida and in the Mountains. For instance, assume a RANGER had two graded patrols in Camp Darby and failed them both. He goes to the mountains with zero for two. He now needs to pass two for two in the mountains to have an even chance in Florida. Assume he fails the first two in the mountains and gets a GO on the third. He has passed his one required in the Mountain Phase but his score is now one for five. He must now be assigned three patrols in Florida and pass them all to arrive at a score of four for eight or an overall 50%. If he fails his first Florida patrol, he now needs to be assigned four more in Florida and pass them all to arrive at a five for ten score. As you can see, failing patrols is something to be avoided because the negative effect is exponential, that is, it snowballs on you causing you to be assigned more patrols and thus work you harder. Another danger is that if a lot of people are in the same shape it may be that there won't be enough patrols available to "save" you all. There is, after all, a limit to the overall number of patrols available. In the case of my class (6-81), my platoon had to be reorganized in Florida and some of our people had to be placed in another platoon which had some "available" patrols. Some of our people went to Florida "down" five and six patrols. I went to Florida with a four for four pass rate.

RANGER School is very specific about responsibility, particularly with regard to the patrol leader. One can fail his patrol because his subordinate leaders in the patrol did not do certain aspects of their job. Oddly enough, individual squad leaders might pass their patrols while the patrol leader failed because of things the squad leaders failed to do. Students are prepared for leading patrols through cadre led patrols so it's not as if one is suddenly thrown into the lion's den so to speak.

During the Darby Phase, highly qualified RANGER Instructors lead the students through practice patrols to demonstrate exactly how it is done. Then the students get the opportunity to lead two un-graded patrols for practice. Now the student is ready to lead a patrol for a grade and from then on, all patrols are graded GO or NO-GO, thus the School evaluates the RANGER's patrolling/leadership skills.

There are five graded RANGER runs during the Benning Phase. The student must pass three of the five runs or be eliminated immediately; one of those passed must be the five-mile run. The rules are simple. You must keep up with your fellow RANGERS. You must not fall behind the man in front of you by more than three paces at any time. The first time you lag by more than three paces, an RI will warn you "You have fallen behind more than three paces RANGER. Close it up!" If you can not/do not close the gap directly you will be pulled from the run and counted as a "drop run". If you are able to respond to the warning and close the gap you may continue the run. You are allowed two such warnings per run and on the third warning (per run) you will be pulled out and counted as a drop run. Failure to complete the five mile run in proper order is an automatic drop from the RANGER School - no reprieve, so you might say then that you have to complete 50% of the runs as you can fail two out of the remaining four. No board action is required in this action and there is no appeal. You simply either keep up or go home. One gets the perception that the school really does not care whether you succeed or not, but in hindsight, that is probably not the real case. What they care about is whether or not the student can meet the standard. No compromise.

The runs are not "killers" but they do eliminate several people from the program. Since we weren't allowed to wear dog tags, belts, rings, or watches during PT, I cannot say how fast the runs were, for sure. The Morgan Team maintained that they were run at an 8-minute mile rate, but having run a few thousand miles in my time, I honestly believe that some of the runs were at a 7-minute mile pace. Marathon runners will probably scoff at that, after all, they typically maintain a rate of 6 minutes/mile for over 26 miles and, of course, a few Bill Rodgers-Types do even better than that. But there are differences to be considered before one concludes that being physically and mentally trained and configured like a marathon runner is the model for prospective RANGERS.

First, there is a uniform difference. RANGER runs in the "last really hard RANGER class" were done in combat boots and fatigue trousers as opposed to lightweight running shoes and non-constrictive running shorts. Combat boots and socks weigh 5 pounds; that's 2.5 pounds per foot that must be lifted and thrust one in front of the other. Running shoes typically weigh a few ounces each. Fatigue trousers are the other big factor in that they constrict the free movement of the legs, particularly at the knee joint. Every time you lift your leg for a step, the material must slide across the knee, and across the buttocks causing the runner to expend more energy to accomplish the task. This clothing, including a cotton tee shirt (light nylon jersey for the marathoner) also increases the heat loading on the RANGER runner.

The footgear presents another important problem besides weight. I don't think combat boots were ever intended to be "running shoes." They are made to be durable, provide ankle support, and general in size to reduce inventory requirements - sizes R (Regular), W (Wide), and N (Narrow).

For running purposes the boot epitomizes the Army supply system and reminds one of the story of the classical supply Sergeant who had signs on his supply bins labeled "Too Big" and "Too Small." The worst part about combat boots on a run is that they tend to create blisters, aggravate latent ingrown toenails, and generally destroy your feet. I think they also take a toll on your spinal column. This is why it is extremely important that prospective students should break in two or three pairs of combat boots by "running" them well in advance of attending RANGER School.

Do your PT and running to condition yourself in boots and fatigues, not in shorts and running shoes or tennis shoes. The boots should be made soft and pliable with a generous application of Neats Foot Oil or equivalent. Don't assume that just because your boots have nine eyelets (9 on new style, 10 on old style, 12 on Corcorans) that you should run your laces through each of them. WRONG! Experiment with various lacing techniques based on "where it hurts" when you run. I found that my left boot should be laced different from my right boot, and that among three pairs of boots, there was a variation required. I wore two pair of wool socks at all times because my nominal foot size is 11B and the narrowest boot I have ever been able to get is 11R. Corcorans are available in 11B, or any size, but I recommend against them for RANGER School. I took two pair of "issue" boots and two pair of Corcorans boots to RANGER School. The Corcorans fell apart, specifically, the stitching failed in the soles and on the narrow vertical strip that forms a junction with the two side pieces and the wrap-around piece that forms the heel; a combination of sewing "thread" that rotted and stitch holes in the leather which enlarged during wet/dry cycling and "ruptured." A final strike against Corcorans is that you are discouraged from wearing them at all in the Mountain Phase because the "standard" sole does not provide a good gripping surface for rock climbing and therefore, presents a safety hazard.

A second important difference between marathon runners and RANGER runners is training. I cannot deny that marathon training is good training, but as I understand marathon training, it is almost a science. One has to dedicate himself to the sport. He eats, sleeps, and breathes running 26-plus miles. His body is specifically conditioned to accomplishing that single task; his diet is designed to provide energy output for a demanding but specific pace and his sleep and rest are closely controlled. A RANGER runner is not afforded any of those luxuries because he must function on practically no sleep or rest, a standard diet, and he must perform a variety of demanding military tasks before and after his run. To summarize the RANGER run then, if you want to be a RANGER and you are a "marathoner," reduce your marathon training and teach your muscles to do other tasks - and do it in the proper uniform.

Terrain navigation is another skill evaluation that RANGERS must pass early in the program. Terrain navigation is no longer taught in RANGER School. As a result of a series of incremental revisions which began in November of 1977, the RANGER Department decided that the time previously used to teach land navigation could be more effectively used for more demanding subjects, so it is assumed that all applicants can read a map and navigate across any terrain, day or night. On day 4 of the course, we were trucked to the Southeastern corner of Fort Benning to an area bound on the West by Jamestown Road, on the North by Lightning Road, and on the East and South by the post boundary. In groups of one, we were dispersed to the four winds with the mission of locating a minimum of 4 points on the terrain. As I recall, we had 5 hours to complete the task or be given a failure. We could earn a major plus spot report by locating 6 points, and some people did. I was quite happy to locate 4 and return to the designated rally point.

The first point was given as a grid coordinate, and of course, I had a grid coordinate of my start position so a quick calculation gave me an azimuth and a distance to my first point. I set my compass, checked my pace cord to make sure there were no knots in it and started walking across the thick woodland. The RI's had made frequent reference to "wait-a-minute vines;" now I knew what one looked like. My first leg or point was 1800 meters distance and it seemed that every step was through those vines. I have walked literally hundreds of miles in the woods in some 35 years of hunting and 25 years of National Guarding, and I don't recall a thicker, more resistant a piece of woods to passage. I did a lot of hunting with an old-timer named Lloyd Davis. Lloyd was a reknown coon hunter and whiskey drinker, both of which he did concurrently. No swamp was to wide or deep, nor night too dark to deter Lloyd from following the wail of his dogs to the tree. He had a term he used; "pulling the swamp", which was his colloquial way to say that he had crossed it. Here I am in Ft Benning, pulling the thickets.

As I tied knot #16 in my pace cord I could see what appeared to be an opening in the trees ahead. I moved on to come out in an area that had been timbered and bulldozed clean. I stopped to take another shot and found a large tree conveniently located within a few yards of my azimuth, so I started walking to it as a guide. I was scanning the far wood line left and right for some kind of marker when two RANGERS came out of the wood line and gathered around my guide tree, and I saw the data board on the tree. It bothered me at first that someone else should be at <u>my</u> point. "I hope it's mine" I thought. "It must perfectly on the wrong one,' I reassured myself. I got to the tree and exchanged small talk with the two people there as I verified my point.

The NAV course has a scheme using lane numbers and color codes whereby you verify whether or not you are at the correct point. Some points are in fact close enough together so that an error in either azimuth or distance may place you on the wrong point and there is no way to relate one point with another. So if you come upon a point that you were not assigned by data at the last point, and you think your pace and azimuth were correct, panic sets in. This happened to several in my class - PANIC! There are only three choices if this happens. You can cast about hoping you can stumble on the correct point. The odds of success are very low but two different students claim they did just that. A second choice is to try to go back to the last point and try it again. This is also risky depending upon how long the leg was and how much time you have left. The third choice is to try to get some information about adjacent points from other RANGER students. This is supposed to be a no-no, but several people salvaged themselves in this manner. It is also risky because each point has information relating to several lanes and color codes and normally one only reads and notes info relating to his own course, so that it would be rare that one person could actually help another more than to say where he has been.

I was shocked to discover that my first point was the second point for the two RANGERS that were there. They left on two separate azimuths and I stood there in a cold sweat. I had been over an hour to the first point. At this rate, 3 more points would be over 3 more hours for a total of over 4 hours. Then depending on the location of my last point relative to the rally point, I might go over the 5-hour time limit. The day was hot and I had drank nearly a quart of water; my heart was beating overtime. "Calm down boy, all the legs can't be this long." I plotted the next point and measured it - 1500 meters. Ceeerist ! I sat down, took a long drink and poured some on my head, then re-plotted the data. It was still 1500 meters. My pace cord cleared of knots, I started off at a near run. The woods were only about half as bad as the first leg for most of the 1500 meters. At about 1100 meters I came out on a small jeep trail and to my right standing in a trail junction was another RANGER. He saw me and said, "The point is down this jeep trail."

"How do you know it's mine?"

"Because, it was my first point, and I have searched all over this sector to find it and it's the only one anywhere around, I guarantee!

"Thanks" I said, and when he disappeared around the bend, I continued my azimuth. Another hundred meters and I crossed the trail he had indicated, and another 250 meters and I came out on the curving trail again. To my right some 40-50 yards away was another marker. I approached it with a mixture of confidence and anticipation. It was mine! Forty minutes to find it! I took the data plotted and plotted point #3 - 1700 meters! Curses!! I filled my two one-quart canteens from my two-quart canteen for convenience and started for point #3.

This was a popular neck of the woods; I must have crossed trails with ten or more people. A couple of them were still looking for their first point. I didn't feel so bad now! This course took me back across the wide part of the bulldozed area. Except for the near and far edges where the treetops were racked up in long rows, the going was easy and I found the third point also in 40 minutes. I plotted point four expecting the worst, but to my surprise it was an easy walk - 1100 meters. I strolled on across the woods, enjoying being out for the first time. I arrived at point #4 at 1640 along with three other RANGERS. Sitting down, I realized my feet hurt. I took off my right boot to discover a small stick had caused a blister. My next point, if I went for it, plotted out as a 1400-meter walk placing me 1100 meters from the rally point. I had less than a quart of water, one blister, and about one and a half hours to get one point more than minimum. In talking with the other RANGERS there, their legs had all been between 900 and 1400 meters. I decided that a bird in the hand was worth two in the bush, and I limped back to the rally point with my passing score.

Upon arriving there, I was immediately "drafted" into a search party that was being formed to go look for an M-16 that a student had lost! I couldn't believe it. How could a man lose an M-16 during a daylight walk in the woods? I never found out who it was but he got one first class cursing from me that day. The weapon was subsequently recovered and the loser got a Major Minus Spot Report. As I said, a few people found six points; some not by navigation but by stumbling on them or by going on information from other RANGERS in the area. I didn't figure it was worth reporting in that manner. Others failed to find four points and still others came in after the time limit, some with 4, some with more, some with less. We at the finish line stood by the check-in hut during the last minutes screaming encouragement to those we could see struggling up the road in the distance. It was sad to see those who were literally yards away when the RI closed his notebook and said, "That's it, RANGERS! Time's up." A Re-test would be allowed for some on Day 18 and even then, some would not make it. It may sound strange to suggest that land navigation should be practiced before going to RANGER School, but that is what I suggest unless you are very strong in that area. Practice will build your self-confidence and put you more at ease when on the course. Luck is also welcomed but it comes in many forms. But I have come to regard luck as the intersection of hard work, opportunity, and confidence.

Another test that you must pass in RANGER School is the Mountaineering Performance Test; actually it is a series of tests, which can be described as knots, belays, and rappels. These, of course, are all given during the Mountain Phase at Camp Frank D. Merrill, Dahlonega, Georgia. Knot tying is something that should be learned and practiced before going to RANGER School to make things easy. If you are not a slow learner, you can learn the knots in School and pass the test, but there are only so many hours in the day and if you are slow to learn mechanical things, you will do like four of our class and fail knot tying and be recycled. Actually we had about a 20% failure rate on the initial test, then after two re-tests, four still failed. The actual tying of the knots is not the problem; it's the time factor and proper "dressing" of the knots that causes the failure. Each knot had a specific time associated with it. On command to start, you would have from 30 seconds to 2 minutes to tie and dress the knot, depending on the complexity of the knot. Dressing meant that the knot had to be very tight and the working end had to be a specific length when finished or, in some cases, both the running end and the working end had to be even - and I mean even; like within 1/8 inch of being the same length. They are very strict on the knot test and in fact, if you cannot pass the knot test, they can prevent you from going to Mount Yonna for climbing and rappelling exercises. Failing the knot test is in itself not grounds to kick you out of the School, but in the end it amounts to the same thing.

The second area of the Mountaineering Performance Test is belaying. A RANGER "on belay" is essentially a safety man whose mission is to catch a climber if he falls by quickly applying brake to the safety rope which normally runs from the belay man through one or more snap links to the climber. The belay man must watch the climber closely if the slope allows this and if not, he can keep a minimum amount of slack in the safety rope consistent with necessary freedom of movement of the climber. The belay man must be instantly responsive to the needs of the climber and he must know the various positions of belaying. To ensure that each RANGER can safely perform belay, he is given a series of tests. First he goes through a ground drill in which he assumes various belay positions on command of the RI. In each position (sitting and standing; upward belay and downward belay) he must respond correctly and instantly to various commands by the RI; up-rope, slack, falling, tension, etc.

The final belay test combines practical failing and belaying. This is accomplished on a near vertical wooden wall, which rises some 30-40 feet high and intersects a large platform much like a sun deck. The base of the wall is a sawdust pit some 3 feet deep. The belay man positions himself on the sun deck and assumes the sitting belay position, downward pull. The climber takes the working end of a 120 foot climbing rope thrown down by the belay man and, making a minimum of 10 wraps around his waist, secures the wrap with a knot known as a bowline-on-a-coil. The vertical wall is constructed of bridge decking materials (3 inches x 10 inches) with 4 to 6 inches of space between horizontal boards. The belay man calls out "On Belay Test." The climber responds "Testing," and he applies his weight to the rope in increments until he is satisfied the rope is secure and taught between him and the belay. This done, the belay man commands "climb" and the climber commands "Up Rope" and he climbs to the top of the wall until he can see the belay man. Now the test begins. He then calls for "slack" and he will pull himself 8 or 10 feet of slack and commands "brake." Then he positions himself in sort of a "U" shape with his hands holding onto a plank 2 or 3 feet from the top (this is so that the belay man cannot see the climber) and his feet planted flat footed some 2 or 3 feet below his hands. The climber then simply turns loose with his hands just like shooting an arrow from a bow.

Just relax the grip and let nature take its course. IMMEDIATELY yell (scream at the top of your lungs) "falling" because you are falling. You will fall at least however much slack you pulled, and if you were shy and only pulled a few feet, then the RI would pull slack for the next practice fall. Always pull 8 or 10 feet of slack! You keep climbing back up and going through the same procedure until the RI is satisfied that the climber knows how to fall and that the belay man can belay, but in any case, a climber must fall at least twice.

The Sergeant in charge of this phase of instruction, MSGT Chenault, said that the School record for climbers falling was 52 times before he got 2 good ones. I thought about that as I heard my falling partner yell "falling" for the tenth time. He was almost half way through. Twenty-two times he fell before he finally got a GO, and he was no small fellow. Then it was my turn to fall. I had felt a growing pain in my right side from about fall 12 or 13, but now as I wrapped the turns of climbing rope around my waist and tied the bowline on a coil, I had a definite pain - low level, but it hurt more if I took a deep breath. It was my turn, "Up Rope" I yelled to the belay man and he began to pull up rope so I could test it. Test complete, I began the climb up to the falling position. Clinging there with a good 10-12 feet of slack I imagined shooting my bow, I needed a good fall because I wasn't sure how many I could take. My fingers relaxed, I was away, falling through the air with the greatest of ease "FALLING!" The end of the rope came quickly and painfully. I muffled a groan and gritted my teeth as I bounced off the wall lightly. It felt good, the form that is. "Good fall, Old Man," yelled the RI, "One more like that and you're a GO." One more like that and I might go, I thought.

Back up I went, through the whole procedure again. "FALLING!" I was away again, dreading the end of the rope ---- Ahhhggg! I couldn't contain it; I quickly followed up with a gruntal RANGER!! to cover up the groan and grabbed the wall to relieve the pressure of my lower rib. "Good fall, Old Man, get down and coil your rope." Two tests down and one to go in Mountaineering Performance. The pain in the rib cage was cause for concern, but I had too much invested to go to a doctor and confirm what I suspected.

The final test in Mountaineering Performance was rappelling which was certainly the most enjoyable training of the course. It is in fact fun. The rappelling site was a shear rock face blasted out of the Mountainside. The total rappel length is approximately 60 feet including the hook-up shelf and the actual vertical drop is 40-50 feet high. The test is simple; one rappel each using left then right hand brake without equipment; and one rappel each using left and then right hand brake with LBE, rucksack, and M-16 rifle for a total of 4 rappels.

The next area of evaluation might be categorized as confidence tests. The first confidence test was given during the Benning Phase at Victory Pond. Day 18 for class 6-81 was a busy one. Actually, Day 18 began on Day 15 at about 1900 hours with a patrol mission briefing. That patrol terminated at 1100 hours on Day 17 followed by a move back from Camp Darby to Harmony Church where we finally got to bed about 2300-2400 hours.

Day 18 began with an 0400 first call and the 5-mile RANGER run. The morning was cold as we fell into formation for a few warm-up exercises before the run. The Morgan Team was in charge again, and I was getting my extra ration of "attention" from several of them. SGT Moore was there trying to get me to answer to the call for "Major Childers" so he could award me a few push-ups. It was a game he played with me. MSGT Peavy set the pace for the run. He was a fine NCO and instructor somewhere in his early 40's, I guessed, with a physique like a classical marathoner about 2 pounds per inch of height. Again, I do not know what the pace was, but it was steady. He got the formation up to speed and maintained that constant pace uphill and downhill for the entire 5 miles except for the turn around slowdown at the 2.5 mile point. The rumor was that they would only run us out 2 miles, that way, when we returned to the start point, we would think we were finished and we would keep driving on for another mile. This was supposed to have some negative effect on us - "psyche us out" so to speak. I was ready to keep on running when we came back to the start point - feeling good!

Another 5 miles would have been OK with me, but we stopped; the last RANGER run was over without spectacle. No one fell out of this, the supposedly hardest run yet and that surprised me, since we had actually not run distance during the previous ten days at Camp Darby. Actually, the last run was a 3-1/2 mile run on Day 7. We had done a lot of walking, climbing, crawling, sprinting, and double-timing, but no distance run at Camp Darby.

After breakfast we moved to Victory Pond for our first "official" confidence test. It was Saturday morning (the day after Friday the 13th). What more could a soldier ask for than to spend his Saturday morning at Victory Pond? A large set of bleachers faces Victory Pond and provides seating for RANGERS and visitors to enjoy a number of RANGER demonstrations, which precede the confidence tests. From the bleachers you look down on a large sawdust hand-to-hand combat pit where the RI's put on an excellent demonstration of disarming each other of various weapons and generally, kicking the hay out of each other. They lay some resounding kicks into each other in a rodeo clown against the bull kind of atmosphere. The class would -punctuate the solid thud of boot against flesh with a loud growl and a few seconds of riotous yelling and screaming. Then on signal, we would cut it off sharply and wait eagerly for the next move. To the left rear of the sawdust pit as we faced it was a very high rappelling tower, which I hesitate to guess the actual height of, but surely it was 60 feet. At the conclusion of the combatives, two RI's came flying down the face of that tower in the Australian rappel firing weapons as they descended. It was a beautiful, fast rappel and a perfect landing. I'll bet they could have heated a canteen cup of coffee water by dropping their snap links in - they were definitely passing some nylon across metal. Next we watched a helo/rappel insertion demonstration and some demolition activity on the far side of the pond, followed by a helo extraction and a fly-by with two RI's riding a climbing rope suspended below the chopper perhaps a hundred feet.

The final demonstration of the day by the RI's was to show how the two tested events would be done. Out of the rappel tower and across the combative pit at a dead run came SGT Finian. Almost without breaking stride at the base of the 40-foot pole, he began racing up the pole literally like a squirrel during rut. This confidence test is called the Log Walk/Traverse/Drop. At the top he again ran across the horizontal 8 inch x 8-inch beam (40 feet off the water). Half way across the horizontal beam is a three-tiered set of steps made from the 8 inch x 8-inch beam, which amounted to an obstacle two feet high, by 4-5 feet long. This he cleared in a single jump, landed at a dead run on the far side and continued to the end of the beam (another 20-30 feet). Now he lay face down on a 2 inch diameter rope and hand over hand, pulled himself out perhaps 15 feet to the intersection of another rope, whereupon he transferred to the new rope, hung by his hands and moved Tarzan-style out to the middle of that rope. In the middle hung a replica of the "coveted black and gold."

"Request permission to touch the TAB, sir," was yelled loud and clear.

"Permission granted," came the response from the ground.

At this he released his grip with his right hand, kissed his finger trips, touched the TAB tenderly, kissed his fingers again, and re-grasped the rope.

"Request permission to turn loose of the rope, sir," was the next exchange.

"Permission denied."

He hung there another minute or so, the cold morning wind (perhaps 15 knots) swaying him and causing a chop on the water. "Request permission to drop, sir!!"

"Are you tired, RANGER?"

"No sir, I am not tired. I want to get wet!"

"Permission granted to drop."

And he was away, hands up over the head for a near perfect water entry from about 40 feet. The water temperature and the wind chill factor showed on his face as he crossed in front of the bleachers and disappeared.

The suspension traverse, otherwise known as Slide For Life, looks like fun to the observer, and can be if executed properly. But with a water impact velocity of some 50 MPH, an incorrect landing can mean a snout full of water, a dislocated joint, or worse. Slide for life is a marvelously simple device. Anyone can make one for their own use. All you need is a beam long enough to anchor and leave 100 feet sticking vertically in the air. Near the top you build a small platform, 1 meter x 1.3 meters, from which to launch yourself and approximately 60 feet above the platform, you anchor one end of a 400 foot 1-1/2 inch diameter steel cable. The other end of the cable is anchored firmly 378 feet (approximately) from the base of the 100-foot high beam -

preferably over water. Now all you need is a small trolley to fit the cable and a handgrip to support your weight.

Our TAC Officer, LT Eckert, was the volunteer demonstrator for this confidence measurer. He looked like a toy way up there on that platform. SGT Swakhammer stood by the water entry anchor with a signal flag in his hand. On signal from SGT Swakhammer, LT Eckert did a chin-up on the trolley handle. As his feet left the platform, the trolley began to accelerate down the inclined cable at the rate of 32 ft/Sec/Sec. A few feet from the platform, Eckert began a loud slow "RANGERS LEAD THE WAY" which he stretched out to last the entire ride. At a particular point down the incline, SGT Swakhammer raised the flag over his head, a signal for LT Eckert to raise his legs and make an "L-shape" with his body. Almost as soon as the legs were horizontal, Swakhammer dropped the flag sharply and LT Eckert released himself from the trolley just as he disappeared from sight of the audience behind a sea wall. A neat plume of water rose above the sea wall, witness to the inevitable collision between water and high speed RANGER. The class gave him a loud applause and a whole lot of growling and howling. SGT Rock then went into action to re-demonstrate the log walk/horizontal rope traverse/drop. He played the part of a reluctant participant to perfection and to our total enjoyment. We howled and growled at his every antic. Probably, it was on this day that the first bond of something other than fear was forged between Rock and Class 6-81. Maybe it was affection - we already had every other emotion; admiration, fear, caution, respect, even doubt. He stood at the base of the vertical pole looking up it, then back at the instructor with that 'I don't want to go up there look on his face.

"Request permission to climb the pole, sir???"

"Permission granted RANGER Rock."

"Are you sure about that now, I don't want to press you!"

He started climbing the pole much like you would expect Lou Costello or Jerry Lewis to do in a movie - one cautious step at a time, occasionally stopping to cling to the pole and stare frightfully down, gauging how far he could now fall.

"Up the pole RANGER or you'll have to do the whole thing over." At this he rushed on up to the top and stood clinging to the two gateposts at the top. Would you believe they have a lockable entrance gate at the top of the pole to keep unauthorized/unsupervised people from playing on the device? A little verbal abuse and threats got him to turn loose of the posts and begin the trek across the "log." One shaky step at a time, he proceeded, knees bent, both arms outstretched for balance. About half way to the steps, the ground instructor yelled, "You're moving too slow RANGER! Go back to the gate and start over!"

"Go BACK!! I'm having enough trouble going forward!"

"Go back RANGER! NOW!!"

At this he sat down, turned around, got on his hands and knees and scurried back along the narrow beam to the gate and clung there. Additional urging by the RI on the ground got him moving across the beam again, this time at an acceptable pace. The class was literally rolling in the aisles. This time he made it to the obstacle steps where he fell to his knees and crossed himself. With the RI screaming at him, he tried to crawl on his stomach up and over the obstacle. Finally, under a threat worse than death, he stood semi-erect and continued on to within three or four steps of the relative safety of the far side - running the last few steps to cling frantically to the upright there. Then I guess he figured he had done enough of the how-not-to act so he executed the horizontal rope traverse quite professionally, touched the RANGER Tab lithely - and turned into a clown again. He hung there looking down and shaking his head vigorously no, no, no.

"Permission to drop granted" said the RI.

"I didn't ask" cried Rock!

Then with a scream that would curdle your milk, he let go and dropped into the cold water below. His face was contorted in pain as it disappeared beneath the froth, leaving only his black beret afloat to witness his passage. A hand came out of the water to grab the beret and pull it under. When he came up, he was wearing his beret and spraying pond water from his mouth as he swam ashore. So the rules were demonstrated. You don't have to go at a dead run like SGT Finian; neither can you inch your way along one step at a time. Simply stand up and walk across like walking a very narrow sidewalk. Demonstrate your confidence.

And it was our time. Who has guts - or who does not? All of the civilian and on-post military observers in the bleachers were dismissed and we were alone, the Morgan Team and Class 6-81.

"I need seven volunteers," screamed the RI.

From halfway up in the bleachers, I made about three leaps down the seats and was the third one in the volunteer line.

"Old Man, I ain't never seen you move so fast! What do you think this group is gonna do anyway?"

"Go first, SGT," I replied.

"WRONG, RANGER! You are going to assist me."

Well you win some and you lose some. As it turned out I think I won because I had the opportunity to watch a lot of people make mistakes before it was my time. These two obstacles had occupied a lot of my thought prior to coming to Fort Benning, trying to figure out the best way to conquer them. This is because everyone that I had ever talked to about RANGER School had described these two confidence tests as though they were the highlight of the Benning Phase. A fellow officer in the National Guard was dropped from the RANGER course several years before due to a back injury received on the slide for life. The back was of particular concern since only 5 months before entering RANGER School I had slipped a disc in my lower back and had been under a doctor's care and treated at regular intervals by a chiropractor. In fact, the last thing I did before checking out of the motel in Columbus to drive out and report in for RANGER School was to remove my back brace and hide it beneath the lavatory in Room #421 of the Airport Holiday Inn. I intended to request that room during one of our breaks and recover the brace, but never did. So, unless the Holiday Inn has a very thorough maid, or plumbing trouble, I suppose the thing is still there.

Once while waiting in an airport lobby back in 1972 or 1973, I got into a conversation with an Army captain about RANGER School. He wore, of course, the Tab and a number of decorations from Viet Nam. Brownley was his name as I recall; an impressive soldier who talked excitedly about RANGER School. He described these confidence tests in great detail as though they occupied a place of prominence in his experience. Major Monroe, a former Regular Army advisor to my unit when I commanded the Cavalry Troop also described the test with some respect. And so I gave some thought to the best way to enter the water off of the two devices. I tried to think of ways I could practice but could think of no way to practice the slide for life. I did walk probably several dozen miles balancing on a railroad track to try and improve my balance for the log walk, and I did improve my balance to the point that I could do a slow airborne shuffle on a railroad track for hundreds of yards without falling off. But of course, walking the track of the iron horse is quite different from walking an 8" beam elevated forty feet above the water. Actually, walking an 8" beam is much easier under ideal conditions because it is flat and relatively wide, but there are also problems. The iron rail, conversely, is very narrow and has a crowned surface thus making balance difficult. So I think that practicing rail walking is a good thing to do because it does improve the sense of balance as well as response to correct imbalance with minimum over-correction. In fact, long rail walks (more than a mile) will improve muscle tone much the same as swimming because a lot of muscles are exercised in maintaining your position on the rail; and you can do it year round at no cost. All you need is a railroad track without train. If you can find a trestle over a river, canyon, or highway you can even simulate the height aspect.

The difficult thing to simulate is that as you are crossing the beam over Victory Pond, other RANGERS are simultaneously climbing the pole behind you, traversing the rope ahead of you, and dropping off of the rope. All of these activities cause movement of the device. In addition, if the wind is blowing, particularly if it is gusting as it was the day our class went through, the problem of balance is complicated. Another complication of the log walk that takes it out of the ideal realm is that prior to climbing the pole, each RANGER goes into the pond in full clothing to verify his ability to swim. Actually I think the real reason is to get him wet so that after a few-people have crossed the beam and rope, the whole affair becomes wet and slippery; and in our case, cold and shivering in the early March wind.

As one of the seven over-zealous volunteers, my post was at the business end of the slide for life. After each RANGER "crashed and burned" I would dash out on the small walkway and retrieve the trolley off of the cable and turn it over to two other RANGERS who would rig it to the body of a continuous line of cold, wet, shivering people in line to climb the 100 foot high pier to the launch platform. I got to watch perhaps thirty or more people execute the slide for life before I dropped a snap link and was switched off to another task. It became obvious that if the trick was executed properly, there was nothing to it.

Properly meant lifting your legs to the right height just above level; properly meant turning loose of the trolley exactly when the signal was given by SSGT Swakhammer; and properly meant to hold the L-shape of the body even after water impact. Those who did it properly would skip along on their bottom and sink slowly, much like a water skier does after he releases the towrope, and not even get their hair wet. An early release meant a high release which usually allowed Mother Nature time to slowly rotate the body slightly one way or the other so that on water contact, the body met the water not as a planing surface but as a paddle (or should I say fan blade). I think fan blade is a more accurate description because the body is spun violently. The arms and legs immediately try to compensate for this unwanted motion and the last thing seen before the flailing body disappears into the spray of water is eyeballs staring and appendages grasping for something solid. Some did more than 360 degrees of rotation - head over heels.

If the trolley is released too late, the potential of colliding with either the concrete abutment, which is the anchor point, or the rebounding trolley is great. The most spectacular near accident occurred due to a late release. This kid did all of the wrong things that could possibly have been done. When he left the platform at the top of the cable he held his legs in the squat or tucked position for some reason, which reduced the aerodynamic drag on his body and allowed him to go faster. He was also a slight person thus the friction drag of the trolley system was less. Together these factors allowed him more than average speed. Standing at the end of the ride, the cable responded to the rolling trolley wheels with a high pitched hum; with this ride the hum was notably louder in fact, I would describe it as a pitched whine much like the sound of a gas turbine starting up. I couldn't tell if SSGT Swakhammer anticipated anything unusual out of this landing or not, he always had the same cold calculating look on his face anyway. Perhaps this ride was not unusual to him as he had probably seen a few hundred, but for me only having seen a dozen or so up to now it looked like an uncontrolled approach. I took two uneasy steps back to get out of his line of ricochet path just as the signal to lift legs was given. He moved his legs from the tuck position to the L-shape; but when he was given the signal to drop, he only dropped his legs.

On down the cable he came; "Drop, Dummy" screamed Swakhammer. He hung there, eyes fixed on the concrete abutment anchor that was fast approaching. "Drop! Drop! God Dammit, DROP!" screamed Swakhammer. "Dummy's" feet suddenly hit the water and I don't know if he was dragged off of the trolley, or if he finally put it all together and released, but the result was the same. His feet suddenly became a moving pivot point which meant his body still had forward motion, but at the same time he was being pivoted about his feet like the hands of a clock gone wild. Splat!! He hit the water unmercifully hard and began a violent, uncontrolled tumble. The trolley, meanwhile, continued to the anchor point, crashed into an old truck tire which acted as a bumper, and rebounded back up the cable a few feet, which is normal. The RANGER, meanwhile is still body surfing toward the anchor point. They (the Dummy and the Trolley) couldn't have missed each other by more than another layer of paint on the trolley - but it wasn't over yet. He did the hydrodynamic tumble all the way in to the tire bumper and SSGT Swakhammer was down on his knee screaming threats and obscenities at him for being born. I rushed out and grabbed the trolley as it started to roll back to the bumper and crack the RANGER in the skull. Both Swakhammer and I were now wet from the splashing we got; the RANGER was bewildered but unhurt. He started swimming the wrong direction to get out. "This way, Dummy! And if you get out, go back and do it again until you can follow instructions!" chided Swakhamner. The RANGER was gasping for breath as he dog paddled to the exit point.

And it was my turn. The first step was to put on the load bearing equipment and plastic M-16 replica and jump backwards off of the sea wall into the pond. God, the water was cold in March! I had been wet in the winter many times before; had even dove naked once in the dead of winter to recover a shotgun dropped overboard during a duck hunt. And I had swam streams many times fully clothed in warm climates, but I had never before swam fully clothed with equipment in cold water. Be prepared to be exhausted because an, awful lot of energy is sucked right out of your body doing that 15-25 meter swim. What's worse is when you climb out of the water into a brisk wind. The climb up the 40-foot pole did nothing to warm me up. I stood at the gate shaking so badly that I wasn't sure how good my balance would be. We couldn't leave the gate until told to. I stood there shaking, silently cursing the guy holding up the show. That may not sound too sporting but in RANGER School where one agony leads to another it is not uncommon to find yourself verbally encouraging a fellow RANGER, even physically Aiding him, while silently cursing him for his ineptness. "Walk Dum Dum, it's only a 40 foot fall," I thought. He finally overcame his fear and got across the steps at the midpoint of the beam.

"All right Methuslum, what are you waiting for, an engraved invitation?" yelled an RI. By now I had learned to respond to a number of names; Old Man, Pappy, Gramps, Methuslum, Chief of the Over the Hill Gang, Week-End Warrior, RANGER "C", and on rare occasions, RANGER Childers.

The hardest part of crossing the log walk is the first three steps. From then on to the middle, momentum is with you. Don't look past the surface of the beam to the water below. Just sort of blur your focus on the plane of the beam, watch your feet line up somewhat with the center of the beam, and keep one foot in front of the other. Going up the steps in the middle is easy, but for some reason going down the steps back to the beam was a minor mental block. Reaching the end of the beam was a welcome point in the travel toward the tab because that meant I would at least hold my destiny in my hands. As cold as they were, I bent down, got a firm grip on the rope, swung off the beam, dangled in the air temporarily while my ankles found a firm latch over the rope. Hanging upside down much like a sloth, I monkey crawled out to the tab, disengaged my ankles from the rope, and again hung in the wind. I had made it all the way to the RANGER Tab on the rope with no visible hesitation or "encouraging" remarks from below.

"Request permission to drop, Sir," I yelled.

"Permission granted," came the reply.

I know that I did not visibly hesitate to drop because I did not receive a ration of abuse, but internally I know there was a short circuit between the brain and the fingers. My mind quickly reviewed with my body how to conduct itself on the way down. Should I hold my nose to prevent water from being forced in by the fall; flat footed or pointed toes; straight legged or bent knees; should I go into a tuck; maybe I should spice it up a bit and do a chin up, release into a half gainer and enter hands first. Oh what the hell, I thought, go! The fingers responded and a few milliseconds later I was shrouded by the mantel of very cold water.

I swam to shore and got into the line to receive my trolley for the suspension traverse, shaking like the proverbial dog passing peach seeds. RANGERs don't go anywhere without their sling rope. It is a length of rappel rope with the ends whipped smartly and is precisely 13 feet long. Carried across the chest from right shoulder to left hip, it stays by virtue that it is doubled and secured at the left hip by an overhand knot with precisely 3 inches of working end extending beyond the knot. The snap link is snapped into this affair so that the student always has the ability to configure a Swiss seat for rappelling, a safety line for water crossing, or any number of other uses. Now we are about to find another use for the snap link and rope. Securing the 50# trolley to your body for the climb to the top of the slide for life tower.

"RANGER Childers!! Why are you shaking; it is not cold out here yet! You don't have permission to shake."

It was Sergeant Rock. "I don't know why your are shaking!! I went into the water and I am not shaking."

Of course he was in dry clothes now.

"Elevate your feet for twenty Old Man, that will warm you up!" Two-zero did not warm me up; it just took more energy out of the body and made me shake more.

The 100-foot vertical climb carrying the trolley and wearing cold, wet clothes is by far the hardest part of the Victory Pond event. Don't look down. Look up. Count the foot pegs as you grab them, not because you know how many there are, but to keep your mind off of how cold they are. Feel your feet as they find their place of the pegs that accumulate below you. By the time you reach the top, the thought is that there must be a better way down than to climb back down the way you came up. Sure enough, there is. You brought it with you. The trolley. The wind was still blowing when I made the last rung on the ladder and stepped onto the platform. As I fumbled with cold fingers to take my trolley off my back, I wondered if my fingers would function well enough to actually hold onto the trolley handles.

"Well, well, look who's here! It's the world's oldest RANGER." It was SGT Reynolds, one of the more "entertaining" of the RIs.

"Well, don't just stand there shaking and dripping all over my platform Old Man; give me your trolley."

My advice is that when you grab the trolley handles, **do not look down**! You'll discover that at the moment of launch, and for several feet thereafter, if you should fall, you will not fall into water, but onto land! (I noted when I visited a graduation in 1996 that they had installed a safety net below the tower) I grabbed the handles and stared intently at the backs of my hands to be sure I had a good grip because I was so cold, I surely could not feel that I was gripping firmly. My knuckles were white so I figured I must have a good grip. I hoped so.

"Do you know what to say on the way down Old Man?"

"Yes SGT Reynolds - RANGERS LEAD THE WAY." I yelled.

"No RANGER Childers! Everybody else gets to say that. You are going to scream 'OLD PEOPLE LEAD THE WAY' - so long and loud that I can still hear it next week!"

"GO!" he said.

I lifted myself chin-up style and I was launched. My gaze shifted from my hands to the figure at the far end of the 400-foot long cable as my trolley began to make the cable sing. "Watch Swakhammer" I said to myself. Don't worry about the chunk of concrete coming at you nor about the water passing swiftly beneath. Good body position and instant response to his signal are the keys. Hope he's not still mad about that snap link I dropped in the pond during trolley recovery! I started the call immediately after I launched: "OLD PEOPLE LEAD THE WAY!" I stretched it out to last most of the way down. When I first began this book, I decided to name it "OLD PEOPLE LEAD THE WAY" after that event. Later on I decided to name it after a principle that followed us through the School, "Driving On."

The signal, and command "Lift your legs." I felt sluggish in response because of the cold. But I remembered watching several RANGER buddies do it wrong and "crash and burn" as it were on the water's surface. I tried to picture my position and measure it in my iceberg-like mind, all the while closing in on the anchor point beyond.

"Drop!"

I released for a near perfect landing as far as I could tell. My face did not even get wet. I swam out quickly and reported to the TAC Officer "Sir, RANGER Childers, 3rd Squad, 3rd Platoon, Roster #10, reports successful completion of the log walk, horizontal rope traverse, drop and suspension traverse confidence tests; SIR!"

You had to get that entire train of events expressed correctly the first try. If you did not, punishment was just a word away; not that it mattered very much. They could always find something to pass punishment for.

"Elevate your feet for one-zero for excessive shaking and shivering RANGER Childers and go get out of those wet clothes. If you die on us it's gonna be a big big disappointment for a very small number of people."

Thus, Phase I, The Benning Phase, was over. The activities that injure most people were all now behind us, along with the Morgan Team, the PT, and the worm pit. I was still there, in reasonably good shape, save the still troublesome major muscle group in my left thigh, and looking forward to the Mountains.

Other tests of confidence would have to be faced and passed, but they wouldn't be categorized as confidence tests per se. They would be hidden under various other labels such as Point Man, Compass Man, Patrol Leader, Navigator, or just plain RANGER. Every hour that one stays in the program is another confidence test passed regardless of the job assigned. There are a number of events, particularly during the Mountain Phase that, again, are not confidence tests per se, but that do require confidence to complete successfully.

The first of these that I recall was the exercise of carrying my buddy down the shear cliff on my back. The scenario was very simple. My buddy had been injured and the only way to evacuate him with the equipment available was to tie him to my back and rappel down the mountain with him as a passenger. The RI assisting in the lash-up looked at my RANGER buddy, Campana; and he looked at me; Campana weighed 215# or more

"Hey Old Man, you can trade buddies for this one; RANGER Campana seems to outsize you a tad."

I looked at Campana.

"Yeah, Gramps" shrugged Campana, "You know, any way you wanna do it, that's okay by me. I can trade and get with. . ." He looked a-round for someone his size. . . . "RANGER Flucker over there." Flucker reminded me of a shorter version of Sonny Liston. I know that Campana did not really want to ride my back down that cliff and I certainly did not relish the thought of having to carry him. But RANGERS are hard-core! RANGERS drive on!!

"Well," I said to the RI, "The ideal solution would be for me to carry RANGER Kelly (who weighed maybe 115) and ride Campana; but nothing is ever ideal so I'll stick with my partner. If I can carry him, I can carry anyone in the class."

The RI just sort of turned away and continued to do whatever he was doing with the ropes. A slight slow shaking of the head said, "OK RANGER, whatever you two want to do is fine."

There was a large rock about knee high there. I leaned over and rested my hands on it more or less assuming the position of a standard load-bearing animal. Campana was draped across my back, all 215 pounds of him, and was lashed to me with his 13-foot sling rope.

"All right Gramps! You got us babe - - - how does it feel," asked my passenger?

"Just don't let go old buddy," I assured him, "and I'll get us to the bottom."

What neither of us knew with any amount of certainty was, how fast I would get us to the bottom!!!

"Let go!" he said. "You realize we are tied together don't you, Gramps!! At that moment I thought about two things, my skinny legs and my vertebrae. If there was a failure of either, which one would it be? I stood up straight. Yep, he weighed at least 215!

"If we fall Campana, it'll be your mother's fault" I said as I laid the climbing rope through the snap link gate.

"My mother's! Why my mother's?"

"For feeding you so #@&*/##! much when you were a pup" I said.

"RANGER Childers, are you positive you can do this" asked the RI.

"No sweat SGT, I'm just making a gut-check with my passenger," and I leaned back and dropped over the edge before anybody including me could think any more about it. Imagine carrying a backpack that weighs 215 pounds' Going over the edge is the hard part because the wall is not flat or even. As I got my body positioned for the first bound, the left foot was at a different depth into the wall than the right one and there was a slight torque on my body. Taking a couple of knee flexes I didn't think the bound would be good. My legs were quivering under the strain; the RI was looking nervously over the rim at me; Campana, I think, had stopped breathing.

"Do something even if it is wrong" I remembered that phrase from Officer Candidate School. If it made sense then, it surely made less now.

I kicked off the wall and released the brake planning about a 10 foot bound, but it turned out to be more like 20 feet. The brake was awkward for me to apply with that body strapped to my back, and the extra load made it worse. The brake simply did not hold solid. We came into the wall at about 20 feet and never really stopped, so I just "walked" on down the face with the rope running through my brake hand. I don't guess anybody noticed at all but I was glad when we reached the bottom. My brake hand was beginning to get warm. Of course what I should have done, and what the RI should have made me do, is to have thrown an extra turn of rope through the gate to increase the mechanical advantage on the brake. I felt Campana breathe a sigh of relief. An RI at the bottom helped to un-tie us - with congratulations.

"Good show Gramps! Good $%#@*&^^ show!" said Campana.

"No, you get the applause on this one" I said, "cause if the situation had been reversed, I don't know if I would have ridden you down."

"If the situation had been reversed" he responded, "I wouldn't have taken me down!"

So we both got a good laugh out of that one and climbed back up to the top for the easy part - him carrying me down!

The next event in the Mountain Phase that measures the confidence is a team effort to get a litter-case off the mountain. The greatest thrill is in store for the RANGER who gets to be the litter-case.

"RANGER Childers, you look more like you ought to be a litter case than anyone else so guess what?" mused the RI.

"I guess I get to ride the litter," I answered.

"Right on, Old Man" said the RI, "And I'm gonna give you about twenty foot of slack."

"Thanks a lot, Sarge."

I lay on the litter while my fellow RANGERS, under the tutoring of RI's, tied me five ways to Sunday to the litter. Convinced that I wouldn't come loose," they took me, bound to my litter, over to the edge of the cliff and positioned me much like a man about to be buried at sea is positioned on the rail. A 7/16 inch nylon climbing rope was tied to the head end of the litter and run through a snap link and over to the belay men. Two rappelers go over the cliff and position themselves 15 feet or so below the rim and offset right and left from the flight path of the litter when it is thrown off the cliff. One "rappelee" is rigged for a right hand brake and one for a left hand brake thus freeing their left and right hands respectively for guiding the litter down the face of the cliff.

"Ready Old Man" grinned the RI?

"Old people lead the way, Sergeant" I replied.

"Well you think about that on the way down Old People," and he launched me straight off the rim. Earlier that morning the class was introduced to the days training with the flying litter case demonstration. We were in a tight formation at the base of the cliff in such a position that we could not see any activity on the ledge at the top. Suddenly two RANGER Instructors came bounding down the face together to stop and spread out. One screamed "ready" and immediately an object shot straight off the ledge, falling in a long graceful arc only to snap violently to a halt at the end of the rope and bang back against the rock wall some 15-20 feet below its launch point. A "Sheeeee" welled up through the class as we realized a live body was tied to that object. "Kee-Riste! Hope we ain't got to do that!" said one RANGER. "Kee-Riste, it's me tied to the object now" I thought, and the sensation of total helplessness came over me. Nothing to do but enjoy the ride I guessed. The RI had just been kidding; he only gave me 10-12 feet of slack. The end of the rope was not nearly as bad as I had thought it would be, and I bounced into the rock face very politely. The two rappelers guided me on down the wall as the belayers above fed slack. At the bottom they started to untie me but an RI came up and accused us of doing it all wrong.

"Go elevate your feet on the red rock for TWO FIVE" he demanded. They started to double time off to the red rock, leaving me on the litter.

"Come back here, RANGERS," he yelled "and take this Old Bald-Headed RANGER with you. I don't want him."

So back they came, grabbed the litter handles and double-timed over to the rock, put me down, and began to do push-ups.

"No! No! No! STOP RANGERS! You cannot have all of the fun! What about this old wore out one laying here on the stretcher?" So they started to untie me.

"No, RANGERS! He's old! He may break if you remove the shipping crate from him. Just turn him upside down on the rock and let him do his pushups strapped in; that way if he craps out he'll be all ready to be carried off."

After twenty-five of the strangest push-ups I had ever done, we turned in our climbing ropes and double timed back to the mess hall for evening chow. This ended the formal instruction in mountaineering techniques. We would move now to Mount Yona for practical climbing and rappelling exercises.

I never knew where Mount Yona was at; or if I have even spelled it right but that is how SGT Rock pronounced it.

"RANGERS! Tomorrow you are going to Mount Yona! I want you to go up there and knock their #@&^*#^ out. Now you're gonna run into some God #@&^*#^ civilians up there #@&^*#^ around with my Mountainside!!" He beat himself on the chest to emphasize the trespass, and paced back and forth on the propane tank. "I don't want you talking to them! If I catch you talking to them #@&^*#^ " he paused, cocked his head looking up and down the formation, giving us time to second-guess what he was going to say #@&^*#^ "I've got sum-thin for you STUDDDS! They say sum-thin to you #@&^*#^ you ignore em like they wasn't even #@&^*#^ born yet! You got that?"

"YES SERGEANT" we responded in unison.

"Ain't nuthing but a bunch of God #@&*/##! hippies with their high speed climbing gear up there. You get the chance you can shove em off the #(*@#! Mountainside for all I care."

"Old Man!!"

"Yes, Sergeant."

"I don't want to get any #@&^*#^ reports on this class not doing a first class job up there, cause if I do," he paused to come up with something new, "I'm gonna come right out of the #@*#/! sky; and I'm gonna have something for you! You got that?"

"YES SERGEANT!"

The next afternoon we were airlifted North to Mount Yona by USMC CH-46's (Marines have 46's, Army has 47's; or is it the other way around? Doesn't Matter; it's a Chinook). I, as company commander, was in the last chalk and by the time I walked down from the one ship LZ at the top, to the bivouac site below, it was almost dark. MSGT Chenault calmly announced that we were all wrong; camped in the wrong area and that I was to straighten it out immediately, if not sooner, or be castrated with a dull rock at dawn. He had a very dry, matter of fact, sense of humor. He was the chief of instruction in mountaineering techniques; no nonsense, no slack, and we were his for another 24 hours.

"When you get them dumb #@&^*#^ where they are supposed to be you 'report back here with your First Sergeant and XO for further instructions. You understand that?"

"Yes, Sergeant!"

"RANGER Childers" #@&^*#^ he paused, perhaps trying to figure out how to ask the next question, or <u>if</u> to ask it. "What the hell are you doing here?"

"Just trying to become a RANGER, Sergeant" I assured him.

"No, I mean at age forty "whatever" he said.

"Well," I said, "If I had come at 20, it would have been too easy."

He regarded that with some deliberation; a slight smile broke in the corner of his craggy face; "Drive On, RANGER!" he said with some doubt.

By now, practically everyone but me had his tent pitched, half of them in the wrong place. I got my three platoon leaders together, walked over the specific areas for each of the platoons tents, and gave them the mission to 'relocate tents as necessary to conform to the allocated bivouac area. Then I grabbed the XO and First Sergeant and reported back to MSGT Chenault. The "staff" was quartered in an old ramshackle Quonset hut which was the only shelter on the entire mountain. I knocked loudly on the door frame (there was no door - just a frame) and requested permission to enter.

"Knock off that city week crap RANGER and get your butt in here. You don't go through that silly routine out here. This is real RANGERS out here; so save that crap for when you get back to "Fort Beginning" Now; you got all them tents in the right place?"

"Yes, Sergeant."

"I'll find out come daylight," he said.

I didn't figure he would because I planned to have camp struck by sunup.

"I want one fire out there. Only one fire. You can keep it going all night if you want. You will have two men up on camp security at all times. No civilians will be allowed in the area. Everybody but security will be in the rack no later than 2300. Breakfast will be at 0700 tomorrow. All duffel will be stacked neatly on that concrete slab there and the troops ready to train at 0800; sharp! The time is now 2130. Do you have any questions?"

"No, Sergeant.

"One more thing, this radio will be monitored all night and hourly commo checks will be made by the security team. You will insure that all of the staff is awakened in the morning at 0600."

"Yes, Sergeant."

The wheels started turning. How can we wake the staff in a memorable way? Maybe there is a cold mountain stream nearby and we can slip into the Quonset hut in teams, grab the staff and haul them screaming and kicking down to the stream and toss them in. That probably borders on mutiny! Maybe just a simple bucket of water on each as they slept! No, that's sort of like assassination. A few other ideas were considered, but finally I decided perhaps discretion would be the better part of valor. Just a small demonstration that might be variously viewed as class spirit, bad judgment, instructor harassment, or whatever. Anyway, at 0600 the next morning, most of the 110 RANGERS stood around the corrugated metal Quonset hut with sticks and rocks in their hands and as the second hand announced the arrival of 0600 sharp, we all started banging on the tin hut. We quit sharply after 60 seconds. No a sound from inside; no cursing, no questions, nothing. We went about our tasks and presently the RI's began to filter out dressed and ready. Nothing was ever said, but we felt good about the little trick.

Breakfast was served out of a mermite can - scrambled eggs, bacon, bread, and coffee. A C-Ration each was drawn for noon meal. A "police call" was made of the area to insure it was left clean, then we divided up into three groups to begin the day's training. It would be a long day of practical exercises in mountaineering. Rappelling, free climbing, and buddy climbing, would be done in a series of round robin stations. The view from the training slopes is fantastic; breathtaking, and there is time to enjoy the view as some considerable amount of time at each station is spent simply waiting your turn. In places we walked across large expanses of solid granite which rose above us and fell off sharply below for hundreds of feet. There is no telling how far one would tumble if he made a slip because not only is vegetation sparse on those exposed slabs, but it's root system is limited to the few cracks that have filled with sediment over the ages. Once I kicked loose about a ten-pound rock and watched it tumble and slide out of sight some 500 feet below. I don't know how far it went beyond sight, but I figured a man would do about the same way. Winston Churchill once said, "Nothing is quite so exhilarating as to be fired upon without success." I don't think he ever went mountaineering on Mount Yona. I have been fired upon without success, but I find mountaineering more exhilarating by far.

The climbing lanes are a canned exercise in that all pitons are already implaced and of course the lanes have been climbed thousands of times. That little fact does not make the task any easier physically, but it does mentally. There is no factor of the unknown. You know it can be climbed because literally thousands before you have done it. Still, it takes more than a little courage to get yourself moving up a near vertical span of granite where foot holds are little more than toe holds and handholds are only blemishes caused by weathering. Each RANGER must climb three lanes. There are 15 or 20 lanes in all. Some are more difficult than others, but I expect the total difficulty of any group of three is pretty much equal. After the climb up each assigned lane, we moved to another lane along the top of the climbing face by hanging onto a cable that was installed there.

Then we would hook up and Aussie Rappel back down the rock wall for assignment to another climbing lane. Each RANGER had to also act as a belay man at the top. Upon reaching the top we would replace the man in the sitting belay position there, he would transfer across to a Aussie Rappel while we belayed up the next man. The next man would then become the belay man; and so on to the end.

We were supposed to have done a 200-foot rappel at night down Mount Yona, but were victims of circumstance and did not get that experience. We were cheated out of this test of courage by a forest fire. It started as another simple training exercise. The entire Company, at that time 110 RANGERS, packed on to five 2-1/2 ton trucks for a convoy, which was supposed to take us to a training area for ambush operations. We knew that in fact we would be ambushed ourselves along the route. We knew because we were told that by one of our "recycles" who had gone through this before. Sure enough, after a long twisting ride up a mountain with the truck sucking dust into the back like a vacuum cleaner, we came into one of those perfect curves; blind until the last moment - then it's too late to stop, no room to maneuver the vehicles, and no place for the troops to go. A drop so steep on the left that we could not even use it for refuge and a slope so steep on the right that the ambush could not be charged. We lost! But through the smoke and grime of that man-made hell, we charged about trying to appear in control and, in fact, after the first two or three minutes (during which time we were annihilated) we turned the tables, outflanked the ambush and set them to flight.

"Unfortunately, RANGERS" the RI began after we were finally rounded up for a critique, "you cannot be reincarnated after the initial two or three minutes because you were not prepared." His speech was soon interrupted by a roar of fire and crackling and popping of dry limbs under searing heat in the gully to his rear.

What happened was that a small brush fire started in the ambush site about 100 yards across a ravine to his rear. In the brush was a lot of blank ammunition and some pyrotechnics from past ambushes. We could hear blank M-60 or M-16 ammo cooking off occasionally, and we could see the aggressors had that fire under control. Then a star cluster cooked off and the candle shot across into the gully behind our RI and quickly started a fire. I and several others jumped up to go stamp out this one before it got away, but the RI made us sit back down. "It's not going anywhere" he said. Famous last words! Within ten minutes we were literally running for our lives and the nearest thing to panic that I have ever seen set in for a few minutes. The wind picked up suddenly, and switched directions several times. Some idiot at some time must have discarded several star clusters because we heard at least two more go off; blank rifle ammo was cranking off sporadically, seemingly all around us. It was all around us; fire now on two sides and smoke so heavy now we could not breath freely. The narrow winding gravel road was jammed with vehicles, a mixture of our five trucks, aggressor transportation, and RI vehicles. Some appeared immobile either because they blocked each other or because the drivers had abandoned them to fight fire, or whatever.

"FOLLOW ME" screamed an RI! Nobody argued; we just hoped he knew where the end of the smoke and fire was. We double-timed up the road away from the standing vehicles that were then being engulfed in smoke. It doesn't take much wood smoke to make breathing difficult, and the loss of oxygen is something that I am definitely opposed to. I think ours was running out because several people began to gasp and wheeze. Suddenly, the wind changed again and we were out of the heavy smoke.

"Everybody drop your rucksacks and rifles," directed the RI. "Leave a buddy team on weapons guard and let's scratch out a fire break down this slope to the creek."

We started scratching frantically with our hands and kicking with our feet.

"Rake the debris away from the fire dummy," scolded the RI.

"You two get your act together! One is raking it back in as fast as the other rakes it out," he corrected another.

"Make the #@&^*#^ thing straight for Kee-Riste sakes!" We made firebreaks for about an hour, abandoning some to fall back to others as the wind shifted back and forth. I had my doubts about how much good we were doing but in RANGER School, one does not ask what is sometimes the obvious. The rules of the game are simple; volunteers don't have rights, and wimps and quitters don't make RANGERS.

Then via radio the RI got the word that a forestry fire-fighting unit was on hand and that we should re-assemble back at the ambush site and await further instructions. Stopping work was definitely no problem for Class 6-81! After recovering our equipment, and making a headcount, we moved back down to where we had left the vehicles. Those that were still there were unscathed so I guess the wind change was favorable to the vehicles also - but not for long.

"Load up RANGERS and get the hell our of here! The wind switched again. The helo driver says the fire just jumped the mountain and is spreading down the valley toward Camp Merrill. It's also coming up this valley we are in at a fast pace." The RI was trying desperately to be cool about a potentially hairy situation and we were obviously not moving with a purpose in his mind. "Move it RANGERS," he belted out, "Move like you got a purpose."

There were only two of our trucks there at that moment so I had one platoon load out on them while the other two platoons started marching out. The other trucks soon caught up to us and I reformed the company adjacent to the airstrip at Camp Merrill. We stood in the sun passing canteens around sharing water because some had consumed all they were carrying and dripping with sweat. Discussing the "what-ifs" of the situation seemed a good way to pass the time and try to look inconspicuous so as to not to draw the attention of an unemployed RI. A helicopter from the forest service flew back and forth overhead with a large bucket of some design dangling on a long cable from beneath the helicopter. Later in the day, from a different vantage point, I could see the bird returning from the fire and flying low enough over a small pond so as to drag the bucket through it and fill it with liquid. It then would lift off in the direction of the fire presumably to dump the water on the blaze. I wondered about the cost effectiveness of that system but apparently the forest service thought it was great, because the bird continued to fly, I know, until nightfall. Someone said that the 'pond' that the helo was dipping from was actually a sewage treatment pond. I don't know that as a fact but there was such a pond in that general area. Some credibility was given to the story by some of our company who were called to fight the fire. Several bucket loads of the liquid were dropped on the fire close to the firefighters. They said it definitely was not clear mountain lake water and their clothes bore witness to that also.

Our company was organized into a fire brigade with two platoons being sent out immediately and the third platoon was held in reserve. The reserve platoon went back to the hooch area and busied themselves with cleaning all of the company's weapons and equipment and performing other "housekeeping" chores. With all the 'chores' done, we basically stood by' awaiting to be called on to relieve one of the two platoons fighting the fire. The sky to the Northwest was a dull orange glow from the fire and I knew that a sizable piece of real estate was going up in smoke. I worried about the two platoons out there, hoping that no one got injured on those steep slopes. In the mountains, ravines and valleys act like chimneys on a fireplace and they can draft the flame causing it to race along the ground much faster than one can move on foot along the steep, rugged inclines. Fire fighting is a grueling business as we were to find out several more times before graduation day. The heat, the smoke, the physical exertion of battling the blaze, and the lack of food, sleep and rest both before and after the fire make the task particularly hard for RANGER students.

The sound of heavy equipment nearby carried through the mountain valleys right to the cluster of houches. The "first shirt" (First Sergeant) and I went out to investigate. It was a forestry service crawler tractor plowing a firebreak at the edge of a meadow some 300 yards from our last hooch. We watched him circle the field silhouetted by the blazing fire beyond him. What a mess it would be if the fire got into the woods around the houches. They were nothing more than old plywood shacks set up on cinder blocks and they would go up like gunpowder. The firebreaks held and the fire at the meadow soon died out but the glow in the Northwest sky showed no signs of diminishing. Finally about 2300, our firefighters began to filter in. The fire was still burning but it was considered "contained."

That unexpected addition to our training schedule cost us the thrill of a 200-foot night rappel. The RANGER School schedule is so full that adjustments are not easily made for ten hours of unexpected events so the Mountain Division decided that the best thing to sacrifice was the night rappel. Well, that was okay by a lot of the class, as they had told a lot of "war stories" about the night rappel. I remember about ten years before, I had an Enlisted Man from the Armored Cavalry Troop which I commanded drop out of RANGER School due to a knee injury sustained during the night rappel. So, statistically, maybe we were lucky; but I personally felt cheated. Among others, one reason I went to RANGER School was the challenge of doing out of the ordinary things.

I chose a so-called "winter cycle" because someone had said "Winter RANGERS don't even talk to Summer RANGERS," and I didn't want some turkey thinking he had done more or better than I have. I wonder if the RANGER Department would let a graduate recycle through the mountaineering phase only? In reality the class got a break because the 200-foot night rappel is one of the performance tests that is normally a school requirement for passing the Mountain Phase.

Class 6-81 was either very fortunate or very unfortunate, depending on your point of view. When we got to Florida we were supposed to do a rappel from a helicopter hovering at 100 feet, but because of circumstances, we did not get to do this trick either. It seems that at the time we were supposed to do this act, the RDF (Rapid Deployment Force) was there on an exercise and they had all available aircraft tied up. So, in lieu of a helicopter rappel, we did extra rappels off of the training tower.

The tower was not 100 feet high, I think it was only 60-80 feet high, but I cannot imagine a great difference there. Once you are 30-40 feet off the ground, any more doesn't really matter. For instance, if you were to free-fall from the helo at 100 feet, the body would impact the ground at about 80 feet per second (FPS) or 68 miles per hour (MPH). A similar slip from a 64-foot tower would slam the body into the ground at roughly 64 FPS or 43 MPH, and a fall from 81 feet would result in an unhappy landing at 72 FPS or 49 MPH. So there is no physical difference worth mentioning between the tower rappel and the helo rappel.

There may be some psychological difference if you are susceptible to psychology. Once on the platform you feel some 'tie' to the ground because you know that the tower "legs go plumb to the ground," to re-coin a phrase slightly. On board the helo, you are hanging in the sky by the grace of a good ground crew, one threaded fastener, and the skill of the pilot. Otherwise, the platform performance is the same in both cases. The tower platform has a three inch pipe installed down and out from the surface to simulate the skid of the helo. Exit from the skid or pipe is the same. Of course going off the tower there is no rotor down wash, no buffeting by the wind, no instability problems. Also, from the tower we only went off of one side whereas from the helo, people go out both the left and right side simultaneously so there is the very remote possibility for students to swing together beneath the helo.

Perhaps the most difficult but least discussed aspect of the Florida rappel is climbing the tower. Climbing is probably, in reality, the most dangerous aspect of the exercise. The emphasis, of course, is on the rappel and on developing the skill and confidence to rappel. But if one watches people climbing the tower, particularly the first trip up, it becomes obvious that the mental obstacle to be overcome in this exercise is the climb and not the drop. This becomes even more obvious when watching the same people do the second climb; it goes much faster, more confidently. The same thing was true of the slide for life. I enjoyed the ride down but the climb up was something else again.

THE PRICE WAS ALMOST TOO HIGH

I suppose that in every great experience of any duration, most everyone will have what they consider their "darkest hour"; that moment in time when you stop and say to yourself "I wish I hadn't done that." And eventually, some level of depression or remorse sets in and you think, "If I could only do that over again." Well, RANGER School is no different and no matter where you graduate in the class, no matter how hard-core you are, you can expect to experience that "darkest hour". For some it may come early in the course; for others, very late. Some cannot cope with the situation and they become quitters. For me it came very late and was the result of such a small insignificant incident that it seems almost ridiculous and yet, it was the kind of stupid act that could have cost me a major minus spot report and my Honor Graduate Status. To be so near the checkered flag and blow an engine is a heartbreak that can be remedied in the next auto race, but in RANGER School, there is no next race for the Honor Graduate Status. You only go around once.

It was the next to the last day of patrolling and we had worked our way up to doing a company level exercise. I was chosen to be the company commander - an honor I supposed, and I had no reluctance about it. Certainly, I had as good of a background as anyone else in the class. Twenty five years in the Guard; Armored Cavalry Platoon Leader, XO, Troop Commander for four years, Infantry Brigade Assistant S-3 and Brigade S-2, Battalion S-3 and XO; making plans, issuing orders and moving people did not bother me. I knew there would be some problems simply because we had not worked as a company before, we had no SOP'S, time was going to be a problem, and the mission would be after dark. So I expected some rough spots but figured I could iron them out. RANGER Kelsey was to be my First Sergeant/Executive Officer, a good man who I knew could work with me and who I could count on. One thing I did not count on was the number of RI's that would be present. Not the normal three for the platoon, but a total of nine for the three platoons plus a couple of 'visiting firemen' who came out to view the first company sized operation.

It would be interesting to know just how much I had left in me at the end of that day but I know I was extremely tired at the beginning of the day. I was so tired and sleepy in fact that I went to sleep standing up while receiving the mission from the RI; so washed out that I thought maybe if I smoked a couple of cigarettes it would alert me some. I had to do something to come alive so after receiving the mission I sat down with Kelsey to make an estimate of the situation.

"Have you got a cigarette I could bum, Kelsey," I asked.

"God, I wish I did" he replied, "I've been out for two days." I looked around. The RI had wandered off down the river. A team of medics were about fifty feet away soaking a RANGER in the river. A victim of the heat, he was laying in the fetal position and could <u>not</u> straighten out due to cramps. The medics had carried him down to the river on a stretcher and set him in the cold stream to lower his temperature before they attempted to Medivac him back to the hospital. One of the medics was holding the patients head above water, and the other one was smoking and holding an IV aloft to ensure flow.

"Plot these coordinate locations on the map, Kelsey," I said, "I'll be right back."

I had been out of chewing tobacco for more than a day, and that is worse than being out of a smoke for two! I approached the medic somewhat cautious because I wasn't sure about the ethics of obtaining luxuries out in the boonies. Well, I reasoned, I did not violate the quota by <u>bringing</u> more than I was allowed. Nobody ever said anything about acquiring goods in the field - or not acquiring them. After all, the helicopter crews pass candy and treats to us during airlifts so what's the difference. I regarded this as resourcefulness; as a target of opportunity.

"How's it going Pappy? It's almost over for you guys ain't it?" said the medic with a smile. Even the medics called me by some affectionate, chronological reference.

"Great," I lied, "If I can stay awake for about 40 more hours it will be all over."

"Well, if you don't mind me saying so Pappy, you just don't look like you can stay awake another 40 minutes," he replied.

"Well, you'd be surprised what old folks can do Doc" I said, "By the way, what's the chance of talking you out of a couple of cigarettes for me and my First Shirt there?"

"Sure Pappy, take a few extra," he offered.

"Sure you can spare them?" I asked.

"Yeah man, I just broke a new carton and we only have a little more than a day left," he assured me.

I pulled off my patrol cap and fished into the earflaps. Long ago a Major Monroe, who was my Cavalry Troop's Army Advisor, told me "if you ever go to RANGER School, carry some money to the field with you. Five, ten, even twenty dollars; but carry it because you can just never tell when some opportunity will arise where you'll wish you had some money."

With only 40 hours left in the field, I figured this must be the occasion that Monroe had prepared me for. It was a pitiful looking five dollar bill, but recognizable. The medic assured me that he would not get into any trouble for selling smokes to RANGERS.

"Nobody ever told me not to," he said. So we struck a bargain for four packs. Kelsey was elated!

My concept of the operation was to assign each of the three platoons a mission which from a macro point of view could be considered an independent mission, thus maintaining unit integrity, and allowing the chain of command in each platoon to perform in an environment that could be evaluated as an entity. My job as the company commander was to coordinate the actions of the three platoons and ensure mission success; thus I could be evaluated in my role as a planner and coordinator, which is what I thought the job called for in this instance. One of the first things that the RI told me when I met him to get the mission was,

"This is not a graded exercise because we don't grade company size operations; but if you do a good job planning and coordinating this operation, I'll give you a plus spot. If you screw it up, you get a major minus. Do you still want the job?"

"I can't think of anybody who could do it any better than me," I said.

"Well," he replied, "we will soon find out about that, won't we RANGER Childers?"

Then I went to sleep on his bumper!

Mission: Company B 75th Infantry (RANGER) conducts a raid vicinity grid 4681012   NLT 2100 hrs to destroy enemy personnel and equipment.

The three platoons were to move by independent routes and linkup at a company patrol base. Enroute to the patrol base, two of the platoons would encounter and capture enemy personnel who would have information about the mission target area. This information would be fed to me in the patrol base and would have some impact on my tentative plan.

My tentative plan called for the third platoon to occupy blocking positions to prevent escape or reinforcement of the objective once the attack was begun; a nice clean mission of security. The First platoon was to have the machine guns from the Second platoon attached to them and they were to make the assault on and consolidate the objective. The Second platoon (minus) had the mission to follow the First platoon onto the objective and provide all search, demo, POW, and aid/litter teams. Three perfectly clean, uncluttered missions, mutually supporting but somewhat independent. I thought it was a stroke of genius. My RI about had a stroke! He could not fathom how I could be so stupid as to come up with such a non-starter plan.

"Did you dream up this genius plan all by yourself RANGER Childers??"

"I strongly suggest that you assault with two platoons on line. The mission for the third platoon is good" he advised; and he went away and left me to continue my planning.

I was about to make my biggest mistake of the eight weeks - disregard his advice and do it my way. If I were to give only one piece of advice to a prospective student it would be to act positively on any advice or suggestion of an RI.

But I had analyzed the situation carefully I thought. The information from two separate enemy sources indicated a very small guard force on the objective; rear echelon troops at best. and we were RANGERS, lean and mean, hard as woodpecker lips, trained to kill, and all that good stuff. One platoon reinforced with M-60's was more than adequate I reasoned. Kelsey was a Special Forces Staff Sergeant in "real life" and no dummy for sure. He still thought I was right. Maybe the RI is playing games with me I thought! So while Kelsey supervised the organization of the company patrol base, I got my platoon leaders together and gave them a warning order. That done, I continued my estimate of the situation, and I sent a team out to pinpoint the objective, to keep it under surveillance and report by radio, to verify the accuracy of the sketch map that we had captured, and to act as guides when we moved out.

The time was passing by swiftly now. OPORD time was coming on me like an F-4 making a napalm run. The last platoon did not make the link up to the patrol base until almost 1400. Naturally they were the one with the most important captured information. With a hit time of 2100 and sunset occurring around 1845, time was a critical commodity again. And once again, rehearsal before the attack was going to suffer. I gave a good OPORD at 1600 which lasted about 45 minutes.

"That was a pretty good operation order Old Man" said the RI with some contempt, "but it is not what I told you to do."

This was the beginning of a long night for me; a plain case of tactician versus tactician. Tactics, like religion, can only be discussed. Religion is verified in death, and tactics are verified in battle. The difference was, he was the RI and I was a student, so by definition my plan was no good. "Not invented here!" The other RI's took sides with him and they all took their turns at me, eating away at my available time; giving me a list of reasons why my plan would not work out and why "theirs" would. I could see that until I issued a change order, I was going to get nowhere. With the two objective platoon leaders and their squad leaders gathered, I gave a frag order to change the plan. First platoon on the right, second platoon on the left, machine guns assault with their platoons, each platoon provide one each search, demo, and aid team; divide the objective up for search. Questions? None! Everybody is pitching in to make things as smooth as possible and the RI's are like a hive of bees moving and milling, creating pressure, trying to generate confusion. That's their job. They did it well. Well at least now they were happy with the plan.

Getting a company out of a patrol base in the dark can be a real fire drill the first few times; this was our first time as a company operation. It was not as smooth as silk, but we drove on to and occupied the Objective Rally Point by force in good form. By the time my recon party arrived at the Release Point (RP), I calculated that I could only allow 25 minutes to conduct the leaders recon and return to the RP. I could hear people on the objective; its location was pinpointed. All I needed to verify was the best direction to make the assault from. There was no need to even check out the far side approach because I knew I would never be able to slip the whole assault force completely around the objective and set up in time, so I sent a two man team to the left flank to check that out. I could now see that the near side was up-hill. I didn't want that, although that was the tentative plan based on captured maps. I took one man to check out the right flank.

The night was extremely well lit by the moon. One thing I noticed about Florida; when it was dark it was dark, but when the moon was up there was a tremendous feeling of vulnerability through visibility. Every bush looked like an aggressor, but on this night I threw caution to the wind and moved swiftly. I could hear them on the objective talking and playing with their weapons and slamming doors; I bent low, kept in the shadows and moved directly to the right flank, crossing a trail as I went. A flare went up and gave the area a yellow cast. As soon as the flare died, I jumped up and ran as hard as I could to a small grove of pines. My recon partner must have still had his eyes closed during that move because from that point on he and I were separated. No time to find him now; I did a complete recon of that flank, moving right up to the edge of the objective itself. Perfect! The only thing that I didn't like was the jeep trail on the far side that the aggressors were using as access to the site, but it was a chance I would take - unless the recon of the other flank had a glowing report. As I backtracked off of the edge of the objective, the fourth flare went up. Hit it! Close one eye. The yellow light showed me an old ammo case. I picked it up to use as a critical marker on the way out. I placed the case off the edge of another trail; now all I had to do was to lead the patrol back along the trail and turn west at the case and move directly onto the assault line. I was feeling good about the raid now; but do I know how to get back to the RP? Reacting to flares had disoriented me slightly. If the company commander can't find his way back to the RP, it is going to be embarrassing to say the least. It's also going to be a major minus spot report! I went back down over the hill on instinct to hit the creek bed where the RP was. The creek was there but no RP! It's simple; it's either up stream or down stream. I could see 50 yards or more in either direction; nothing looked familiar. My watch said 6 minutes to return. Don't panic! I think it is downstream. Move upstream for two minutes, if you don't find it, turn and run back to here. That will give you approximately three minutes to search downstream.

It was downstream.

"Well RANGER Childers, I was beginning to think maybe you were lost," said the RI as I gave the countersign to the sentry.

"Sometimes I have to walk a little extra, Sergeant, but I never have been lost" I replied.

"Drive-on, RANGER."

With the final change in the assault plan issued, I led the two-platoon column back to the RP. The third platoon was enroute to their blocking position. The security team reported no change in the enemy situation. I crossed the creek with 69 RANGERS in a modified wedge behind me and moved up the gentle slope to the trail; paralleled the trail to the ammo case and filed into the assault line. Everything was going perfect; we were on the assault line with about one minute to go to make the strike time perfect. Then Mr. Murphy showed up; the one thing that could go wrong - did. A vehicle without lights was approaching slowly on jeep trail. I cursed the moon and gave the hand signal to go prone. The jeep passed along the trail and on up towards the objective. Did they see us? No indication that they did; no change in speed; no firing; no excitement. I jumped up and ran the

20 yards to the center of the trail to get a view of us from their position. Crap! They could have seen us plain as day. The surprise may be over! I could hear some muffled excitement on the objective now.

Apparently the aggressors had been set up for an attack from the East, and when the jeep came by and spotted our assault line on the North, they had to scramble to re-orient. In real combat, security would have been placed on that trail, and such a jeep would have either been quietly stopped or we would have been warned, but in this training situation, there really isn't any reasonable way to stop a vehicle that doesn't want to be stopped; and time was against us. But for me it was obviously decision time!

"DROP YOUR RUCKS AND ASSAULT" I ordered, and I started down the line getting action. My two platoon leaders were doing their job moving their platoons especially RANGER Flucker. He was everywhere. As we broke cover on the objective, the most fantastic firefight erupted that I have ever seen or heard tell of. No scene in "Apocalypse Now" could compare to this one; flares, smoke, machine gun fire, grenades, star clusters, and trip flares everywhere. RI's were everywhere too, "killing" RANGERS. My RTO and I were among the first; then my First Sergeant. Flucker took charge. Someone came over to give me aid, "I'm dead" I told him. SGT Lovett happened to be standing there amid the smoke and screaming and machine gun fire. "You're dead RANGER Childers, lie down and shut up!"

This happened twice more before the objective was secured and the search teams began their job. So I thought, I'm going to do something to show I'm dead, that I'm out of the problem. Lying on my back, I stuck both feet straight up in the air - the symbol of the dead. Then for some dumb reason I decided to light up a cigarette, a definite sign that the problem is over. So there I was, like an opossum in the highway - smoking a Marlboro and watching the show; and along came SGT Lovett. "RANGER Childers, what the hell are you doing in the dying cockroach position - smoking?"

"Trying to look out of action, Sergeant Lovett."

"You are definitely out of action, RANGER Childers, and that action is going to cost you!"

I put my legs down and the cigarette out, and he's chewing on my hindquarters unmercifully. About then, RANGER Flucker hollered "fire in the hole, fire in the hole " the signal to evacuate the objective, and RANGER Codero comes along and jerks me into the fireman's carry while Lovett is still chewing me out.

It must have been a little comical; Codero double-timing with me on his back, smoke and flares still burning brightly, and Lovett right behind us trying to make Codero put me down.

"RANGERS don't leave their dead" Codero told Lovett.

We would all read about this dedication to fallen brethren RANGERS in Mogadishu and RANGERS refused to allow RANGERs in a fallen helicopter be taken by the rebels. The action ultimately resulted in 18 KIAs, but no RANGER was abandoned on the field. Amazed at the dedication and sacrifice, reporters inquired of the survivors and the answer was simply part of the RANGER Creed:

> . . . . I will never leave a fallen comrade to fall into the hands of the enemy. . . ."

"All right by God, BANG! Now you're both dead. Put! Him! Down!" he ordered.

Just then the problem was called off; control was passed back to the chief RI for a problem critique, but SGT Lovett took a parting shot at me.

"RANGER Childers, I'm gonna have a talk with the Colonel about your class standing."

"Yes, Sergeant" I replied. What else could I say? Most threats rolled off me like water off a duck's back but that one hurt to the quick. Had I let my guard down in the final hours and "blew it?" Inside I was tormented, but I had a job to do; no time to feel sorry for myself now; spilled milk, water under the bridge and all that rot - but damn I felt rotten; betrayed by myself. And what was it for, the cigarette or the cavalier attitude or the fun we seemed to be having at the brief comedy event? At this point it didn't matter much. The only thing to do now is to put it aside and drive on.

I never heard another word about the incident, nor did I ever get counseled as company commander for the problem. During the critique the RI's were highly complimentary on the actions on the objective; "Maybe the best I've seen" they said, "fire and maneuver between platoons - outstanding, "everyone knew his job." But the deal I was offered by Sgt. Parker; a positive or a negative spot report - was never closed as far as I was concerned. Maybe it was neutralized.

Perhaps I was tired, I know I was! We now had just about 30 hours left in the field; but the next day seemed like an eternity away now. We had a 4 click cross-country to a patrol base from the critique site. I was attached to the second platoon for the move since my own platoon had been in the blocking position 2 clicks away, and had moved from there to their patrol base. I would be linked up with them the next morning during the RI changeover. I didn't know it now, but the next day I would be in the Platoon Sergeant slot from morning until late afternoon.

Those words kept haunting me, "I'm gonna talk to the Colonel about your class standing." It was nearly 0500 when we got to the patrol base after a very long, wet, miserable 4 clicks of Florida swamp. I had plenty of time to think over the last leadership position, the actions on the objective, and the fantastic job that RANGER Flucker did in assuming command when both I and my First Sergeant were "killed by the RI." And yes, I thought plenty about having tangled horns with Sgt. Lovett. Those thoughts were heavier than my rucksack. The swamp had been merciless then we got off into a dud bomb area by error and had to relocate. When we finally settled, the RI gave instructions for everyone to go to sleep and awake at first light.

I curled up under my poncho amid the palmetto's and was out almost immediately. "Putting it aside is not easy but that is the object of RANGER School; to place the student under physical and emotional pressure, by whatever means, and see if he can or will function. I was glad for the nearly one hour's sleep, which followed, the first I had gotten in two days. It was cleansing. The assignment as platoon Sergeant that morning was totally unexpected. I had done my share of leadership positions! Looking back, it was probably a Godsend too, because it gave me a cause; something to keep my mind occupied. I never thought about the dying cockroach act again - until I started writing this book. I only thought about "driving on." Now I wonder what happened.

Well the lesson I learned was simple; one I had learned before actually, but now it seemed to take on more meaning. When things get as bad as you think they are, and most of the time they are not, it doesn't do any good to fret about it; it's too late to prevent it from happening. All you can do is to work hard to cancel it, and that's called "driving on."

TAKING A BREAK

Break time was always a welcome period to our class, and I guess to all classes. There are only two breaks; after the Benning Phase, and after the Mountain Phase. 'Typically' if I can use that term for only two events, we would be assembled about 1600 or 1700 by SGT Rock for a lecture on how to conduct ourselves on break.

"All right, RANGERS, you've earned a little break. Well, you ain't really earned it, but out of the goodness of my big heart, I'm gonna let you go until". . . and went into a long pause and held his watch arm aloft and stare at it . . . "2300 hours tonight. OLD MAN; for the National Guard, that's 11 o'clock tonight; for you Marines . . . when Mickey's little hand is on the eleven and his big hand is on the twelve. That's the first time the little hand gets on the eleven after the sun goes down - tonight. You got that?"

"Now; I wanna tell you sum thin! Columbus, Georgia has been just outside the gate there for a hundred years! You can not tear it down in one evening RANGERS. You cannot drink all the beer in Columbus, RANGERS! You cannot whip the whole 18th Airborne Corps, RANGERS!"

"Now I'm gonna tell you sum' thin STUDS! I don't wanna get no calls from the fuzz, to come down and get you out of jail! I'm onna come get you all right! In about three weeks; and RANGERS, I'm onna have sum thin for you! You wanna see me mad; you have some Sheriff come drag me out of my favorite bar to get you out of jail - and RANGERS; I'M GONNA BE MAD.

Six or seven hours is a very short break but I suspect the School has a lot of good reasons for making it so short. Give a guy too much time to think about it, and he may not come back. I looked forward to the break, as did my wife. She took the opportunity for a little travel, an airplane ride, living out of a suitcase, and of course, checking on me. She was more worried about me than I was. After graduation she confided that she didn't think I would survive the Florida Phase. "You looked like death warmed over on that second break," she said. "So much worse than on the first break that I went back home and prepared myself for the worst; I did not see how you could stand another step down the ladder of debilitation."

After travel time to and from Harmony Church, we had about 5 or 6 hours together; dinner, shop talk, school talk, and renewing old ties. Not necessarily in that order. She insisted on me getting some sleep, but somehow it never worked out that way.

Dayle always gave me a "go get em tiger" release back to the school. Our house could have burned down, my job abolished, and both kids kidnapped the day before break, and she wouldn't have let on. She understood one thing by just looking at me; I did not need anything to worry about right then, including her own fears about my condition. That kind of support is extremely important in a course as demanding as RANGER School.

Many people simply go to the barracks and sleep for the whole break. Some wash clothes, shop, and take care of personal things; then sleep. Others go out and gorge themselves on food, especially sweets; then sleep. A few go and drink beer and get a buzz on, but they are an absolute minority. So those few who would get no sleep during the break were really not much behind the power curve so to speak.

THE DOUBTERS

The 'doubters.' They stood in line to tell me I couldn't make it through, not in so many words, but indirectly and maybe even unconsciously. Certainly not maliciously, but with some coveted curiosity. Questions like "why did you wait until now to try it" really translated to "don't you think you are too old?" Or maybe, it was an opinion, "I don't think you are going to make it!"

"You're a National Guardsman!!" translated into "Now I know you can't do it."

"What do you do for a living" really meant "what condition are you in." I suppose on the first day of my arrival, only two people in the whole world knew that RANGER Childers had what it takes to complete the course that was my wife and myself. But completing the course was only a part of the goal. The ultimate goal was to be Number One and that was in the back of my mind from the beginning. I did not launch rockets and announce it loudly; not my style. I just decided surreptitiously that I would be going for the gold. On graduation day it occurred to me what a coincidence it was being No. 1 in Class 6 of RANGER School 1981; I had also been No. 1 in my OCS Class, Number 6, in 1964; and had been considerably older than my classmates in both cases. Maybe 6 is my lucky number.

I had never been superstitious about lucky numbers, black cats, walking under ladders, four leaf clovers, or the rest of the long list of possibilities. But such a coincidence was almost too much to ignore, so I use the digit "6" in a lot of things that call for digital input. When the 29TH Division first began to be fielded with Mobile Subscriber Equipment (that is the Army equivalent to cellular telephone communications), I went with my driver to the Signal Battalion to get my equipment "affiliated." We were in the field at the time conducting tactical operations and the Battalion had a one way trail into the affiliations site and there were several vehicles in line to be affiliated. When it came my turn, the soldier announced that I would have to give him a 3 digit number as my affiliation code. So I gave him 666; my lucky number three times. Easy to remember. He gave me a very strange look and was alternating his gaze from me to obviously someone who was standing behind me. I turned around to find my Chaplain standing there with a worried look on his face.

"Excuse me sir," the Chaplain began uneasily, "I couldn't help but overhear the code number you chose; and I must advise you of the religious sensitivity of that number."

Well that event was good for several retellings and some imaginative modifications over the next few days.

The first day I almost felt harassed by the "attention" I was getting. All I wanted was to dissolve into the crowd and become just another shaved head, but when you are 42 years old, you cannot dissolve into a crowd of 20 year olds. A 42 year old, balding head does not look like a 20 year old head, even when both are shaved.

Sergeant Duty (that's a real name) was my first contact with the RANGER Department, and as it turned out, was also my very last. I flew to Columbus the day before reporting day and early the next day, got up and started looking for a barber shop. As soon as I walked into the "style" shop across the highway from the motel I knew I was in the wrong place. There were empty chairs with "stylists" standing by, but the young lady by the appointment desk said, "I'm sorry sir, you have to have an appointment."

I stole a glance at her appointment book, which was almost barren before 10am, "OK. Make me an appointment."

"What time would be convenient for you, sir" she inquired very professionally.
"How about" ------ I glanced at the wall clock, "Now, or say thirty seconds from now?"

Still serious, she studied her book and said; "Fine sir, I think we can work you in; which stylist do you prefer?" and she listed three or four.

"Which ever one is best qualified with electric clippers, and can take off all of my remaining hair," I replied.

"Electric clippers!"

I thought she was going to have a baby or something!

"Sir! We don't use such tools here. We do styling, not butchering!"

"Well, can you tell me where I can find a butcher shop with a - red and white stripped pole out front that goes round and round" I asked?

After a poll of the customers and employees she came back with directions and eventually I found a good old-fashioned barbershop; a two-chair shop manned by the owner/operator.

"Yes sir" ---- he stared at my collars without no rank nor insignia trying to figure out how to address me ---- "uhh, Colonel; I cut hair for twelve years for the exchange in Benning. I can fix you right up." I accepted the promotion graciously and chit-chatted with him as the electric shears began to grind away.

"Sure you want a RANGER haircut, sir" he asked?

"Well I don't want one but I can't get into RANGER School without one" I replied.

The shears went silent.

"You're kidding me aren't you sir" he asked? He didn't smile; he didn't move; frozen with his arms up in the cutting position looking down through his bifocals like Mr. Whipple scolding Charmin squeezers.

"Nope, you're not kidding are you," he said, "This haircut is on me!"

The taxi driver that took me to Harmony Church had taken scores of people there before and knew exactly where to drop me.

"Just line your bags up neatly along that sidewalk and report in at that building" he pointed out. "Good Luck! You'll need it!"

Inside fifty or so people were seated; some on the left side of the building filling out forms and some on the right side - waiting. I had my orders checked at the door by a recycle and joined the group on the right. SGT Duty was in charge, making everyone fill a myriad of forms, block by block. He did sort of a double take on me as I found a seat, but didn't say anything at the time; he just stopped in mid-sentence for about 10 seconds, mouth open, motionless; then his eyes did a slow scan across the room and back to me; he exhaled the rest of the breath that he was caught with, and shook his head just slightly and continued his spiel. One thing many RI's have in common is an aptitude toward being stand-up comics.

While the students were catching up on block filling, SGT Duty did a tour down the isle inspecting haircuts on the waiting side of the room.

"You!" He pointed to a guy a few rows ahead of me. "Out the door, left, down the street, PX, haircut, MOVE!" "You, go with him; you, Goldilocks, go with him!"

He passed by me about a half a step and stopped. I could feel him looking at me. "You, what are you doing here?" I looked up to make sure he was talking to me. "Yeah, you; I'm talking to you! What are you, lost or something?"

"I've got orders for RANGER School, Sergeant" I replied.

"HAAA!" he shouted with joy. Finding that out was like Christmas. I was now a certified free fire zone. His tone changed from one of inquisitive rudeness to a Morgan-Teamer!

"Well get the #@**#! out of here and get a #@*%@! haircut then, Baldy" he screamed.

Well, I had forgotten to ask that veteran barber how long it had been since he gave his last RANGER haircut. I was glad the initial encounter was over, but several more introductory encounters would occur before I would have the feeling that I was just another shaved head. If I had to pick one experience out of my life and label it, the hardest thing I've ever done,' mentally, it would be "reporting in" to RANGER School and becoming a student during the first two or three days. Embarrassment is a terrible thing to face mentally. I don't know why I felt embarrassed; maybe I wasn't. Maybe I was just self-conscious. Guilt?? Maybe I was afraid down deep inside that I would fail and then everyone would have been correct and I would have them to face.

Failure is a terrible thing to face mentally. I could almost feel the snickering behind my back or at least I imagined it. "What's this old relic doing here!" If it was happening maybe it was justified in the minds of others. Had I finally tried to reach too high? I looked around that black and gold decorated classroom and everyone I saw, except SGT Duty, was literally young enough to be my son, who was 22 at the time. I think doubt is a very natural reaction and I point out these things because I think that no matter how much self confidence one has in himself, he should not be shocked, appalled, or discouraged if doubts begin to creep in.

Success is measured in terms of how much self-confidence triumphs over doubt and there is, I think, a constant internal battle between these two forces. I would be a liar if I said I never had a doubt. Of course I had doubts, but I had more self-confidence. This self-confidence was the result of months of preparation and training and a desire to do it, which went back years. My decision to attend RANGER School was not made over a few beers at the Officers Club, and I would caution most people against waking up some morning and deciding to go. They are the ones who will face failure and the resulting embarrassment. For Regular Army personnel, this is probably mitigated a great deal by the fact that they go back from washout to a different environment than a National Guardsman or Reservist does. The Guardsman/ Reservist goes back to his home, his hometown, his daily place of employment, and to his unit and for the rest of his life he lives with his failure. For a Regular Army wash-out, he may not even return to his sending unit; or at best, he may not stay there long after he returns, but in any case there is-a fairly quick dilution of people who he has daily contact with who know that he washed out of RANGER School.

So, for me, at my age, the decision to go was perhaps bold. There were so many circumstances beyond my personal control which would have sent me home tab-less and people would only have thought "Dumb cluck! He should have known better! Never did have any sense!" or a dozen other uncomplimentary opinions.

The haircut only took five minutes or so in the chair and probably would have taken less time but for the inquisitive barber.

"Well, I admire your guts" he said with a laugh, "but I don't know about your judgment."

By the time I returned to the classroom, SGT Duty knew how old I was and that I was a Major.

"Childers, as soon as we get through with these forms you post over to the Colonel's office at 3rd RANGER; he wants to have a talk with you," and he told me how to get there.

By the time we got through all of the forms, and I found the right building, the Colonel was not in, so I was admitted to the S-3's office to talk with the Major. He wanted to make me feel quite at ease, but actually I felt ill at ease because I was there to be a RANGER student and he immediately established a Major-to-Major atmosphere.

"It's our policy to bring in all Field Grade Officers for a little chat before you get into your first day" he began. My first thought was "whatever you're going to say does not matter; I can't go home with this haircut unless I have the RANGER Tab.,' I refocused on his conversation . . . "It's rare that we get Field Grades through here; it's rare that we get National Guardsmen through here; it's rare that we have anyone over 40; so you can see we have a special concern for you. It's hard out there and I want to be sure that you really understand how hard it's going to be. You can expect no slack because of your age. Your rank has no meaning whatsoever."

"Yes, sir" I interrupted, "I understand that completely. I would, in fact, resent any special treatment. I feel that if I don't get injured or sick that I <u>will</u> graduate."

"Well, he continued, "Injury and illness are going to be perhaps your greatest problems. There are a lot of activities in the course that can cause injury and a lot of exposure that can cause illness, and there is where your age is going to be a liability. You will not recover as fast as a 20 year old. <u>I</u> can, and do, get out there and 'run with them for a day or two, maybe even a week, then I've had it. You've taken on a task that few people your age would even think of taking on."

We chatted on for 15 minutes or so more, giving me every opportunity to gracefully withdraw; and also to ask any question that might still be unanswered. I was anxious to be dismissed, not because I didn't enjoy his company, but because I felt that I was already getting something that the other RANGER students were not getting and policy or not, I did not want it. He dismissed me with the warning that the Colonel would probably still wish to see me later.

Sure enough, the next day in a class the RI announced "RANGER Childers will report to the Colonel during the next break." I felt like a neon sign. Jesus, I thought, I wish they didn't feel that they had to do this for me.

He was a very congenial person; did his best to make me feel at ease. I accepted his offer of a very comfortable couch and assumed the relaxed position, but, I felt the same way as I had before. I went there rankless and that's the way I wanted to be treated. We chatted amicably for maybe 15 minutes; me telling him some of the reasons why I was there and him telling me how difficult it was going to be for me.

Frankly, I think in the short run, the Department would have been relieved, if not elated, if I had withdrawn immediately or had quit or failed during the first few days. Their concern, naturally, was for my health and safety. On graduation day, the Department was elated; because I had not died on them during the course of eight weeks. RANGER School is #%*!@$^ tough; but they don't discriminate because of age and for understandable reasons they are not enthusiastic about people beyond 30 showing up. They depend upon the "war stories" to discourage the half-hearted, and the over-the-hill bunch.

During the Mountain Phase, I was talking one evening in the planning hut with RANGER Hague. He was a Regular Army Captain before entering the RANGER course and had been our RANGER company commander during the Benning Phase. He confided in me something that occurred on Day #1. I had wondered why the TAC had not made me the first company commander since I was the senior officer in the class.

"Boy, am I glad I did my tour as CO in Benning instead of here", he said, "You've got the tougher job up here. By the way, do you know why you weren't CO in Benning?"

"They were <u>saving</u> me for here" I ventured.

"No" he laughed, "that might be fortunate, but that's not the reason! I overheard Eckert, England, and Rock discussing it that first day; Eckert wanted to appoint you as CO because they <u>always</u> appoint the senior man as CO. But England and Rock talked him out of it because they didn't figure you would "last more than five days then we'd just have to start all over anyway."

Well, that was like a shot in the arm to my ego.

I recall during the later days of the Florida Phase, RANGER Campana and I were acting as guides/OP/LP for other members of our platoon in a link-up operation. This was supposed to be a grand scale operation in which the non-airborne qualified RANGERS would be helo-inserted in to secure and mark a drop zone and the airborne types would then parachute in from C-130's. Class 6-81 had a lot of bad luck, hard times, and sour experiences; this operation was to be no exception. Our first hint of a long fruitless day came when the helicopters did not show to lift us non-airborne personnel (NAPs). - No sweat; the RI's initiated their backup plan and we NAPs were trucked to the vicinity of the LZ and we patrolled into and set up contact teams and DZ markers for the drop. And we waited; and waited. We knew when the sun went down that there would be no airdrop. Hint #2.

Meanwhile the chute bunnies were having troubles of their own. After finally getting loaded aboard the aircraft, one of the aircraft could not get off the ground - engine trouble or something. The one that did get off the ground got almost to the DZ and had to turn back due to mechanical trouble - then, when it started its approach back at Eglin main, the landing gear would not drop. Finally, all of the jump jocks got back on the ground, plumb across Eglin Air Force Base from the link up point.

Now it is understandable that the RANGER Department could not foresee such a series of difficulties and have a standby plan to execute, so it took a while to coordinate ground transportation and make the linkup. They started arriving in the vicinity of the DZ by truck and patrolling in around 2200 hours. Meanwhile, we, the NAPs without glory, occupied a patrol base in the drop zone for several hours. The area reminded me very much of the New Mexico desert around Socorro and Albuquerque; vast, quiet, low scrub-like vegetation, and sandy. Although Campana and I were RANGER buddies, I suppose we talked more during this time than I talked with the whole class combined over the entire course. There just isn't much opportunity for casual conversation in RANGER School. Anytime a student gets to talk is always while he is doing something else. So this was a rare treat and Campana passed on to me some of the impressions that I had made on the class. Well, by this time everybody who knew the rules of choosing the Honor Graduates (and that did not include me) were saying that I was the only contender in the selection for Distinguished Honor Graduate; not that I still could not or might not yet screw up and drop out, but, that right now I was it. I didn't put much store in that at the time because quite frankly I was really too tired to care one way or the other. One of the more humorous things that he mentioned was his own first impression.

"I remember that first night in the barracks" he related, "I was stuffing my locker and I looked up and saw you coming in. At first I thought you were part of the staff; then I thought, no, this sucker is lost. Then, when you started occupation of a locker I thought maybe he's some shell shock victim that they're humoring. I have to admit Gramps, you fooled the hell out of me. "

The RI's generally regarded me as somewhat of a curiosity piece. Many would make a point of recognizing me to the class, which I classified as the "indirect" method; or by taking some opportunity to engage me in conversation, which I classified as the direct method. In general, it was the younger, E-5's and E-6's who took the direct approach while the more senior ones used the indirect approach, if at all. It did not really matter to me if I was specifically ignored, but it was an interesting study in human nature. I noted some few reactions that bordered on perhaps a blend of resentment, disbelief, and envy at one end of the spectrum.

There were two instances during the Florida Phase that were unusual with regard to the RI's reaction to my presence. The first occurred about ten seconds after I got off the bus. I never knew if my "fame" had preceded me and this RI was waiting for me or if he just spotted me and reacted on impulse. I was helping get baggage off the bus when that familiar tone sounded.

"RANGER! ! "

By the end of two phases one becomes very adept to determining even with his back turned when an RI is paging. The sonic sensors send the dB level to the brain which quickly computes back azimuth, range, and urgency and automatically causes the body to wheel and lock at attention in the proper direction while the vocal chords respond with "YES, SERGEANT!" I was looking square at the coveted black and gold on an RI patrol cap.

"How old are you RANGER?"

"Forty-two and climbing Sergeant."

"That's the lowest number I would believe RANGER! Get down for one - five," he said with kind of a dare in his voice.

I dropped and did 15 very sharp, crisp pushups for him-and one for Class 6-81, and one for THE BIG RANGER IN THE SKY; and popped back to attention and reported

"PUSH-UPS COMPLETE, SERGEANT!" He stood there with his hands on his hips and looked me up and down slowly from head to toe a couple of times without saying a word. Maybe he was killing time to check my breathing. Then in a very quiet, convinced kind of a voice, he said, "OK, RANGER; Drive on!" But that was the one and only time I ever had an RI do his own personal one-on-one evaluation on me nor did I ever see it done on any other RANGER. I don't know what his criteria for passing was but whatever it was, he was satisfied and he never repeated the test.

The second instance involved a Sergeant Major. I will remember his reaction for the rest of my life because he, more than anyone else who ever paid me a compliment, knew more than any of the others what I was really going through. He was RANGER qualified, of course, having done that in his 20's. But what gave him a special understanding was that he had waited until he was 45 years old to become airborne qualified.
He made a special point of looking me up that first evening in the chow line; walked right up and grabbed my hand and shook it heartily.

"I just wanted to shake your hand" he beamed, "I don't believe you!" I enjoyed talking to him for several minutes then, and several occasions thereafter. In fact it seemed that every time we came in out of the swamp, he would come around to "check on" me.

The point of this discussion is not to count the times I blow my own horn, but to refute an age-old lesson that most of us are taught from early childhood. "First Impressions Are Important;" "First Impressions Are the Ones That Last The Longest-" and other variations. I don't think there has ever been a more unfair social practice in the history of mankind that to teach such utter nonsense.

<u>NEVER!</u> Never judge a person's ability or potential solely by his looks, his physique, the strength of his handshake, his mannerisms, his speech, or his personal habits. Never judge a person too quickly or under limited circumstances. And of course, never judge a person by his chronological age. Each of us have so many false values by which we judge people: he wears glasses; white socks; greasy hair; drives a pickup truck; smokes a pipe; has broad shoulders; big hands; looks you in the eye while talking; and on and on. So what!! All of these things may be indicators that will aid you in assembling a complete picture of the person later; or may aid you in "improving" this person later. Meanwhile, "how does he perform the required functions" is the important thing.

"Everything that can be counted, does not count; and everything that counts, cannot be counted."
Albert Einstein

WHY

There is no single reason why I went to RANGER School nor is there any one reason that I can single out as most important. The decision was based on a complicated and long-term series of experiences. I don't know how long I'd passively wanted to be a RANGER or RANGER-Type, but I remember precisely when I acquired an active desire for those qualifications. It was in 1968 when I returned from Viet Nam. Four months in the Mekong Delta with Task Force 116, the Navy's Riverenne Force, exposed me to a little known (at that time), elite group of super-combatants known as SEALS. Now we think we know a lot about them. A movie has been made about them. Numerous books have been written by and about the SEALS. I was a mechanical engineer for the Naval Weapons Laboratory and had volunteered to serve in Viet Nam as a field engineer to evaluate weapons and equipment in the combat zone; to determine what was good and bad and make design improvements, or to act as liaison to accomplish that task.

It would be the first of four times over a 30 year career that I would go to a war zone as a civilian employee of the Department of Defense. I was back in Viet Nam for my second four months in a combat zone, serving with the Marine Corps operating out of Danang (I Corps) with conventional Marines as well as the elite Marine Force Recon units. Then in 1988 I would be again serving with the Navy and with the SEAL Teams during the oil shipment crisis in the Persian Gulf – Operation Ernst Will. Finally, I would go to war as the Science Advisor to LT GEN Walt Boomer, Commanding General of the First Marine Expeditionary Force; OPERATION DESERT SHIELD/DESERT STORM, to liberate Kuwait in 1991.

I'll have to admit that when I arrived during the TET Offensive in 1968, I did not know a SEAL from an orangutan. About a week after I got to Saigon, the war quieted down so that I could get transportation out of the capital and down to the small Delta town of My Tho. About the same time that I arrived in the country, so did 6 each Smith and Wesson Model 39's equipped with a silencer system. It was called the "Hush Puppy" because ostensibly it was designed to meet the requirement of silencing village dogs who tended to give to barking when they sensed American soldiers/SEALS lurking around. My first assignment in the field was to run a combat evaluation of the 9mm "Hush-Puppy" using SEAL Team II as the evaluating unit. To describe the SEALs and their operations, even what little bit of it I know, would be the subject of a book in itself. Besides, the last time that was done, a publisher was sued heavily by one of the SEALs who was the central character, by name, without his permission, in their story. Now, of course, there are dozens of books on the Teams

That SEAL is now out of the Navy and a widely known author named Richard Marcinko. Dick is the epitome of the "silent option," a warrior without peer, and a rouge by his own description; a genuine American hero of the Viet Nam War that I greatly admire, and a man who I am proud to call a friend.

Dick teamed up with a talented writer who was able to convert his colorful experiences and lifestyle into some very interesting reading to which I commend you. In 1998 I had the good fortune to meet John Weismann, the writing talent for the Rogue Warrior series of books, which features Marcinko. After chatting with John a few minutes, I inquired about Marcinko. His reply was, "I wouldn't know; I haven't seen him in three years." That was an incredible reply to me as I had always thought the two created these adventures for Marcinko. I could imagine Marchiko sitting around chugging beer and telling stories with Weismann taking notes and later perhaps putting it all together. "Yes," John continued, "I have a contract for 8 books and I have one and one half to go." So much for legend.

But, SEAL exploits in Viet Nam are more than legend; they were real, dangerous, taxing exploits by some very bold and capable warriors. There is no group of warriors that has my greater respect than these. There is no single individual that I either know or have read about who has my greater respect as a warrior than Dick Marcinko, and I have met quite a few real warriors in my convoluted career.

Needless to say, I returned home thoroughly convinced that they, as a group, were the most fantastic warriors in modern history; and I wanted to be one. Perhaps the answer is that I was too busy to try it right then. I came back with a requirement, and a design concept for something that the SEALs needed - a larger (than 20 rounds) magazine for the M-16 Rifle. Perhaps I was being logical again as I had been in 1964 when I received my OCS commission as a second lieutenant and wanted to go active duty but decided no; "in the Army I would be just another butter bar while here at Dahlgren I'm doing a critical engineering job; and after all, I spent four and a half years for that education. To discard it now on a whim would be just plain foolish." Now, in 1968, the logic was that I had the design in my head for a device which could help a group of people who I admired very much. Perhaps it was because someone said, "thirty is a little old to start a career as a SEAL." Now I know better than that.

Perhaps it was my wife's less than enthusiastic appreciation of the change in life-style; although she never said no. But she has never said no to anything I wanted to do. She was always ultra supportive, but then I was able to sense when I was probably being more stupid than practical. Probably, it was a combination of all of these factors that ultimately led me to do what time has proven to be the right decision.

I began work on the magazine and within a year, I was back in Viet Nam again, this time assigned to the Marine Corps Third Marine Amphibious Force (III MAF) in DaNang. In my baggage was 85 magazines for the M-16 Rifle; 50-round magazines. During the next week I traveled the length and breadth of Viet Nam distributing the magazines to various units of SEALs and Marine Force Reconnaissance Units. Some of the magazines ultimately fell into the hands of various Army units such as MAC SOG, CCN, CCC, and CCS.

There are some acronyms for you to choke on. And since they were among the not-so-well-known organizations of the time and, unlike the SEAL Teams where everyone and his brother is publishing books and making movies about them, little has been written about these acronyms. MACSOG is Military Assistance Command Special Operations Group. CCN is Command and Control North; CCC is Command and Control Central; and you guessed it, CCS is Command and Control South. But that is all I can tell you about them at this time. Sooner or later someone will write a book on them.

But back to the magazines; the magazines were "experimental" by normal development standards and both I and the user expected some failures. They were willing to take the chance. As the months passed, the good reports far outweighed the bad, and I took great pride in having invented and produced a device, which went on record[4] as having saved specific lives through its superior firepower.

---

[4] Brief explanation of this claim provided in Appendix H

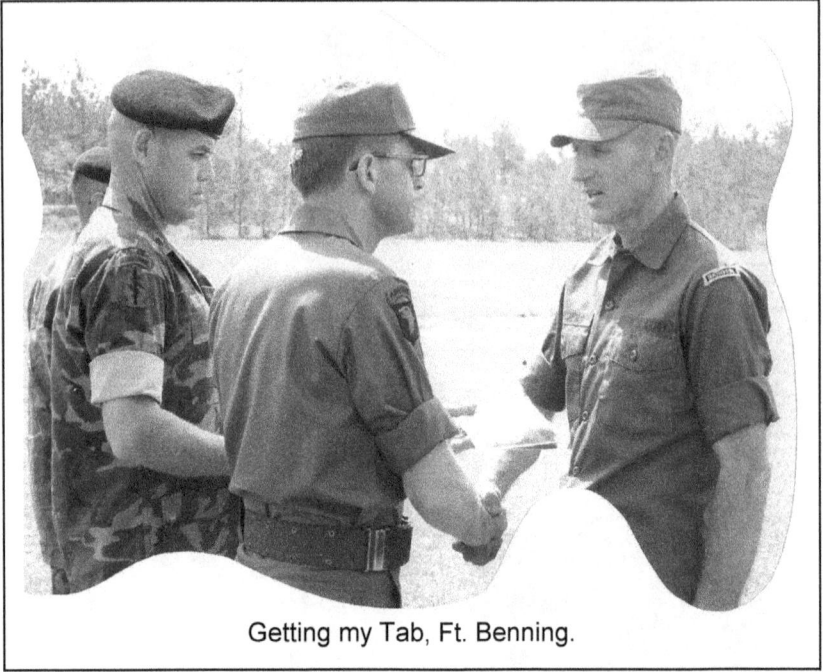

Getting my Tab, Ft. Benning.

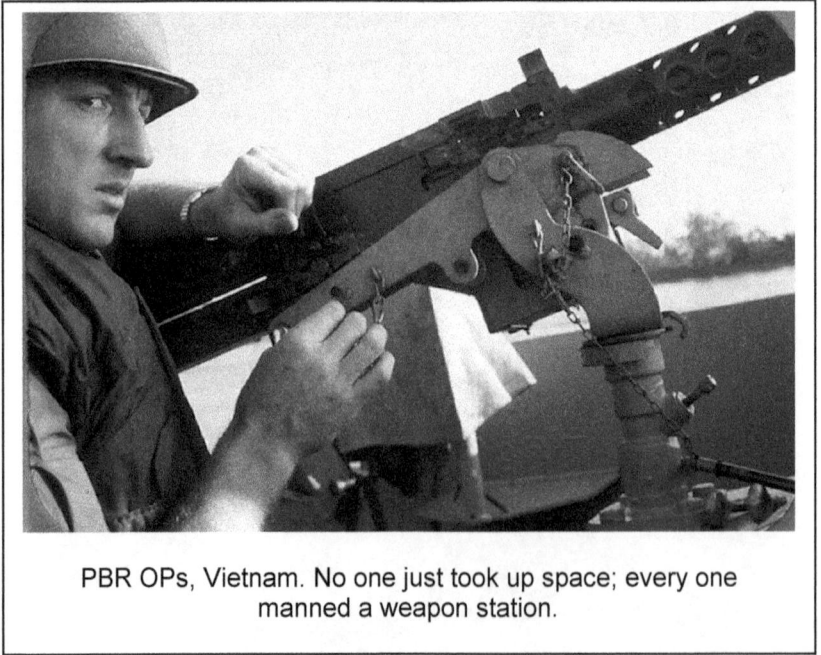

PBR OPs, Vietnam. No one just took up space; every one
manned a weapon station.

Bar armor we installed on "Brown Water" navy vessels. Today the Stryker vehicle utilizes this same 40year old concept. Armored LCM, Vietnam.

Picture of me in my shop in Vietnam with the Hushpuppy. The background has a version of the 50 round M-16 magazine plus a few collectibles.

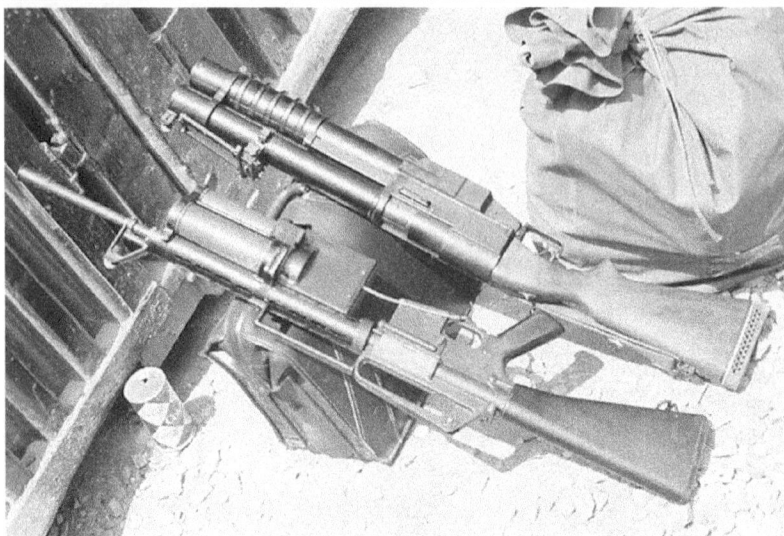

Weapons introduced by VLAP: pump action 40mm grenade launcher and a 3-round grenade launcher under the M-16 barrel.

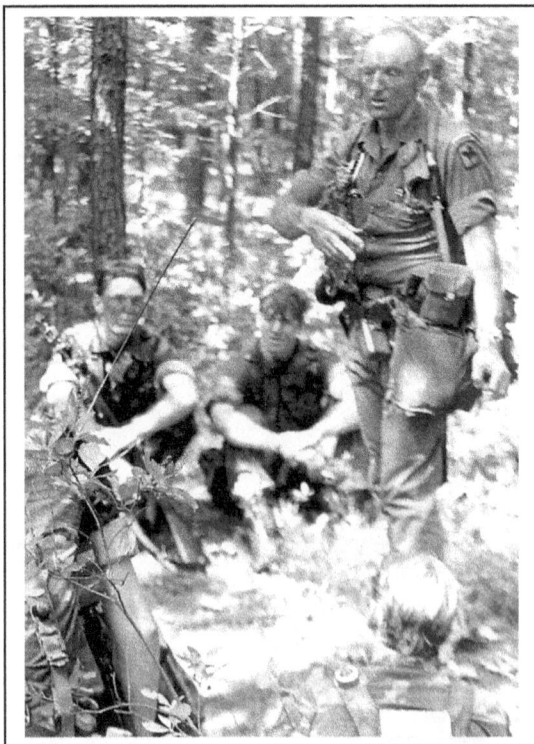

Passing it on. Teaching patrol tactics and planning.

During these evaluations I made frequent visits to the using units and in some instances was honored by accompanying the patrols on operations. My horizons were broadened during this tour and I discovered that the Force Recon Units (at least in the Viet Nam conflict) did the same exciting kinds of things that the SEALS were doing. Once again I was excited about upchucking my engineering career and turning to the call of the jungle literally! But by the end of this second tour I had uncovered another equipment need; once again the challenge of engineering and the illogic of change won out.

I returned home to begin designing what I then called a Special Operations Weapon (SOW). The SOW concept encompassed a family of ammunition and a weapon to fire it. Basically it would be a 12-gauge select fire gun fed from a top mounted 10 or 20 round magazine and would be configured much like a sub-machine gun. The basic round of ammunition was to be the buckshot but the "family" would include frag grenades, flares, signal smoke, CS, fleschette, discarding sabot, and anti-material rounds. In the end, two concepts were prototyped and they are described in a book published by CWO Tom Swearengen (USMC RET) entitled "World's Fighting Shotguns." The final design was worth two patents for me, and a third one that I never got around to pursuing. It was a most unique gun concept. Pistol grip and forward hand grip with extensible or folding wire stock. Select fire, automatic or semi-automatic. Fired either standard length shells (up to 3") in select fire or longer rounds (ostensibly 6 inches long) in a single fire mode. For single fire of the long rounds, the weapon would "break open" similar to an old M-79 Grenade launcher or double barrel shotgun so that the breech could be accessed to manually insert one round at a time. When the long round was fired, most of the round went down range leaving a standard length empty shell casing to be ejected by the normal mechanism.

The feed system was based on a four bar linkage that accepted a shell from the magazine and held it in readiness to move in line with the bore for insertion as the barrel oscillated back and forth by propellant gas action. The feed system and magazine were part of the upper receiver. When the breech latch was moved to the release position, all of this would pivot intact to expose the chamber of the barrel. This arrangement allowed the long rounds to be loaded without interrupting the mechanical sequence of the auto-loading mechanism. I mentioned the oscillating barrel; this gun concept did not have a moving bolt like most weapons, rather, the barrel moved forward against a recoil spring upon firing. As the barrel moved past the magazine and reached the foremost point of travel, a spring-loaded tab popped up in front of a new shell in the magazine. As the recoil spring returned the barrel toward the rear, the tab pushed a new shell out of the magazine and into the waiting four bar linkage mechanism. Cam surfaces in the exterior of the barrel interacted with the four bar linkage to shuttle shells in alignment with the bore and to be back in place to receive new shells from the magazine at the precise moment required. Trouble with this great idea is that the war was over and nobody wanted to invest in such a "radical" idea. So we still don't have a combat shotgun; just another commercial hunting gun painted black with a few cool attachments.

Someone advised that by the time I could have gotten through all of the training required by the SEALS, the war would be over and I'd be just another warrior with no war. They turned out to be quite right. The programs that sent me to Viet Nam withered and died; so did the SOW project. The M-16 50-round magazine project was popular in the bush but not in the Pentagon. It died also of benign neglect with a population of 85 hand made models. And eventually, the US began to turn the war over to the Vietnamese ("Vietnamization" was starting when I was there in the summer of 1969), and finally ceased wholesale overt participation.

But those two tours in Viet Nam had shown me a side of the military that I had never known before, made me a few life long friends, and gave me a burning desire to be qualified to creep around the jungles doing clandestine and covert things. The natural service for me to try was the Army, since I had a commission there already; but I still could not logically drop out of engineering and put on the green suit. Logically then I should apply for a leave of absence with the Naval Weapons Laboratory and apply for RANGER School through the National Guard. After all, the National Guard Bureau had just established a policy of encouraging at least one RANGER qualified officer per company.

My Department Head at the time was a civilian named "Chuck" Bernard. My application for leave was in the approval chain (or disapproval chain) for several weeks; finally it came back to me with Bernard's initials on the routing slip. He neither approved nor disapproved the request, rather, he had stapled a Xeroxed copy of my position description (job description) to my request and returned it. The message was clear; if I could do my job at Dahlgren while I was in RANGER School, okay.

Funny how things turn out. Chuck left Dahlgren in the late 70's and moved on up in the Department of Defense to become a Senior Executive Service kind of a guy and eventually retired to become a private consultant and owner of a small chain of contractors serving the Department of Defense. He and his wife Judy are both holders of Doctorate Degrees in the Washington DC area and were doing great; now on a ranch in Texas somewhere . Chuck's son retired as a Major in the Delta Force in 1999. Chuck and I were very good friends and frequently had lunch and discussions. Chuck asked me to meet him for lunch one day. When I linked up with him, there was a third party with him which turned out to be (then) Major General Jones, USMC; the same Jones who moved on up to become Commandant of the USMC and then Commander of the European Command. So Chuck moved in influential strata inside the Beltway. He was one the most remarkable engineers that I ever knew. Always thinking out of the box, (he invented the term) it was his concept to install the 105mm howitzer in the AC-130 aircraft for the USAF. I was honored that such a remarkable man would take the time to attend my change of command ceremony wherein I assumed command of the 29 TH Infantry Division (Light), Virginia Army National Guard, headquartered at Ft. Belvoir, Virginia.

During the time that my request for leave was being "processed" two other things were happening. At Dahlgren, we were getting into the Guided Projectile business and it really looked challenging. I was asked to join the design team as the control section engineer. The other event was my National Guard unit; I was about to inherit command of the Armored Cavalry Troop, which in the Guard is a rare opportunity. The time was just not right for RANGER School.

By the summer of 1976, the guided projectile empire at Dahlgren had been taken over by the Army and I was about to be promoted out of the Cavalry Troop. My new assignment was initially as the Assistant Brigade S-2. At this point, I should like to be able to scribe "The time was now right. I decided that I would not commit myself to anything that would interfere with RANGER School." But I cannot write that. RANGER School did not even occur to me. Viet Nam was in the distant past and there was nothing on the near horizon to whet my appetite except a possible fight for oil in the sand dunes - and they had just moved me out of Armor and made a ground-Ponder out of me.

Three things happened in 1978 that rekindled my fire. First, I was moved from the Brigade Staff down to be the S-3 of an Infantry Battalion. In my view of readiness, training drives the battalion. So I was, in my view, back in a troop leading position again and was no longer a "staffee." Second, our Brigade received a new Army Advisor, LTC Ed Yaugo; RANGER! He came to us from commanding the RANGER Battalion at Fort Stewart, Georgia, and we all felt it a real honor to have a man of his background and credentials as our advisor. I coveted the knowledge that his black and gold represented, but, well, I wasn't in the shape I was ten years before when I wanted to be a SEAL. The third event of the year was the introduction of the Army's new PT test for the Guard - a four-mile "walk." Our new Brigade commander, BG John Castles, encouraged it into a four-mile run - a contest.

Over the next several years, BG Castles became the Adjutant General of the State of Virginia and served quite successfully for 12 years. During this time he led the state of Virginia to the highest pinnacles of success as measured by the National Guard Bureau, achieving the honor of being the number one rated state in terms of readiness for mobilization. I owe General Castles an incredible debt of gratitude for the leadership and challenge he gave me over the years between RANGER School and now. He conferred on me command of a Battalion, sent me to Army War College, broadened my experience by assigning me command of the Troop Command followed by command of a Infantry Brigade. He made me a General Officer and the Assistant Division Commander for Maneuver, which postured me to assume command of the Division after his retirement. Sometime during this period of time, his son, John Junior, read one of the early iterations of Driving On and got inspired; went to RANGER School, earned an CIB in Panama, and is making a career of the Army. Last check in 04, he took command of a RANGER Battalion. I look for him to make General officer and perhaps, with that intersection of hard work and opportunity, become a CINC or Joint Staff General.

Being a great admirer of General Castles I figured I had best get in shape, challenge my battalion and lead them to victory over the other battalions. Well, I didn't win the race; it was won by a 23 year old Captain; a marathoner. (Captain Young later became a Brigadier General in Virginia) But I won a victory, coming in fifth in the entire Brigade, and I was 40 years old. I won a victory because I knew then that I still had the stamina to hold my own with younger, supposedly stronger men. I went home, talked it over with my wife, and we committed ourselves to getting me through RANGER School. So when someone asked me why I waited so late in life to go to RANGER School the answer was not a simple "one liner;" but if I were to try to simplify it I guess that all I could say is that I just never got around to it; or that I felt a greater obligation to do other things first.

And, of course, "late in life" is a relative term; totally perspective in nature. Many people like to think of themselves as complex, multi-faceted, or perhaps mysterious. Perhaps that gives them a feeling of sophistication. I regard myself as a rather basic person, believing in simple things. "You are as old as you feel" is a timeworn phrase; simple, basic, and to me; believable. And as I began my impromptu speech at Todd Field on graduation day I had that principle in mind.

"I appreciate the opportunity to speak to you today, and I'd like to share with you two secrets that I have held throughout this course. The first one is about my age; you see, the truth is there is a 19 year old man trapped inside this 42 year old body."

I think that is the essence of life; you are what you think you are, or said another way; you cannot be what you don't think you can be. You are what you do. The lesson here is simple. Determination and desire are factors to be reckoned with. It may not be too late in your life to try something that you always wanted to; to change careers - or even start a career; to get an education; or whatever it is that you want to do but that is so often discouraged by those who think that chronological age is a key factor. Age is a factor when you allow it to be. And I am reminded here of an accomplishment by my good friend Chuck Bernard who I mentioned earlier. Twenty years ago when he was my boss, and a very sharp technical guy, he only had a Bachelor's Degree. With that basic degree and a lot of practical smarts and political guile, he advanced to the SES level of government and retired. Last year, his Doctorate Degree was conferred on him. He didn't need it; he just decided to get it. Determination has no bounds but that which is self-imposed.

The reason why I went to RANGER School at all is as complex as why I waited until the chronological age of 42. I can list them one by one without any conscious order of priority.

> I always wanted to be a RANGER-Type.
> To measure myself.
> Self-satisfaction.
> For the knowledge and experience.
> To set the example.
> To be all I could be
> And let's be honest, to get the TAB!

And I could express these in many ways and add a few more also, but perhaps the most important one is to set the example. As a Guardsman I believe in something called commitment. In my view, commitment to anything must be total. I feel obligated to be totally committed because the Guard plays such an important role in the overall defense plan of this country. Preparation for and the defense of this country must be the bottom line in my life because if we lose our freedom through weakness, we lose all of the things that make freedom so precious. Von Moltke said it so aptly :

"The army is the most outstanding institution of every country for it alone makes possible the existence of all civic institutions." A man who has nothing for which he is willing to fight; nothing he cares about more than his own personal safety; is a miserable creature who has no chance of being free unless made and kept so by exertions of men better than himself."

Many Americans do not realize the nature and importance of the National Guard. Some in the past have thought of the Guard as poorly-led and they point to everything from Kent State to the failure of the 24th Infantry Division to take it's "Roundout" National Guard Mechanized Infantry Brigade to Desert Storm with it as evidence. Others think of the Guard as being a haven for draft dodgers even in the absence of a draft. Still others over the years have regarded us as little more than a Boy Scout troop. And there are those who know nothing at all and have no opinion. Wake up America, your Army National Guard comprises over 50% of the Total Army strength. Your National Guard provides your Army with the following (1999 data):

63% of all Infantry Battalions are National Guard
63% of all Field Artillery units are National Guard
70% of all Engineer units are National Guard
21% of all Medical units are National Guard
45% of all Aviation equipment is in Guard Units
55% of the Total Army Combat Units are National Guard
46% of the Total Army Combat Support is National Guard
25% of the Total Army Combat Service Support is National Guard

The old phrase which was once an advertising phrase relegated to mockery, "Sleep well, tonight your National Guard is awake" is not a joke. The Guard has a critical role in the overall plan of survival, and they play that role in a highly professional manner. We are evaluated continuously by the Regular Army to the same standards that Regular Army units must meet. Even though Guardsmen only train formally for 39 days per year, they meet the Army's challenge and repeatedly impress the Army's evaluators with performances that surprise and delight these evaluators.

The Guard is a true voluntary force made up of people who really want to serve their country. The cross section of America is revealed in no other organization like it is in the Guard. We have Privates and Sergeants whose civilian professions range from executives, to professional engineers; from laborers and lawyers to proprietors; likewise we have Colonels and Generals whose professions range from judge to farmer; from senator to car salesman; and every kind of job in between. On Friday you may be the "big cheese" and on Saturday you may be a jeep driver for a Lieutenant who on Friday was a "go-fer" in your company.

Is the Guard a good value?? I think so. It is relatively inexpensive to procure and maintain. The total Army Guard only consumes about 5.5 Billion compared 54.1 Billion consumed by the Army (FY-97). This $5.5 Billion represents only about 2% of the Department of Defense budget. The Light Division, which I commanded from 1996-1999, only costs $119 Million annually to operate which is about one third the cost to operate the next most expensive Division in the Reserve Components. Though it is apples and oranges, compare this to the cost of operating an active armored division...about $1.6 Billion.

What can the Light Division do for that investment? Good question! And the answer is, we don't know for sure because it has not been tested as a Division on the ground in war. But it has passed a lot of small-scale tests. It had been through the world famous "Warfighter" at Ft Leavenworth on three occasions prior to my retirement and in all cases has beat the "world class OPFOR" by every measure used by the Army. It was responsible for the land defense of Iceland for 3 years. It has deployed a command and control cell to act at ARFORICE (Army Forces Iceland) in the joint forces Northern Viking 95 Exercise and performed with distinction. It put together a Battalion (80% Reserve Component/20% Active Component) and deployed it to the Sinai for a 6-month peace keeping mission. This was declared a highly successful deployment. It has deployed battalion task forces to the Joint Readiness Training Center (JRTC) on 3 occasions and sent the first Brigade Task Force to the JRTC when the JRTC was first stood up at Ft Polk. It has sent company and battalion task force units to all of the major combat maneuver training centers to support active component and reserve component rotations. All have been thoroughly successful. We have successfully deployed and brought home three separate units to Bosnia; a 46 man Fire Support Element, an infantry company (Charlie Company 3-116th Infantry Battalion), and a target acquisition detachment. All three units did a superb job and have been applauded by every level for their professional and flawless performance. These are some of the accomplishments of the Division before I retired.

Since I retired, 9/11 occurred and with that attack, all National Guard units across the nation have proven their worth on every front; homeland defense and deployment to combat zones. There is simply no task yet given to the 29TH Infantry Division (Light) that the Division has not stepped up to and performed in a magnificent manner. Based on the performance of the various components of the Division as I outlined above, I firmly believe that the Division could be mobilized and deployed to function successfully in any military operation for which it is designed to accomplish. The other seven divisions in the Army National Guard have similar success stories. My bottom line is that I firmly believe that the Guard is the best investment that the nation can make in its security.

The Guard occupies a special spot in my life; it is high on my priority because America and all that it stands for is high on my priority. I believe in the simple concept that a country that is prepared to fight and who has the national will to fight is far less likely to have to fight than a country who has no capability or will. As a leader I want to be able to meet the ultimate challenge with the best training I can acquire. I am committed to that. As a concerned leader, I want all of my troops to have the best training and the best leadership that is possible for them to have. I feel that I am obligated to demonstrate to them that I am doing my best to do my part in preparing myself to train them in peacetime and lead them in combat. What better way could I demonstrate my commitment to that end than to tackle the US Army RANGER course?

As fallout to this I had hoped also that my performance would challenge many of our young officers to attend, and ultimately that was the case. One very special example was that of a soldier named Daniel "Chip" Long. Long was a Combat Engineer his entire career through his command of the 29th Division Light Infantry Engineer Battalion. It so happened that I was a Brigade Commander and was in need of an Executive Officer. I interviewed Long, was impressed with his record and demeanor, and offered him the opportunity to be my XO; but on one condition; that he attend RANGER School. He took the challenge. He was I think 45 years old at the time. He did not make DHG but he did clearly earn the Tab.

He took over the Brigade when I left it, later moved in to be my Assistant Division Commander (Brigadier General), and later commanded the Division. He was the ADC(M) when the unit deployed to Bosnia. Then upon completion of successful Division Command tour, he was activated by the Army to serve in Iraq as the Deputy for Reconstruction there. Note this; this is truly unique. A National Guard two-star general is tapped to come on active duty and go to Iraq to manage a $18Billion program of re-construction in a combat zone. He and I both believe that having earned the RANGER Tab, and all that comes with that earning, was his key to the great follow on success he had after the course.

RANGER School, among all of the other things that it is, is an exercise in leadership by example.

One of the "Principles of Leadership" is to "set the example." I believe very strongly in being able and willing to do anything that I might ask of a subordinate. So one of my strongest motives was that of setting the example for not only the people in my unit but for the National Guard throughout the country. I think the Guard needs a boost in morale and I was willing to go through the most challenging program the Army has to give hope to those who would be reluctant; to be the model to which they could compare themselves and say "If he can do it, so can I."

At the beginning of our two week annual training period (AT), 1981, I assembled all of the officers and NCO's for a pep talk and told them what I expected of them for the AT period.

"For the next two weeks I want you to bust your bunns for the Virginia National Guard! I firmly believe that one should not ask anyone else to do anything that he himself is not willing to do. On 23 April 1981, just 37 days ago, I stood on a hallowed piece of ground at Fort Benning called Todd Field; that's where they pin RANGER Tabs on the survivors. I got to Todd Field by busting my bunns; and I did it for you, and for the Virginia National Guard. "

Well, "busting your bunns" became the Battalion motto for that AT period; and a daily greeting. I would meet an enlisted man in the field and he would salute and sound off with "B-Company is busting their bunns, sir," or I would visit a period of instruction and the assistant instructor would report with "A-Company busting bunns, sir." The final proof of the pudding, though, was when our Battalion was rated an overall "1" by the on-site Army evaluator. That is the highest rating that a unit can get, and no other unit among the other seven "gradeable" units within the Brigade was rated that high.

PUNISHING THE BODY

The body sustains a lot of damage while going through RANGER School. With the proper knowledge and care, much of it can be guarded against. Some of it can be prevented or minimized by conditioning before arrival at Benning while other types of damage is just plain rotten luck.

The most common type of damage is to the skin and assumes a wide variety of forms. Blisters on the feet leads the pack; on the back of the heels, on the balls of your feet, on the instep, and on the sole of the heel. Whether or not blisters can be blamed solely on a bad fit of the boot is debatable. Certainly a bad fit will accelerate the problem but I think the real answer is that the foot is simply abused beyond its limits. The Mountain Phase is particularly bad on the feet because you are carrying heavy loads up and down steep grades, shuffling sideways on steep slopes, stumbling, falling, slipping, and sliding in the dark because a large part of your movement is after dark. Be aware that the feet are abused more than any other part of your body. Awareness of and care for the feet is absolutely essential to graduation. Learn the proper adjustment for each boot of each pair; under load. Carry twice the number of pairs of socks (minimum) that is recommended, and change often. Clean, air, sun, and powder your feet whenever you can. If you discover something in your boot besides your foot, stop as soon as possible and remove it. Always carry foot powder, a sewing needle (in your patrol cap) for draining blisters, "mole skin" for relieving pressure on tender spots, and dry socks. A prophylactic is an ideal device to carry a pair of socks in to keep them dry; and believe me, there won't be any other use for it. Go to the medics at the first sign of foot trouble; they are good on feet. My feet developed a layer of skin a full 1/8 inch thick on the soles on both heels and on the balls of my feet which took between two and three months to return to normal. I remember my battalion was doing a 12mile forced march to EIB standards (combat loaded) in early June (following graduation in April) and at the end of the move I sat down to remove my boots and air out my feet. As I pulled off my socks a crowd began to gather around "gee-whizzing" at my soles - and they were a terrible looking mess.

"Great God Major" said one second Lieutenant, "Maybe I don't want to go to RANGER School after all!"

Another common skin condition affects the hands. The hands take a lot of abuse anytime of the year, but the winter is particularly bad. All ten of my fingers were cracked open in at least one place from the weather. The tips of all the fingers plus the top of the middle joint of some of the fingers were open sores. A crack, which looked like a two day old cut, would suddenly appear; typically about ¼ inch long and deep enough to be painful. I think it was a combination of cold and loss of oils from the skin. These "weather cracks" as I called them, coupled with additional damage due to gouging through the brush, climbing up and down hills, falling and crawling, and simply being dirty much of the time caused me a lot of concern and a low grade pain or irritation during much of the Mountain Phase.

Months after the course was over, my fingernails manifested a most unusual form. Wrinkles formed in the fingernails. Imagine "waves" emanating from the root out toward the end of the nail. This occurred on three fingers of one hand and 4 fingers of the other hand. It took over a year for these waves to completely disappear. One fingernail still retains a distorted appearance from this experience. Now I know that it was caused by a level of malnutrition and the body attempting to make up for losses by drawing from the peripherals. In RANGER School one doesn't have a lot of time to sit and examine his ills and figure out how to cure them; he just keeps driving on; sometimes too far and too late. Some people actually neglect themselves, in their zeal to drive on, to the point where they go beyond the recovery stage and they find themselves in recycle.

There are a few things one can do to reduce the overload on the hands. First, wear gloves as much as you can get by with. Gloves fall into the same category as ear flaps on the patrol cap - not to be used just because it is a little cold. Gloves, with or without inserts (liners) not only keep your hands somewhat warm, but they protect the hands from all manner of abrasion, from thorns, from cold weapons, and from sharp sticks in the night. I suggest taking two pair of shells and four pair of inserts to the field. Secondly, hit the medics up for plenty of Keri-Lotion. They issue this lotion in small one ounce plastic bottles. Yeah, I know guys; your father never used hand lotion. Only your mother and sister did. Well, nobody is going to see you except a bunch of animals with cracked hands. Use it liberally at least once a day. Thirdly, I found that chapstick was a good treatment for the cracked fingers. Rub the chapstick directly into the cracked skin. The medics have plenty of that and yes, you'll need it for the lips too. Finally, carry a few Band-Aids on you. Sometimes you don't see a medic but once a day or maybe every other day out in the bush. If you are sick or injured, they are only minutes away, over the next hill, but believe me, you do not want to request a medic to put a Band-Aid on a cut finger. There is nothing more irritating to an open sore than wool fibers from a glove insert so a fresh Band-Aid at the right time is a real blessing.

In Florida, there is a bacteria (I suppose) which causes inflammation of the skin, which the RI's warned us of as "cellulitis."- It has been known to cause RANGERS to recycle. Several of our class had a bad case of it, but stuck it out.

Then there is poison oak/ivy, insect bites, and the normal wear and tear of sliding down mountains, sunburn, dragging your battered body through the brambles and wait-a-minute vines, the inevitable collision in the night with objects that don't move, and soaking in water for long periods of time, all of which take their individual and collective toll on your "hide."

Finally, there are two more areas that don't really amount too much in terms of harm to the body, but are interesting to note. That is the cumulative effect of constantly "taking a kneel' and assuming the prone position. Both the knees and the elbows develop a thickening of the skin as a result of this constant and unusual action. I have very sharp elbows and they got so tender that it was extremely uncomfortable to lay in the prone supported position for long periods. I solved this by applying patches of "mole skin" to my elbows.

Next to skin damage, bone and joint damage took the greatest toll on our class. Knees and ankles were the most common culprit, but we did lost two RANGERS to the hand to hand combat training. One sustained an injury to his back and was carried off to the hospital and we never saw him again nor did we ever get the full story on exactly what the nature of his injury was. This is not to say that he never recovered or anything like that, rather, that in RANGER School, when someone drops out or is taken out for whatever reason he simply becomes a mystery to the rest of the class. He is no more; in fact for all practical purposes, he never was. No good-bye's, no nice to have known you's; he's just gone!

The other hand-to-hand casualty was a young Marine officer. The class felt - compassionate, I suppose when we lost him. He had injured himself on the last day of hand to hand combat while being thrown by his buddy, but did not know how serious it was, and he did not want to go on sick call. Pride I suppose; or fear of recycle. Anyway, he struggled through some rather rigorous exercises with a cracked collar bone. At Victory Pond, he made the swim test and made it all the way to the middle of the horizontal rope to touch the tab. There the strain of hanging vertically was simply too much. A loud snap signaled the start of another recycle. He fell rather like a guided missile with a bad gyro; but still managed to swim out with one arm trailing. An x-ray revealed a broken collarbone; and he was the only exception to what I have said about how people disappear. He did drop by the company area and chat with a few of us as he processed out.

Then there were several people injured on one of the RANGER runs one morning. We always ran in close formation, four abreast. Typically this made a formation 30-35 people in length. Our speed was somewhere between seven and eight miles per hour, and always in the darkness before sunrise. On two occasions, someone fell and was run over, stampeded if you like, by 20-30 people. This fall by one person would cause additional people to fall and on one occasion, four people were trucked out by the medics and treated for boot marks up their back, plus various and sundry cuts, bruises, and abrasions from falling and tumbling on asphalt pavement. The main formation did not noticeably slow up. Some RANGERS lithely jumped the human obstacle, others side-stepped while some were able to recover themselves from the pile-up and continue the run. The first time it happened was the worst because no one even allowed for the possibility. We were just running along like a herd of animals and suddenly someone hits the deck. Calamity!

The second time we were observant; aware, and for all of the runs thereafter, which was three, we put the weaker runners on the outside of the formation so they could fall out into the ditch, or we put them in the rear. In Officer Candidate School, we used to help weak runners by getting a guy on each side and physically aiding him down the road. In RANGER School, that is not allowed. You must keep up on your own, and you must stay within a tight formation.

Hand to hand combat drill is called "combatives" in Army lingo. To really enjoy combatives one needs to be a Neanderthal in stature, have rubber bones, a brain that is insensitive to shock, and total disregard for the integrity of his opponent's skeletal system. On day 2, 4, 6, 7, 8, and 14, we engaged in combatives for two hours at a stretch with a short break between hours which usually consisted of running around the pit at full tilt a few times, then out of the pit for a short formation. The exercise pit was configured as two concentric circles, the inner one being the area where the Morgan Team put on demonstrations on how to bring bodily harm to an enemy.

Typically, hand to hand was scheduled from 0400 to 0600. This meant a wake-up time of around 0315 so that we could dress, secure equipment, do some straightening up of the barracks, and be ready to move when the Morgan Team arrived. We tried to keep lookouts to spot their approach and warn us so that we could go roaring out of the barracks and fall in just as they arrived. This never seemed to work, and I am not sure why we did it. The first thing they would do was check each RANGER for belts, watch, dog tags, or anything in the pockets. We could have none of these due to the danger they posed in the pit, but of course, there was always one or two items found. RANGER pushups were the order of the day. "Elevate your feet, dummy!" After harassing the class unmercifully long enough so that we could not possibly get to the pit on schedule, they would hustle us on down there. And of course, upon arrival we were hassled for being late, for not being loud enough, for facing the wrong direction, for being born of the wrong parentage, or just for practice. It took us a couple of days to figure out how to get the company into position to receive training properly. After we learned how to do it, we would enter at D (4) in a column of platoons, march too I do a column left then a counter march which would locate the company, when halted and given left face, facing the RANGER tab with the first platoon on the right, second platoon center and third platoon left of D. The company commander would then move at a dead run to the tab while we all screamed at the top of our lungs. He would slow from the run to a fast walk, six paces and no more (no less), stop and report our availability for training. When he finally got the report right; when we were finally loud enough to be heard; we were allowed to enter the pit.

"All right RANGERS, when I tell you to move and only when I tell you to move, you get your bag of bones through that gate - do not step on my grass (Off Limits Area); do not step on my cinder block wall - you will run, not walk, as fast as you can. You will move at a dead run three times around the pit and assume your assigned locations. You will not touch any of my RI's in this process. The last twenty RANGERS in position will do remedial training. Do I make myself clear?"

"YES SERGEANT!!" we would scream in unison.

"MOVE IT! "

And the stampede would begin. Twelve score and more screaming RANGERS funneling through the narrow opening beneath the tab at a dead run - pure pandemonium! It was every man for himself here; no teamwork in sight. It is now a few minutes after 0400 in the morning, still very dark and very cold but it doesn't matter; the huge floodlights around the pit cancel the darkness and the physical activity which is beginning will hold back the cold. The outside diameter of the pit was, as I remember, about 150 feet with a 50-foot diameter demonstration circle concentric to that. The rules of running around the circle, always counter clockwise, were-.

Don't be last.
Continuous vocal noise.
Don't let a Morgan Team RI touch you.
Don't run behind a Morgan Team RI.

None of which made much sense except "Don't be last." The others were self-defeating in that if we did either, it was down for ten or twenty pushups and that was a guarantee of being last.

The last twenty or so RANGERS got to do something different like low crawl around the outer diameter at high speed and if you were lucky you got to do it on the stomach and not on the back.

To complicate things, the Morgan Team RI's would position themselves like spokes on a wheel, radially out from the demonstration circle so as to make us run a larger circle. Then they would change their positions, moving out or in along the spoke. Naturally, we runners are looking for the shortest path, to run so as the various RI's moved in and out, so ran the "herd" such that our path looked like a sine wave whose zero line was a circle. Sometimes they would give us a time limit.

"You've got just 2 minutes to make 6 turns around the pit and be standing tall in your position, and God help the RANGER that is last."

When everyone is finally in position, training begins. First we would practice what we learned the day before; left side fall, right side fall, front take-down, rear take-down, whatever. We would do it by the numbers as called from the center -ring; first I would wear the white hat so to speak, and toss my buddy to the ground and simulate killing him. After six or eight repetitions of by-the-numbers drill we would do it at our own speed for half a dozen times. Then it's the buddy's turn, and the time of truth. Did I hurt him when he was the dummy? This training cannot be faked because the Morgan Team is wandering all around looking for sandbaggers. SLAM your buddy into the ground, don't ease him onto it. Give him a resounding open handed blow and a blood curdling scream, not a light tap or even a sound slap. It has to be on the threshold of pain to be acceptable. But don't get carried away and kick him in the spinal column while he is down. We pulled the punch on that one for safety reasons although the RI's did not in their demonstrations. Incidentally, if the throws, falls, and punches are not being executed with vigor and realism, the RI's will step in and demonstrate the proper techniques to both buddies - on them!

By the numbers drilling is a grueling experience; one fall after another. Wipe the sawdust out of your eyes and fall again. Slam your buddy into the sawdust, beat him in the chest, scream, fake a kick, on guard, and stand by - it's the buddy's turn to "get even" now. Then of course, the RI's have a variety of techniques that they employ to make the RANGERS make errors like face the wrong direction, sound off at the wrong time, go into the wrong stance, etc. All of these things are punishable by pushups at least, or a turn around the pit.

My first two days of hand to hand, I was paired off with a RANGER that outweighed me about 50# so that throwing him was not easy, but when he landed, he impacted with a thud! He sounded like the proverbial sack of s--- hitting pavement. I admit it made me feel good making that sound. He was not well coordinated so when he threw me, it was disastrous. We were, I think, in the process of killing each other when we mutually agreed to find more suitable partners. The secret, if there is one, is to get paired off with someone of equal height and build and learn how to throw and fall correctly early in the game. If possible, get a copy of FM 21-150 and practice before going to the course.

After punishing each other for 40 or 50 minutes, the command would be given to "take three laps around the pit and form up in the assembly area." Sometimes it might be 10 laps; or three laps over and over until we got it right. Another wild race would begin amid a din of noise; screaming, yelling, running, dodging other RANGERS, avoiding the "RI touch," and crashing through slow groups in a wild attempt to not be last. Running in sawdust, by the way, is not like any kind of running I had ever done before. It is extremely tiring. We would form three ranks deep in the prescribed area. "First rank, SEATS!" And the entire company would sound off loudly, crisp, short; and the first rank would literally drop to the ground as one. If that wasn't done with Blue Angel precision, it was "Sloppy RANGERS! Take another lap. MOVE!!"

And we would try it again! "First rank, SEATS!"

"OK, that's better. Second rank, KNEEL!"

"Third rank, STAND AT, EASE!"

That all finally done acceptable (never right, just acceptable), two Morgan Team gorillas would charge into the center and face off. As the MC narrated, the two demonstrators would go through new moves, first by the numbers; then at speed. The class would punctuate their moves with an appropriate "growl," particularly the coup de grace kick in the back that the RI's always gave. The demos were impressive; the combatants were tough, precise, practiced, and obviously enjoyed what they were doing. There seemed to be some good-natured contest between the demonstrators as to who could deliver the coup de grace nearest to the threshold of actual injury. The class enjoyed the contest immensely and cheered them on.

After the demonstrations of new ways to have fun killing your buddy, it was "take two laps and fall into your assigned areas," and of course, the now understood rule, don't be last. Whatever remained of the scheduled two-hour period would be consumed in practicing what was learned in the demonstration. The two hours goes by surprisingly fast, perhaps because it is fun in a sadistic sort of way. I had a great deal of concern that my lower back would not be able to take the punishment. Each time I would impact the ground, my mind would send out an inquiry to my back, "You okay buddy?" Each time I was impacted in a right side fall, I could feel it in my bad ankle and I had some concern for it. Both of those worries were for nothing. Then on day six, the third turn in the pit, the unexpected happened. During one of the many laps around the sawdust pit, in an attempt not to be last, I heard and felt a loud snap; as loud as could be made by snapping the fingers. A tremendous pain seared through my left leg and I slowed to a hobble for the last lap. The RI's were on me like rats in a garbage dump.

"You falling apart Old Man?"

"Give me two zero, wimp!"

"Yeah, you and my grandmother!"

"Oh crap!" I thought, "What's this? I've never had one of these before." Fortunately, it happened very close to the end of that two hour period of instruction, and I did hang in there through the end. Basically, I could not bend the left leg, without pain, nor could I load it heavily. The end of the two-hour hand to hand is culminated by a two or three lap race and exit under the tab. The last twenty or so RANGERS in the ring are only to be pitied, and naturally with my new handicap, I was one of those last 20.

Two RI's will stand near the exit and when it appears that twenty or so RANGERS are left in the ring, they will start screaming to "hit it!" Everyone facing these RI's will dive, from the run, into the sawdust and lie there awaiting the next command. It might be a minute before the next command comes, meanwhile the remainder of the company is lined up out on the road starting a chant of encouragement for those remaining in the ring. The "outsiders" know that the "insiders" are about to get the most grueling grilling that anybody will get in a short period of time. For those outsiders who have been insiders before, I know that they can have nothing but pure pity; not anything as sophisticated as compassion, but just plain raw pity.

The name of the game about to be played is the "two second rush." It is played with two commands; "Move" and "Hit it." On "Move" the insider springs up and dashes on a straight line for the exit as fast and far as he can before the "Hit it" command is given. Generally this is about two steps! On "Hit it" you dive into the sawdust. If you didn't move swiftly; if you didn't dive like a P-38 and plow into the sawdust like a D-10 caterpillar; if you didn't scream loud enough; if you look non-motivated; if you look like you're not enjoying the game; then you may be stopped, given push-ups, or even turned to go the other direction (away from the exit) awhile. Generally, the command to "Move" is given while you are in midair; just before impact. Or another way to measure it is that the command to "Hit it" is given about half way through your effort to rise out of the burrow that you have made on the last impact. However one views the phasing, that 50 yards or so is a very <u>demanding</u> 50 yards. Somehow, I managed to put the pain out of the equation and get through the exit in about the middle of the group, because having seen this act before, I knew I did not want to be the last of the last. As people "escape" and the RI to RANGER ratio increases, the remaining RANGERS come under extreme pressure for a short period; like, they (the RI's) will get in the way so that the short path to the exit is blocked.

The injury turned out to be a pulled hamstring in my left leg. So I now had a sensitive fifth lumbar, a left sprained ankle, and a pulled hamstring; and the five mile run was only a few days off, along with the Darby Queen Obstacle Course, and the Victory Pond event. I had serious doubts that the BIG RANGER IN THE SKY wanted me to continue my vacation in Georgia. Certainly I had plenty of excuses to quit if I wanted to, but I didn't want to. Quitting is not something that I can live with, and a quitter is someone that I have no use for. No, there had to be something more compelling than mere pain. Death would do it!

KING OF THE PIT

Years ago, I heard stories about the King of the Pit game. As described to me, it appeared to be a free-for-all, no-holds-barred slug-fest at the bottom of a slime-filled pit wherein the winner was declared to be the RANGER who could not be thrown out of the pit up onto dry land. Supposedly the entire company would be marched into this pit, which was nominally about six feet deep and was ankle to knee deep in stagnant water and mud. Either by platoons or squads or buddy teams or whatever, they would then try to throw each other out of the pit up onto the rim until there was only two left; then they would fight until one could eject the other, leaving a victorious King of the Pit.

Our last period of hand-to-hand combat was dedicated to crowning the King of the Pit. To my great joy, the pit was not six feet deep nor partially filled with stagnant water. Rather, we played the game on the hand-to-hand combat sawdust arena. We were randomly paired off and lined up under the RANGER Tab. Initially, about ten pairs were dispersed throughout the arena so that each pair had plenty of maneuver room and the contest began. The idea was to beat your opponent using the takedowns and throws that had been taught during the previous ten hours of instruction. The RI's were there to make sure that there was no karate, kung-fu, or back-alley moves used. Military combatives only, executed with vigor amid blood curdling screams of the combatants and the lusty roar from the onlookers eagerly awaiting their turn. As the initial ten pairs wore each other down one by one and winners were declared, the winner would be set aside and a new pair sent in. In some cases, if someone won quickly, or easily and the RI's thought he had not been through a hard enough workout, they would send in another combatant and make him fight again. This of course broke up the pairing scheme under the Tab and suddenly, I was in the arena -not with my RANGER buddy and combatant partner Rienick; but with my future RANGER buddy (by coincidence), the biggest guy in the class, a former football lineman and true brawler - RANGER Campana.

I've got to beat him quick, I thought, while he's still wondering how or if he ought to manhandle a man twice his age; before I get too tired trying to move his mass from the upright position to the prone position; and before he realized that I was out to kick his bunns. A few feint to get him off balance then over the hip. We squared off knees flexed, bent at the hips, arms up in the ward off position and circled each other a couple of times. I never realized what a mean face he had. A double stiff arm thrust to his chest rocked him back only a little before he reacted with a thrust upward with both arms to break the thrust. A second thrust into the chest, this time less movement of his body to the rear as he dug his powerful legs in. We circled. A third thrust, this time he was anticipating my move and I met a stonewall as he moved to meet my stiff arm thrust. Good! Now for the fake out. I started a thrust forward punctuated with a kung-fu scream and as expected he started to meet it. I redirected my right arm, under his left armpit and around his back, turned and threw my right hip into his stomach, straightened my legs, and lifted him for the throw over my hip. My faith in fancy throws and take downs dissolved in a cloud of sawdust as we crashed to the surface in a tangle of arms and legs, squirming and straining for an advantage.

"Break it up, RANGERS! Get Up! GET UP!" It was an RI separating us to restart which I was glad of because I could not get out from under him.

"You hurt Gramps?" Campana whispered as we separated. I didn't answer; didn't want to tell him a lie. We circled each other again grimacing. To end the match the take down must be by one of the methods we been taught, followed by the coup de grace to the chest. Or, after a period of time when the two opponents have fought until they can hardly stand or move quickly, the RI will declare a winner and put him aside for subsequent elimination rounds.

"Make him mad, Old Man," screamed the RI! "He ain't trying to hurt you."

Good idea I thought. Maybe I can make him lunge forward, then I can grab his shirt, fall on my back and kick him over my head. We circled. I gave him a stinging slap right across the chops and faded back; that did it. Here he came, eyes glaring, teeth grimacing. I grabbed his shirt and fell back, raised both legs to engage his abdomen for the toss. That was it; that was as far as the classical maneuver went. He was having none of this. Instead of sailing over my head with the greatest of ease, he crashed like a mad bull right down on me. The pulled hamstring in my left leg made me essentially one-legged and I could not redirect his trajectory with the strength of only my right leg. Forget that theory about using the opponents weight against him. When you are overloaded, you are overloaded. The laws of physics must be honored. He made accordions out of my legs and crunched them into my chest. We rolled locked together changing top and bottom several times until we cracked into the outer ring of the cinder blocks.

"Break" screamed the RI.

We separated and got up to face off, more slowly this time. Wiping the sawdust and mucus from the face and chin we circled again and drifted away from the wall. I did one thing right, I made him mad!

He charged right in and after some barroom scuffling, he got me in a crude bear hug and fell on me.

"Break! BREAK! Damit, this ain't tackle football! Get Up!"

We rose again and glared and circled eyeball-to-eyeball, bending ever lower to strengthen our defensive posture. I am convinced that the Army needs to re-evaluate its hand-to-hand training program. These tricks only work against a man standing up right and not resisting! The remainder of the fight was a series of imprecise attempts to throw each other that degenerated into two tired people squirming in the sawdust locked in a hopeless standoff.

"Break! That's it, Old Man" shouted the RI, "OUT. Campana to the center."

That was it. I didn't feel like the loser, but at the same time, I knew I would never throw him. That kid was strong and heavy. I limped out of the pit exhausted and walked around taking in air. Exhaustion from this event is complete, but temporary. I watched the remainder of the contests. I only saw one or two classical throws during all the time I watched. The rest were like Campana and I, a simple fight to exhaustion. It's not like you can actually kick the opponent in the crotch or destroy one of his kneecaps or run your finger into his eye socket up to the second joint. No real stuff. Only the throws and holds taught by the school. It is moves and technique, enthusiasm and effort, and aggressiveness and determination that they are looking for. And that cannot be faked.

Finally, the elimination's had worked down to the final pair who by now had fought five or six times each. They were tired as we formed a triangle of bodies in the arena to bound the area where they would go the final round. Among a lot of lusty cheering and chanting, they squared off to determine who was King and in the end, it was RANGER Kilipia, The Finnish Captain.

The myth of the King of the Pit game is revealed. Though it may have been done in a muddy depression at one time, and may be again in the future, today it is done on a sawdust arena.

THE DARBY QUEEN

"The record time for completing the Queen is 27 minutes." It was Sergeant Rock starting to lay on the challenge. He put on his broad smile, stuck out his chin, hands on hips, took a few paces one way then the other; "Most 'Queens' don't take me that long" he bragged as we catcalled his innuendo. He turned, dropped his arms, "Cut it!" he screamed. "By God it don't!" he asserted.

"AAHHH UURRAAHHH!!" we responded as a chorus that would shame any tribe of baboons.

"All right now, I want this XX#$@(**&! record of 27 minutes broke! Class 6-81 is gonna set the record to stand as long as the Queen stands."

"AAHHH UURRAAHHH! AAHHH UURRAAHHH!" We believed we could do it.

"Hot Dam; if my Old Man hadn't pulled his hamstring! He'd set the #$#X@**! record! Now, I want somebody out here RAT NOW that can do it!!" About 20 or so people rushed out to give it a try amid a whole lot of howling and growling the rest of us.

"At ease #X@&&%*'; I ain't through yet! Now, I'm own tell you sumpin. I'm gonna hold the Old Man back till last! And by God, you better not #$X@&*%! let him pass you. Anybody that comes across that finish line after the Old Man; I got sum thin for ya, RANGER!!"

"Old Man, I want you to pass ever son-of-a#^@*!% on that course cause I feel like bein real mean today. I'm hungry!! I want raw meat!! You got me Old Man??"

"Yes Sergeant, I got it!!!"

"Let me tell you sumthin; you don't pass anybody....I'll be watching ....I'm gonna come out of the $@#&@^@% sky and I'll have sumthin for you RANGER!!"

A team of four people set a new record of 22 minutes. I have always wished that I hadn't had the hamstring then; because I felt I could have done the course in less time. It was not nearly as difficult as I had been led to believe by RANGERS from several years before. Then of course, it could have been changed somewhat too. The History Channel on TV did a special on a manly military event called Best RANGER. Part of the 3-day competition to declare Best RANGER team each year is the Darby Queen. I have attempted to sketch the course in the following figure, but of course so pencil sketch can do justice to the difficulty of actually committing the self-destruction of attacking the course.

I never did learn the rules to the DARBY Queen. A lot of people did not go through every obstacle but to my knowledge, no one was dropped from the course for not completing it. I heard one RI tell another that "25% of the obstacles were not completed by everyone and that 30% of the people did not complete all of the obstacles." The penalty for failure was not clear.

In all, I passed about 20-30 people going through the course. I never heard what Rock did to those who came in after I did. Several of the obstacles required just plain guts as opposed to strength and agility; and most of those involved height above ground. Some people are just plain afraid of height. My answer to that is just don't look down!

YOUR BODY IS A WHAT?

Preparing your body for RANGER School is not an undertaking to be considered lightly, and don't forget the mental attitude. I remember back in 1970 when I first attempted to go, I made a phone call to the RANGER Department to ask a few questions about the course. Then as up until now there was very little published information, and all I had was a few rumors and "war stories." God only knows who I talked to, but it was a Second Lieutenant; very eager and daring sounding on the phone; had that "come on down and try us" kind of a tone.

"Well, I guess you must have some initial period of physical conditioning" I asked?

"You might call it physical conditioning, sir" - he called me sir and I was only a First Lieutenant - "but I would call it physical destruction!" And he laughed crazily like someone out of a Vincent Price movie.

Things haven't changed much in ten years. The first few days are physical destruction and to get through it one should be prepared either through deliberate training or by virtue of his natural state of condition. Most people will not meet the latter category so they will have to prepare themselves. I practice the belief that one should train under the same conditions he will be tested under, i.e., I did all of my training in combat boots and fatigues rather than running shoes and shorts. It occurred to me during training what really great exercises the Army has evolved and I wondered how many civilian exercise addicts might find a military style physical training program interesting and challenging. The Army's Physical Training Manual is known as FM 21-20 and it can be accessed on line at the Reimer Digital Library by following the instructions at **Appendix E**.

Good physical training requires no special equipment, no gadgets, no flashy uniforms, and no memberships; it does take a measure of dedication. And of course, it is always recommended that one should consult his physician prior to entering any kind of exercise program that is a departure from his normal routine. I think it is important to say that a rigid exercise program is simply not for everyone - regardless of their health and physique. A rigid exercise program necessarily involves a state of mind that harmonizes family, friends, commitments, obligations, duties, and relaxation with a viable program of physical training. Experts in the field are beginning to consider seriously the alleged "high" that runners/joggers get from daily runs. They become addicts to running. A similar addiction develops for vigorous exercise. If something interrupts it, a level of resentment is felt and I have little advice to offer which will counter this feeling. I suspect that each person must seek his own level of tolerance to frustration which results from such interruption.

I solved the problem largely by not tying myself to a rigid, repetitive schedule. I did not impose upon myself the requirement of running "X" miles every day or to do "Y", repetitions of a set of calisthenics, rather I allowed myself an extremely flexible schedule. I laid out a number of different runs which I could choose from depending on how much time I had and how much I had been running versus how much I had been doing "grass drills" or whatever. My runs were 3, 5, 6, 10, 12, and 14 miles in length. More than one path existed to make the 6-14 mile runs. These paths included secluded roads, power line rights of way, logging trails, and cross country alongside a streambed. With such a variety of paths, running did not get boring and most of the surfaces were relatively soft on the knees, ankles, and spinal column. Typically, I would run two days in a row for three miles, then jump to 10 or 12 miles on the third day and back off to 3 or 5 on the fourth day. Or maybe I would run a 3, 5, 10, and 14 in four consecutive days and lay off one day. I tried never to miss more than one day of running at least 3 miles and usually I would only run the 12 or 14-mile track once a week. On rare occasions I might run both the 12 and 14-mile track in one week, but the idea was to train, not kill myself. And yes, it did occur to me that I might drop dead on one of those backwoods jaunts, so I had superimposed color coded routes on a USC&GS map so that my body could be located if I did not return in a reasonable time.

The point is, design yourself a flexible program, one that isn't boring; one that is challenging, and that won't frustrate you if you get home from work one evening and find that your wife has obligated you to entertaining friends or whatever. You just spin the dial the next day and "drive-on," because you are not hung up on specific things each day.

Prior to and following the runs I went through warm-up and cool-down exercises. I think each person needs to design his own warm-up exercises simply because they can be boring and there are some exercises that various people do not like. The important thing to remember is to stretch each major muscle group and get them warm and flexing. Do it slowly (5-10 minutes) and deliberately. Side straddle hop (15), bent leg sit ups (40), deep knee bends (20), push-ups (50), squat thrusts (25), chin-ups (10), and inverted crawl (40 yds) is the sequence that I used. On cool down from a long run (10 miles or more), during that last half mile I would alternately stop and do 10 quick push-ups and running deep knee bends. From the finish line I would walk swiftly for another quarter mile, stopping every 100 feet or so and do deep knee bends and squat thrusts. Finally I would terminate with 40 slow sit-ups, 20 push-ups, and 10 chin-ups and walk around for 10 minutes sipping water.

A running deep knee bend is an invention of my own. While running in mid-stride you suddenly go into a broad jump attitude and land in the squatting position on both feet. Naturally you have some residual momentum stored there somewhere that needs to be released. It can be released either by leaping up and continuing the run or by diving forward into a shoulder roll before springing up. Either solution is good exercise and it sharpens your balance and control also.

Another variation that I often applied to a short run was to take a jumping rope along on the run. While running at an 8-minute mile pace I would put the rope into action and jump rope while running, alternating between jumping the rope on each foot; with jumping on a leading foot; jump rope for 100 yards and carry it for 200. This gets strenuous and you'd best have a good heart for sure before doing this.

As I approached the time to report for RANGER School, and I repeated this three times before everything was finally right, I modified training somewhat and concentrated on passing the entrance PT test. I trained under the impression that I would be tested upon arrival with a five-event PT test; the bent leg sit-up, the inverted crawl, the run dodge and jump, the horizontal ladder, and the two-mile run. As it turned out, Class 6-81 was the first class to be tested with the revised PT test, which was the sit-up, push-up and two mile run.

On 5 January 1981, just seven weeks before my final scheduled reporting date, I sprained my right ankle so badly that I was off work for three days.

"Four or five weeks and you should be back to normal - if you take care of it," advised the doctor.

Talk about cursing! I was enraged; what had I done to deserve this? I looked back over my history of trying to get admitted to RANGER School with utter disbelief. Someone up there did not want me to go.

With permission from my employer to take off nine weeks leave; I made application through the National Guard to attend a spring course, 1979. "No news is good news!" WRONG! No news is simply no news. Complacent, trusting me; I was in my own little world of training; thinking that somewhere in that vast bureaucracy there is some devoted soul making sure that my paperwork is moving through the machine on schedule. Okay, so I didn't really believe that; I just wanted to believe that.

About a month before the scheduled class, I called our schools section to check the status; and I can't recall the details of the excuse now, but it was another foul-up by "they".

Everyone, even "they," deserves one error of administration so I quietly requested a slot in a fall 1979 class. I was sure of one thing, I did not want to go during the June-August time frame. I was then targeted for mid-September but on 21 August 1979, I slipped a disc in the fifth lumbar while exercising. One month was not enough time to recover I knew, so I called my schools section again to discuss the status and "beg-off." No need to beg-off though; "they" had done it again! "No slots available." So I applied for a March 1980 class. It was mid-December before I fully recovered from the effects of the slipped disc so I began an intensive training program to meet the March schedule. In February, the schools section called me - "there are no slots in the March class for Reserve components because of the Iranian Hostage Crisis." In March, I decided that Lady Luck was finally on my side; the cancellation due to the Iranian Crisis probably saved me a failure because in early March I went to my doctor with a nagging little pain in my lower right side. After a "second opinion" examination by a surgeon, a very small femoral hernia was discovered.

Since RANGER School was now off until the fall at least, I decided that a fledgling hernia is no thrill to enter bodily punishment with. I can say that only for something like RANGER School would I ever be admitted for repairing a hernia again! Now, I told myself, nothing else can happen; I'm on for October 1980. It was July, I had-a new physical examination, the paperwork was "in," my new employer was agreeable, and I was getting back in shape.

August 21, 1980, exactly one year to the day; I could not believe it except for the pain (that was real enough); my back went out on me again. I recalled the scene from the movie PATTON where he was in that splendid old European mansion bedroom on the evening he got word that he might lose his command after the slapping incident. The way he delivered those lines---   "Tonight I feel so --- LOW!" haunted me. And I felt so low; but I said, "I will not be beaten by this!" If I had known the term "driving on" then, I'm sure I would have said "Drive On!"

I went immediately to my chiropractor for relief, and let me say that I have the very highest regard for a good chiropractor. After the initial adjustment and relief of pain, I explained my dilemma to him. His response was not encouraging.

"I don't think there is enough time between now and October for you to recover under normal conditions" he said. "I have recently read about the apparent effects of massive doses of vitamin and mineral supplements on such problems, but there is no real proof of results" he continued. "I'll give you a copy of the article I read, but you ought to consult your family doctor before you begin taking pills."

I didn't bother with asking an MD. I just started taking the list of pills in the article on combating lower back trouble - zinc, calcium, magnesium, and vitamins E and C; and doing specific exercises for the lower back. Whether it was psychosomatic or real I do not know, but the apparent result was improvement. The program I followed was outlined in an article by Roland Evin Horvath in the February 1979 issue of The American Chiropractor/Patient Edition.

In summary it called for:
Vitamin C: 2000 mg/day, with as much as 20,000 to 30,000 per day for the first four or five days;
Calcium:1500 mg per day;
Magnesium: in the form of magnesium oxide, 250 mg per meal;
Manganese: 60 mg, three times a day;
Vitamin E: 400 units, three times a day.

Within a month I was back up to full pace even though I did still have an occasional "twinge" in the back when doing certain movements. I learned something important out of this experience and that is that the back is a complicated structure that many people totally disregard. It is estimated that as many as 30 million Americans suffered a "bad back" condition in 1970, and 70 million today. A National Health survey in fact has recently found an incidence of back trouble to be 28.3 per thousand for men and 25.8 per thousand for women, rating third in the cause for lost time at work after arthritis/rheumatism and heart trouble. But that is another subject and I would recommend reading Living With Your Bad Back, a Bantam book by Theodore Berland and Robert G. Addison, for an education.

The primeval urge to kill had to be suppressed. I imagined the phone and the chair arm were his scrawny neck as I squeezed till my knuckles were white. "I don't want to talk to SGT Delay, I want to talk to whoever writes his inefficiency report," I said calmly as I found out that my October 1980 class had met with "administrative problems." Colonel Brightman was called to the phone.

"Colonel, let me say in the beginning that if I should sound insubordinate, that it is not personal. I AM JUST TOTALLY DISGUSTED WITH THE PERFORMANCE OF YOUR OFFICE IN GETTING ME A SLOT IN RANGER SCHOOL." And I related to him the series of events leading to my outburst. In closing I tried to make sure he understood a critical problem.

"Colonel Brightman, you must understand that I really appreciate your people persevering after repeated failures but they must understand that a six-month delay is no small thing when you are over forty. This intrigue began when I was forty; I am now forty-two. Do I have to be fifty to get in?"

Even with his assurances, I decided to get involved in this process directly. The control loop is from the State Adjutant General's Office to the Chief National Guard Bureau to the Schools Branch at Fort Meade to Fort Benning and back again. The RANGER Department at Fort Benning said there was plenty of room in the class starting 24 February 1981; the Schools Branch said, "what they say doesn't matter." The truth is that the loop is not closed properly by anyone!" "They" are not doing their job, whoever "they" is. Class 6-81, for instance, could have easily accommodated an additional 25-75 starters and I would bet that somewhere around the country there were a number of people who, on a weeks notice, could have packed up and attended if the "loop" had the proper controls; a simple stand-by mode would suffice. I was in standby for two years! Under the current system one thing is for sure, and don't let anyone mislead you; no one, unless it is the President, can "promise" a slot in RANGER School to a Guardsman.

The doctor's prognosis of 4-5 weeks recovery time on my ankle looked like a tremendous roadblock in light of having only 7 weeks until reporting day. But I was determined to go come hell or high water. And I thought of one of my favorite people's favorite jokes. One of my role models and former cavalry officer (MAJOR Alvin York Bandy) used to tell this story about the Fredericksburg Flood of 1930. It seems that some little kids were lined up on a second story balcony watching something in the rising water below. Some firemen came along in a rescue boat and offered the kids safe haven, and as they declined, the rescuers noticed what the kids were so intent on a hat protruding out of the water and moving methodically back and forth, back and forth, across the yard. "What is that" asked the rescuers? "That's Daddy," responded the kids. "He said he was gonna mow the yard come hell or high water." And that's the way I felt about the doctor's prognosis. "He doesn't realize he's talking about a future RANGER," I reasoned. "RANGERS do the impossible; that's why they are RANGERS and not ordinary soldiers!"

Then I got serious. This was a situation that needed a strategy and a plan. The strategy: pass the entrance test, run about the middle of the pack during the first few days of "physical destruction" and survive; then pull out in front of the pack during patrolling; resist temptation and don't do anything foolish, i.e., fun but possibly crippling. The plan: develop a detailed day-by-day training program to ensure passing the entrance test. I worked backwards from reporting day, allowing one full week at peak performance; that being defined as being able to make a score of 500 on the entrance test; a perfect score. Working back from there I estimated the time required for a build-up to maximum performance at a rate that would not damage muscles or cause shin splints and the like. Taking in to account that there were some things that I could probably start doing within a week or so, I made a matrix of day by day goals to be reached, peaking to 500 on 15 February 1981. The best schedule I could arrive at had me starting to run one mile on 28 January, or about three weeks after the sprain. It was still swollen, and it hurt; but I didn't see a choice because in addition to the 500 score I was calculating, I was also imposing upon myself the added requirement to run 5 miles in 35 minutes.

Finally, I was disregarding the age charts, i.e., my score calculations were based on that required of a 17 year old rather than a 42 year old. Oddly enough, the charts did not go beyond 39, nevertheless I was under the impression that everyone must perform to the lowest age group. To accumulate 100 points in each of the five events I practiced for what was not an easy task as is indicated by the extracted chart below which shows the accepted "handicap" based on age differential. Some of these may not seem to be significant, but I guess that you have to be over 39 to really appreciate the small handicap allowed.

Age	Inverted Crawl	Run-Dodge-JUMP	Horizontal Ladder	Bent Leg sit-up	2-Mile Run
17-25	14 sec.	19.5 sec.	83 rungs	54 14:09	14:09 min.
36-39	17 sec.	21.0 sec	69 rungs	51 reps.	14:43 min.

On 15 February, I went to the PT field at Fort AP Hill, Virginia, to test myself; the ankle still had some swelling and a blue streak just below the anklebone. This would be the first time that I had pushed myself for the 500 points or the five-mile -run in 35 minutes; and truthfully, I had some reservations, particularly about the run-dodge-jump score. My two mile run time was 13 min. 15 sec., five mile time 34 min. 40 sec. All is well; sit-ups -54; inverted crawl a close 14; horizontal ladder, 83 and not shot. I dreaded the last event - the run-dodge-jump - because it placed a tremendous load on the ankles and because I had not made any of my goals in this event so far. I checked the course, it was dry. Behind the start line, I positioned myself for a good start; GO! I ran the course as fast as I dared and clicked the stop watch as I cleared the finish line; walked around breathing deeply, almost afraid to look at the watch. 22.5 seconds! I had the charts memorized by now; that was worth only 80 points in the 17-25years of age <u>column</u>, a minimum acceptable level for this event. TRASH!!

During the next week of training, 480,was my top score. I could not beat the 22.5 seconds on the run-dodge-jump, and some days I would drop to 23.0, which according to the rules I was practicing to was a NO-GO. I was peaked out. I couldn't do any better. The <u>minimum</u> entrance score was 400 with the <u>minimum</u> allowable individual event score of 80. I could easily make 400-but that one event, run-dodge-jump, was marginal. What to do?

GO! Or as I would later learn, DRIVE ON RANGER! Well there has to be a point here somewhere; a lesson to be learned. I guess the lesson is that if you want something (reasonable) badly enough; if you are willing to work hard enough; if you have faith enough in yourself; chances are that you can reach your goal. My grandfather used to say that "if it's too easy to get it ain't worth having noways." You were right Granddad.

I was never so glad in my life when I arrived at Ft. Benning to find that the RANGER Department was testing the validity of the Army's proposed new three-event PT test in lieu of the five-event system to which I had been training. The entry test for Class 6-81 was composed of only three events; the two mile run, the bent leg sit up, and the push ups with a <u>minimum</u> of 80 points in each event; no run-dodge-jump. I did not know the details of the scoring system, which was some disadvantage to me, so I was torn between trying to run middle of the pack and maxing the course since I did not know what "middle of the pack" was on this test. If I had done only three more push-ups (which I could have easily done), 58 instead of 55, I would have maxed the test, 300 instead of 290.

We called it the worm pit but I don't know why. It was too cold for any self-respecting worm I ever heard of. Until I was introduced to the rucksack, I dreaded the worm pit most of all. The worm pit was under the management and supervision of the MORGAN TEAM. They were happily open for business immediately after the RANGER run every other day during "city week" of the Benning Phase with the motto "We Aim To Please Even If It Kills You." The last of February in Georgia was ... BRISK. As we double-timed into the field that first morning from the first RANGER run amid the noise of cadence and the screaming of the MORGAN TEAM, a cloud of vapor visibly rose from our ranks like can be seen coming out of a city storm sewer (only a coincidence I'm sure) when the temperature suddenly drops. I felt like I was in another world. For a few moments after we halted in formation before the PT platform, there was complete silence. We stood steaming from the run under flood lights so bright that we seemed isolated, small, lost in the void of darkness beyond the reach of the lights. We had just done a left face and sounded off in unison, 128 strong, RAN-GER!! It echoed back and forth between the tall pines flanking the field and drifted off on the crisp predawn air and fell silent. The Morgan Team were all standing at parade rest, sinister, in carefully selected positions all around our formation; watching us. Their uniform was black nylon windbreakers with RANGER in yellow letters placed prominently over the left breast; fatigue trousers starched to perfection; and Corcorans shined like paten leather, gleaming in the yellow light. I didn't know what this place was then, but I had the strange impression that it must surely be patterned after hell.

I cut my eyes to the right just a little bit to get a better look at our situation.

"You want to buy this place old man!!!" screamed a MORGAN TEAMER in my ear and I do mean IN my ear. "Find yourself a light pole and get your feet up and I'll tell you when to stop counting."
And that seemed to be the signal for the rest of the team to spring into action. The Morgan RANGER on the PT platform was screaming for the report and the company commander was under attack from three sides. Then I lost track of what was happening in the formation as I was getting a lot of personal attention at the time. I found a light pole but quick; but I didn't know what I was supposed to do with it. I had not seen a RANGER pushup yet. I was trying to climb the pole; what else do you do with a light pole?

"NO! NO! NO! I did not say to make love to the pole RANGER, I said to elevate your feet."

So I fell to the ground, laid on my back and put my feet up on the pole. He went into an absolute tantrum! Flung his hat to the ground amid a long string of inquires into my family lineage. I didn't know what he wanted! Sit ups?

He recovered his hat and paced a couple of quick little circles fixing his headgear and gesturing to the heavens as though requesting divine guidance. Then he knelt quickly on one knee and in a clam, quiet, comforting voice said "Uhh, RANGER Childers, excuse me please. I know that you are a much older model than I am used to seeing, but I know that the more recent model humans cannot do pushups while laying on their backs."

I was scrambling to turn over. He was screaming and I was discovering how hard it is to do a RANGER pushup; or pushups. I don't remember how many I did, but I did them until I could not do another one. The chest would get 3 or 4 inches off the dirt and no more. The arms trembled and I could feel the blood vessels in my neck and forehead swell then my feet slipped off the pole and I flopped in the dirt.

"I didn't tell you to stop yet RANGER."

Back up with the feet. I strained out one more pushup and fell back to my chest; one foot slipped off the pole and caused my mouth to bury in the dirt and I discovered the dirt was sawdust.

"One more RANGER. You ain't tired yet!"

What does he know? I bowed my head, gulped a deep breath and pushed the planet earth away from my body; "AHHHhh!!" The scream helped me get almost to the full extension of trembling arms before the foot slipped again.

"One more RANGER. You ain't tired yet. You might be old but you ain't tired."
Wish he'd stop saying that. I gulped and strained and screamed again and I felt the chest leave the ground slowly; I visualized Cape Kennedy; the arms trembled and the trunk burned from the strain of keeping the feet on the pole. The elbows would not lock, I could go no further. I hung there stalemated.

"Don't you go back down till your elbows lock RANGER," he threatened, and I could feel myself losing; shaking, sinking back down in slow motion. I guess they can tell when you are really trying and realize when certain tasks are manifestly absurd! A hand grabbed my collar and tugged me just a little and my elbows locked straight.

"DOWN."

I dropped my chest to the ground and lost my footing again.

"One more RANGER! I know you've got one more hidden in that old body somewhere now let's see it. "

Somehow that was hysterically funny to me and I started laughing and I could not keep my feet on the pole.

"You think that's FUNNY RANGER? Maybe you've got TWO more hidden away somewhere?"

Suddenly it wasn't funny anymore; just hysterical, but I think the brief three second reprieve helped. My feet in place, I started another pushup. The arms would not straighten, they trembled under the strain. I felt a pain in the area of my hernia repair and thought "Oh Crap." The arms were losing; I was sinking.

"Scream OLD MAN.' GET IT UP.' You go down and you're out!"

I think I was going down though I had no reference with my eyes squinted straining so hard I could feel a cold shudder pass through my body like a charge of electricity. Then the tug on the collar.

"You don't deserve my time old man. UP OR OUT!"

And I felt the elbows snap in and I hoped   he wouldn't demand another.

"All right, fall back into your platoon! You're not gonna make it RANGER!!"

My platoon was just beginning to move out to their starting location and I caught up to the rear.

The worm pit consisted of eight events. They differ from anything I ever encountered in my life before. Obviously designed by a group of like-minded (warped) individuals seeking a means to measure the metal in all RANGER students. A text description seems like an inadequate means to attempt to paint a picture of the worm pit but here goes.

Since our company had 3 platoons, we started at three locations; one for each platoon. Then on subsequent mornings, the whole model would be rotated clockwise so that by the end of city week, each platoon had gone through the worm pit in comparable sequences. The first morning my platoon lined up at the ROPE CLIMB to begin the course.

ROPE CLIMB is a marvelous piece of sadistic ingenuity. The layout here was vertical ropes hanging from a elevated horizontal beam. These vertical ropes hung centered in a, guess what, trench of water. In addition to the hanging ropes, at the point at which each rope was secured to the support beam there was a second rope; secured to the beam and stretched on a angle down to the far side of the pit and anchored to the ground. With the advantage of a slight running start, you leap from the edge of the water filled pit and grab the vertically hanging rope much like an ape might do. The ape probably won't even get wet .... you will. You then lithely climb the rope some 15 to 20 feet (depending on, whether you are standing on the bottom of the pit or clinging precariously to the wet rope) and touch the knot at the top. There are only two knots in the rope; one at the bottom, which keeps it from raveling, and one at the top for touching. The first RANGER up the rope on the first day is the only one who gets a break, the only one who finds a dry rope. From then on, it is wet, and eventually muddy as the RANGERS from the low crawl make the circuit and transmit mud from their clothes to the rope. When the knot is reached and touched, you transfer from the vertical rope to the inclined rope and return to earth. Believe me, an inch and a half wet muddy manila rope is a bear to climb on a cold Georgia winter morn.

Upon exiting the inclined rope we ran across the sawdust pit with a full bore run of about 50 yards, to encounter a wooden laddered structure that requires a running climb up increasingly higher horizontal timbers until there is a sudden vertical climb of some 5 feet. Shorter RANGERS have a harder time here, but once up on the last rung, the only way down is a jump into a sand box. The drop is probably 15 feet. Of course a loud Hooahhhh or a RANGERS Lead The Way with suitable enthusiasm must accompany the leap or you must do it all over again.

The next obstacle was the chin-up bar. You arrive at the chin-up bar surprisingly winded because running (not double-timing) in sawdust when you are cold and soaked just takes it out of you. If a chin-up bar is not open, you get a breather? WRONG! You get to do push-ups to "keep the circulation up RANGER." A MORGAN RANGER is there to make sure you do a minimum of six chin-ups on the first day and progress after that. I was shaking so badly and my hands were so cold I could hardly do them, but I strained out eight. The bars are polished jade-smooth by thousands of hands slipping on them. Six properly executed chin-ups are required. This means a complete extended arm, full hang at the bottom, a slight pause – but not too long or you will be accused of resting – followed by 5 more chin-ups that pass the RI assessment. Of course he is screaming at you all the while. None of the moves are correct. Every chin-up has to be repeated at least twice. Now remember, this is done after a 50 yard dash, a climb and jump and another 50 yard dash.

Finally the RI will tire of harassing you and release you to enter the belly-down low crawl under a barbed wire net. Here you figure out why it is called the worm pit. It is mud, strewn carefully with hand selected granite rocks. . Mud is soon to be oozing between your fingers, running down your shirt collar, and into your ears. Mud in the ears is actually a secret defense to abate the noise of the screaming MORGAN TEAM who of course are waiting on you at the end of the crawl. It is unlevel, with a harmonic wave subsurface profile (that's where the rocks are). But you are not alone. Depending on which of the 5 lanes you are in, you can have a fellow RANGER sliming his way through on either side of you, which adds to the wave action of the liquid mud that inundates every orifice on your body. For winter RANGERS, it is also cold. God it's cold! But take heart, the next segment offers an opportunity to wash some of the grime off. And another good thing about this low crawl is that the RI's can't scream in your ear because they can't get to you until you emerge from the 20-yard crawl. You arrive at the far end with red mud soup clinging to the front of your fatigues the full length of your body

With a MORGAN RANGER in your hip pocket chewing the mud out of your ear, you run to the next obstacle---the HORIZONTAL LADDER. A short dash from the exit of the belly crawl you encounter what at first appears to be a long covered picnic area; vertical piles supporting a gabled roof with no sides whatsoever. Then you note the "floor" is not a floor, but a water filled pit. You are beginning to contemplate the depth and what it is that you are supposed to do. The screams in your ear cause you to look up where the ceiling should be to discover long horizontal ladders that stretch from your side of the pit to the far side. Immediately, with the help of your friendly RI, you break the code; this task is to climb up to grab a rung of the ladder in your lane and do the monkey walk from your side over to the far side. Remember, you just came out of a pit of mud. You probably have 25 pounds of mud and water in your clothes. How many rungs do you really think you can handle before your cold, mud-slick hands release you into the water pit?

Their ladder was unlike any I had practiced on. First, the rungs were a little larger in diameter to make them harder to hold on to. The rungs rotated freely, almost like they were mounted on bearings. They were steel, and cold. The hands were cold, wet, and slimy from the crawl; and the body now weighs maybe an extra 15 # or more due to the parasitic mud and water. Altogether these factors make rung hanging difficult at best and if you slip off, naturally you fall into the pit of water beneath the ladder which I am sure was put there as a safety feature (tongue in cheek here). Finally, the RI tires of your repeated attempts and send you to the next phase of this misery.

Beyond the LADDER is another low crawl under barbed wire.... this time on the back so that both sides are symmetrically covered with mud. With your faithful MORGAN RANGER nipping at your backside, you drag yourself under the last strand of wire and run to the CONFIDENCE CLIMB. The confidence climb was simply constructed; 4 vertical power poles with horizontal timbers spaced at about 3-4 feet. Eight rows put the top of the climb at some 24-32 feet above mother earth. . No big deal unless you are afraid of heights or unless someone steps on you in the process or slips and falls on you. You climb up, roll over the top timber, climb down and assume the horizontal back position for the next crawl.

The last obstacle is the inverted crawl or crab walk in the mud from the CONFIDENCE CLIMB to the ROPE CLIMB. The muddy ground is like a giant heat pump, sucking the precious heat from the hands with each "step." The first time around, I did not know if we would make the circuit again or what. But here we were, lined up on the ROPE CLIMB again and I think I can speak for Class 6-81..... cold and exhausted. Then a whistle blew down field and RANGERS were running from various obstacles towards the obvious formation area where a small knot of black jacketed MORGAN RANGERS were pacing and screaming. Those of us behind the ROPE CLIMB pit didn't even bother to go around; the shortest distance between two points is a straight line so I jumped right in. In mid-air my brain did a quick analysis of the situation. ..... may as well take advantage of the situation and get some of that mud off while in the water so I went down neck deep and scrubbed furiously, briefly. GOD it was cold! Then the RI was on my case BIG TIME.

"Get out of my pool old man! What are you doing? Every time I turn around you are trying to relax on me! GET OUT!!"

And I was scrambling toward the edge along with several other RANGERS who had the same idea.

"NO RANGER! We do not get out of the water that way. What are you doing? Trying to cheat me? UP THE ROPE GRANDPA!"

Talk about shooting yourself in the foot! I thought I had done it. I couldn't climb that rope again not now! I didn't tell him that. I grabbed the rope with a RANGER growl and started pulling. The hands were like two lumps and I could hardly feel the rope. Straining and grimacing I inched my way up the rope. Reaching up about head high I grabbed the rope and drew my water-logged body up until my grip was on the chest, then holding with the feet and one hand, I would move one hand up to get a new purchase. Then the other hand up, grab, and draw the body up again. Two more draws and I could reach the knot The RI is outputting a continuous stream of verbal abuse; instructions. Straining I made another draw, and locked the feet and legs on the rope. As I made the last reach, my feet and legs could not hold; I slid back about a foot. With all my concentration I gripped the rope in my hands, released my feet, bent the legs lightly and got a grip on the rope slightly higher with the feet. With both the arms and legs I tried to lift the body. Slowly, quivering, I made it back up to within two pulls again of the knot and hung there struggling with my feet and legs to get an anchor point on the rope again. Finally I had as good of a lock as I could and reached up to make one more draw with my arms. The entire right hand thumb suddenly went into a cramp and I could not close it around the rope. I began a slow, slow slide down the rope and once it started, as exhausted as I was, there was no stopping it. I managed to keep the decent under control but the cold water below was as inevitable as was the hassle I was about to get from the MORGAN RANGER. During all of this I noted that I was the only one trying to climb the rope as a route out of the pit. The price of fame I suppose.

It was another half hour or more before we were finally released to fall into the barracks and clean up for breakfast, and thaw out. I stood at the door of our barracks with a garden hose to flush everyone down before they went inside dripping all that mud and ruining the barracks. This entire exercise might be fun in the summer, but in the winter it is a bear to endure.

MORALE

"RANGERS, the next eight weeks are going to be the most demanding eight weeks Of Your lives. Many of you are going to discover a reserve of energy, of will, of desire; of determination," he paused to scan about the black and gold classroom filled with freshly shaven heads, "... of whatever it is down there in that reservoir that you have never called on before. You will learn how deep that reservoir is and how to reach into it. And for those of you who learn that secret about yourselves - and only you can learn it - when you think you are cold and hungry and tired; when you think you have taken the last step and uttered the last command; when the pressure has long since passed the unbearable mark; you'll reach down inside where you have never been before; and you'll overcome those mere human frailties. You will drive your body forward even when your mind is saying stop. ONLY those of you who find this reserve and learn to call upon it will be on Todd Field to earn the coveted RANGER Tab and join the fraternity whose very name - is a way of life! RANGERS LEAD THE WAY! "

You could have heard a pin drop throughout his speech, except for the sound of his voice. Not a chair squeaked; not a paper shuffled; or a pencil tapped; not a throat was cleared. But with that last word, the roof must have raised on that large butler hut as 132 RANGERS went into a howling and growling frenzy; everyone screaming something different, totally uncoordinated but LOUD. After a few minutes of this an RI took the stage and began a chant which was picked up almost row by row until the whole building reached a crescendo. RAN-GER! RAN-GER! RAN-GER!

Within a few days, we were organized in our noise making. We had a morale officer, a few chants, and were experimenting with a class motto.

"You will have a class motto, RANGERS!" SGT Rock was pacing back and forth reeling off an impossibly long list of things that we had to do immediately if not sooner. "And it better be one that THE BIG RANGER IN THE SKY would approve of. You got that?"

"Yes, Sergeant," we replied in unison.

"I can't hear you RANGERS," he replied in a sing song chant.

"YES, SERGEANT!!"

"Now!" He paused with his index finger held at the ready, "AM onna tell ya agin #@&^*#^ that's I am going to tell you again, in Southern dialect . . . "I don't want no trash mottoes. It's got to be short and sweet; and socially acceptable - in case I want to bring my girlfriend out to listen." And he stuck out his chest and strutted a bit as he gazed from under his black beret to measure his humor.

Then the whole class broke into hysteria as SGT England offered an X-rated comment about the kind of girls that Rock ran with. The two of them then had a good natured exchange in X-rated mockery of each other's off duty attributes and tastes in everything from cars to women which kept us entertained for several minutes; then back to business.

"First thing you need is a Morale Officer; someone that's loud mouthed" and he was interrupted by Marines sporadically from all over the room screaming some traditional Marine battle cry III-EEEE-YAAHHH; and by the RANGER Battalion people uttering UUHHH-RRAAA. Altogether sounding very much like two warring tribes of apes suddenly thrown into the same cage. This went on for a minute or so until Rock's magic arm made a swift horizontal sweep like a scimitar and the room was silent.

"We need someone that's about half crazy" ---- And with that several people jumped up and started doing crazy antics; one RANGER jumped up on the stage and started walking on the back of his hands in a crouch like an ape, grunting and scratching; one ran over on his hands and knees and started trying to untie Sergeant Rock's boot laces with his teeth; and that's all I had time to see before I was knocked out of my chair along with three or four others by the falling body of a Marine.

"He's the winner," declared Rock, "Hell, he's all crazy." The "winner" had jumped up on a desk, screamed a few X-rated phrases throwing doubt on the parentage of the other "candidates;" then he launched himself in a swan dive out across the class and came crashing down among us.

I can't recall his name as he did not last long enough for me to learn it, but here was the classic example of judging someone using "standard" criteria. A powerfully built man he was; deep, strong command voice, aggressive, eager, witty; but he couldn't run! I simply could not imagine someone showing up at RANGER School who could not do that most basic of tasks - running.

RANGER Nathan fell heir to the job of morale officer and he did an outstanding job throughout the course and was an absolute clown. He had been in Special Forces prior to RANGER School so he had a broad range of chants, jingles, and cadences to use in harmonizing the class. Prior to each period of formal instruction the class would stand at attention beside their desks and begin a loud chant to the direction of Nathan.

"RANGER! RAN-GER! RAN-GER!" We would do this continuously until the instructor made his appearance. Nathan would pull off his oversized patrol cap and begin twirling it slowly about his head, whereupon we would stop the chant and begin a low but forceful "WHOOAAAA!" As Nathan raised his arm higher and higher and twirled the cap faster and faster, our noise got louder and louder until finally we reached a peak just before running out of breath. Then he would fling his cap to the ground and we would yell RAN-GER!! at the top of our voice. Silence. Inside a butler hut the noise was deafening; it seemed to echo for several seconds and you could actually feel the sound pressure level on the chest cavity. The Company Commander would then salute the Instructor and sound off with,

"Sergeant; RANGER Hague;

RANGER Company Commander, Class 6-81;

RE-PORTS; 132

He would pause and the class, in unison, would scream "RANGERS!!"

"Assigned" he would continue;

"132" ......

RANGERS!! (we would fill in again) ....
"Present for instruction, SERGEANT!"

Then generally the instructor would toy with us for a while; we weren't loud enough, the numbers were incorrect, the commander boo-booed in his report, or something. This choreography had to be perfect or it was a "NO-GO". Sometimes it would take two or three tries to satisfy him then finally, "Have them take seats!" Then the commander would do an about face and command "Take! --- SEATS!"

Whereupon we would respond in unison and at the top of our lungs, our class motto. In its final form, it was simply, un-originally,

"RANGER Class Six eighty-one;

If we can't do it, it can't be done."

It took us eight days and as many tries before this one was accepted. Actually we had at least one new one every day and some days we would try two or three. On occasion, everyone would not have gotten the latest change yet, and some would be screaming one motto and others a different one.

The RI's would just go high order at this and we would all be down for "one-zero." I have a hard time remembering jingles so I have forgotten most of the ones we tried. One was a modification of the McDonald's Hamburger jingle. Another one that didn't fly but that I liked was "Class 6-81; Mobile-Agile-Hostile-Fertile".

Everywhere we went as a platoon or company, except of course not on patrol, we either marched or double-timed; and always to some chant or cadence call. There is something magic about a group of soldiers moving to cadence. One gets so absorbed in this ritualistic maneuver that pain can be forgotten, sleep dispensed with, and rest delayed. Chanting is a binder that pulls individuals into the group; compelled to be absorbed by those genetic memory cells that link modern man with prehistoric man and take him back subconsciously to a time when chanting and rituals were the center of life.

Airborne RANGER Airborne RANGER, where have you been?
Around the world and back again.

Airborne RANGER Airborne RANGER, how did you go?
In a C-130, flying low.

Airborne RANGER Airborne RANGER, how did you get down?
In a T-10 parachute, big and round.

Airborne RANGER Airborne RANGER, what did you do?
I killed Commie #@**/#!, just for you.

Airborne RANGER Airborne RANGER, how did you kill?
I cut his @#*&#! heart out for the thrill.

Airborne RANGER Airborne RANGER, how will you get back?
Using skill and daring; and I'll give no slack.

Airborne RANGER Airborne RANGER, where will you retire?
In the middle of hell when I've put out the fire.

Airborne RANGER Airborne RANGER, how do you make love?
Standing up in a hammock, with the moon above.

And it can go on and on; and there are many many others
exposing the lethality of RANGERS, promises of bodily harm to
commies, the life and times of your favorite First Sergeant, etc., etc.

And there is the Airborne RANGER –

Stand up, hook up, shuffle to the door.
Step right out and count to four
If my chute don't open wide
I've got another one by my side
And if that one should fall me too
Look out ground, I'm coming thru.

RANGERS place themselves above mere Airborne troops with
the quip that Airborne is just a mode of travel, RANGER is a way of life."
But chanting and cadence are important. They are first of all indicators
of class espirit, and cohesion. Is everybody responding as loud as he
can or is he just moving his lips? Is everyone sounding off because he
wants to or because he is under peer pressure to do so? Is he really
putting his soul into destroying his vocal chords or is he 'sandbagging?'
After about three or four days, many of us had strained our throats so
badly that it was almost impossible to give a good account of ourselves
during howling and growling. I finally rediscovered what I knew from

long ago but forgot - bring the sound from way down in your stomach. Try to do everything with the throat and you are in trouble. We also discovered a new term, and a source of "free candy" through having throat trouble. The medics issued us huge quantities of throat lozenges which we termed "RANGER candy." RANGER School would be impossible without "RANGER candy." I kept RANGER Candy in my mouth almost continuously during my waking hours during the Benning Phase to soothe the throat.

I don't think an individual, a "loner," can make it through RANGER School. Everyone has to pull together as a unit whether it is the buddy team unit, the squad unit, or the company unit. Many people try unwittingly to go it alone; they are a ball of fire when they are in a graded position and they 'sandbag it' when they are not in a graded position, but eventually they will pay the price. No man runs level forever; he has his ups and downs so to speak. The importance of a cooperating unit is that the average of the group is up most of the time and that group average will cover a man's bad days.

After I completed RANGER School I went back to my unit and began to encourage others to go for it. To help them, I initiated a "Pre-Ranger Training Course" within the Battalion. One of four soldiers we sent off to Ranger School was a SSG out of our Engineer Battalion. He was an incredibly strong, powerfully built soldier. PT and long marches were not a problem for him. He was a very bright, quick learner, and promised to be an outstanding RANGER Student. He was. Probably would have been the Enlisted Honor Graduate if he could only have made higher peer ratings; if he hadn't been somewhat of a loner. His metabolism demanded a lot of caloric input. Three days before the end of the course in the Florida Phase, he was accused of stealing rations from, of all people, an RI. He denied it. Then he had a confrontation with his RANGER buddies over the issue, got into a fist fight with one buddy, and was kicked out of the course.

During the Benning Phase and on occasion in the early part of the mountain Phase, the class would put on some kind of a "skit" prior to a formal period of instruction. The concept of skits is to check class spirit and imagination, build teamwork and espirit, and I suppose to entertain. All of the ones we did were a "take-off" on some previous periods of instruction or on some instructor. We thought the skits were terribly funny but occasionally they bordered on insult. But of all the ones we did, the ones that were always simply hysterically funny, were done by Ranger Milton and a small supporting cast.

Many of the classroom lectures were introduced with a stone faced reading of an official military account of some combat action involving RANGER operations that failed because of some oversight or that was successful because of good planning or some divine act of providence. The instructor would use these short stories to launch into their period of instruction. Milton would get up and mimic this. With thumbs hooked in his belt and lower lip obtrusively extended he would scowl and strut back and forth across the stage reeling off an endless story that made no sense at all. Then he would hit us with a punch line that also didn't fit but somehow was funny. He would mock SGT. Rock often; "RANGERS," he would say stiffly as he cocked his Head and squinted his eyes, "I got sump thin for ya; but you ain't gonna get it cause you ain't earned it yet STUDDDDSS." And someone was sure to say "That's what I'm talking about!" I don't know what that meant but for some reason it was always funny.

We also had a song that we adopted as the class song and SGT. Rock must have loved it for some reason as he was always calling upon us to sing it. We sang it on the graduation field "Oh Lord it's hard to be humble, ..." and we sang it just like it's copyrighted version except for the line that goes "I must be a hell of a man---" we would sing "I must be a hell of a RAN-GER."

SLEEP - SO GOOD!

Sleep, or the lack of it, was a terrible enemy to all of us. We spent a lot of time moving across country but when we were not moving, generally we were on our stomach in the prone security position. I don't think there is any worse position to be in when you are sleepy but must stay awake. We would lie there guarding our sector of the perimeter, usually in buddy teams, kicking each other occasionally to wake the other. I was determined not to be caught sleeping by an RI, and up until the very last hour of the last operation, I was successful in that. We had made our way across the Santa Rosa Sound after dark by rubber assault boat and moved inland to set up an ambush. We occupied a linear ambush site up on a high sand dune paralleling a hard surface road. I didn't know Florida could be so cold; but it was as cold as the proverbial well diggers rear in Alaska.

The crossing had been into the wind and the chop on the water created a fine mist which covered us each time the blunt bow fell from a small crest. I was the number two man in the crew, thus the pacesetter. The moon was up and it had only been a day or so that we had a full moon, so the other boats were in full view. It looked like a small armada gliding across the moonlit sound noiselessly; sinister, deadly, and ruthless. A chill of excitement ran up my spine; then reality. The chill was pain; my shoulders burned with pain as we struggled against the wind. Noiseless! Except for the labored breathing, the dipping of paddles, and the slap, slap, slap of choppy water against the rubber structure. Still it was exciting; shades of World War II!

We lay there in position, wet from the crossing and wading, chilled by a stiff wind blowing off the sound, and nothing to break the wind whatsoever. An hour passed, still no target. I was fighting to stay awake. I started emptying my magazines, quietly, carefully cleaning each round of ammunition just to try to keep busy; to keep my mind off of the cold, and the sleep that I wanted so desperately. I spit on my fingertips and held the hand up into the wind to chill the moisture, then wiped it across my drooping eyelids. It helps. Heavy snoring to my left; I'd toss small sticks, whatever I could reach, to wake up my buddy. Two hours passed, the wind was steadily causing an odd roar in my ears. Sometime shortly after my fuzzy watch told me I had been there over two hours, I must have dozed off, although my mind was playing tricks on me to make me think I was still awake; but I must have been asleep.

Your mind is very clever in trying to take care of your ravaged body. It knows that your body needs sleep and it knows that sleep is not on the schedule, so it creates a situation that fools that portion of the brain that is supposed to control conscious functions. The situation created by this caretaker portion of the brain is never a controversial situation, nothing that would draw attention or scrutiny; always a low key, passive, believable activity such as cleaning your rifle in a rainstorm, but never anything like having dinner with your wife at Steak and Ale. I don't remember what trumped-up situation I was in, but suddenly a terrific pain was searing through my lower right rib and in my state of semi-sleep, my mind flashed me back to the practice fall in the mountains. That computed unbelievable; but it was real enough that my breath was being forced out of me. I groaned "AAHHHH!" And I was awake. An RI was standing with both feet in the middle of my back! Sgt. Lytle as I recall.

"You're not asleep are you RANGER?" he said as he stepped off and continued striding down the ambush line. I felt really bad about it for a few minutes, getting caught that is, then I said "Oh, what the hell, I'm only human." I don't think he even knew who I was, or cared. Everybody was asleep in that sector and he was trooping the line to get us ready for our last firefight of the course.

Usually I managed to keep myself awake by not lying down for very long at a time. I don't know how the other platoons were, but we had plenty of 'sleepers' in the third platoon. When I would begin to get groggy I would get up and ease around the perimeter waking people up. "I'm not sleeping" they would say, sometimes quite resentfully. No gain in arguing the point; their mind was playing tricks on them. They really thought they were staying awake. They were so earnest in their denial that it would have been believable, but for the snoring. Sometimes it would almost be humorous to sit there and listen to half a dozen snores, almost harmonizing with each other at times. If they just didn't snore so loud I think I might have left them alone sometimes, but snoring sooner or later will attract an RI, then we're all in trouble.

On more than one occasion my platoon would have to go back to the last halt and locate someone who went to sleep and somehow got overlooked when we moved out. Sometimes these halts would only be for literally one minute. Take half a step off the trail and "take a kneel' while the PL checks his location on the map and in that brief interval someone is so tired and sleepy that he flakes right out. He might even hear the patrol get up and move out, but his caretaker generates a situation that is perfectly logical and acceptable to him. He sleeps on content, blissfully; until he is rudely awakened by an RI who has had to back track and find a "lost RANGER." I remember once in the mountains, we moved into the attack position to make a raid about 0300 in the morning. God it was cold! We had been on the move continuously since noon the day before up over the Tennessee Valley Divide and down again. The unexpected little 'blizzard' that blew in on us just about 2400 hours had not helped matters any at all; and just to blow our minds, the 'target' had a warming fire going the size of a Georgia mansion. I could tell right away that we were going to win this battle and capture that fire!

When you're cold it is even harder to stay awake. The body is perfectly willing, even anxious, to curl up tightly and shiver itself to sleep. Maybe it's a desire to return to the safety of the womb but whatever the psychology of it all is, that's the urge that must be resisted. Many an unwary traveler to the other side got there by curling up against the cold and never waking again.

Eventually we did attack the target; and you bet your sweet bippy that we captured that fire! Spoils of war and all, what! The RI decided that we had done a fair job, so he allowed us what we would call an admin break to the war and critique the action in the warmth of the aggressor fire. We heated water for coffee, ate some portion of a C-Rat, and generally relaxed for nearly an hour. This is when I first began to realize that no matter what we did, sleep is not on the program.

Lack of sleep is the cumulative stress factor that works on the mind and the body in a mutual disintegration pact. We could as well have posted a guard and slept most of that hour; but that's the rules of the game and one does not change the game rules in someone else's park.

The fire was beginning to die out and the circle shrank tighter and tighter as each RANGER maneuvered for a share of the glowing coals. Hot on one side, cold on the other - that's the trouble with fires; then no matter where I stand, that's where the smoke drifts to.

"All right RANGERS, time to move. PL get me an equipment check before you leave this lounge."

The procedure is that the APL digs out the equipment list and as he reads it off, whoever has it sounds off and shows it to the RI. It must be either physically seen, or felt if it is in the bottom of a ruck sack.

"PRC-77?"

"Here.

"2 M-60 's?"

"Here" and "here.

"TA-1 and wire?"

SILENCE

"Who's got the God damn TA-I?'"

"McDonald had it last."

"McDonald! Where the hell is McDonald?"

McDonald is not around the fire! So we begin the inquisition; who saw him last? Where? His RANGER Buddy! Who is his RANGER Buddy? How can this happen?

"AT EASE!!" bellows the RI.

All movement ceases; I think even the fire stopped burning. You could hear the snow melting, that was all; nothing-else, no wind, nobody moved. The RI had his head cocked, listening. When it first broke, it sounded like one might imagine a bear would sound if he stuck his nose into a beehive. A tremendous snore floated up out of the thicket on the crisp morning air. McDonald!

"Follow that snore," directed the RI, "and get him up here before he attracts some lovesick bear or something"

Anytime I think of sleep anymore, I shall probably be reminded of an incident in Florida, which was - what else can I say - appalling to me. The night was moonlit so bright that you could almost read a map. We occupied an ORP about midnight and settled in to await the completion of the leader's recon. With the moon so bright, we had to make the perimeter a little larger than normal and we occupied one-man positions essentially; although our buddy was in plain view, he wasn't within easy reach.

It was Florida all right, but not the sunny beaches of Miami or Fort Lauderdale that normally come to mind with the mention of the word. The cool night air was beginning to chill the skin, moist from gouging through the palmetto thickets for the last four hours. The scourge of sleep pestered me mercilessly, relentlessly; stare left, stare right, shift positions silently. Take a fresh chew of tobacco; count the starts; snoring to the left; O.K., walk the perimeter! I was enroute to the second "snorer" when I paused to step over a pair of feet, and I noticed a rattling noise in among some palmetto fronds; I was staring into the shadows intently when a slight noise to my rear startled me. Wheeling, I faced a form coming out of a shadow.

"Kilipia" the voice said. "RANGER Haynes is there," he pointed to the noise, "he is, I think, very sick."

I knelt in the shadows, touched Haynes' shoulder and nudged him gently awake. He was shivering so badly that his teeth were literally chattering.

"I'm freezing" he said! "I just can't stop shaking!"

"How long have you been like this" I asked?

"Ever since we set up here" he moaned.

That was about an hour before. I looked over at his RANGER buddy laying about ten feet away. The moonlight was clear enough for him to read the look on my face; he gave a helpless gesture with his hands.

"He didn't want me to tell the RI's; wanted to make it through this problem."

"Give me your poncho" I whispered, and I began to search Hayne's rucksack for his poncho. With the two ponchos, I fashioned a sandwich of poncho/straw and leaves/ poncho and tucked him in tight to hold his body heat, if any, in. Then I quietly cut some foliage and camouflaged him so that the RI's would not come along and find him.

"Move over here closer and watch him close', I told his buddy, "if he doesn't start to warm up in two or three minutes, you'd better call an RI. I'll be back shortly."

About 10 minutes later I came back by to check on him and his shaking had subsided and he was feeling warm, but a little nauseous.

"I'll be okay now" he said, "Thanks, Pappy, this blanket really did the trick."

"Just stay under there as long as you can; sip water slowly if you start to sweat. A good sweat will do you good." I don't know if that was good advice or not, but I know when I was a kid and used to feel a cold coming one; chills and feverish feeling; I would wrap up and get just as hot as I could until I 'sweated it out.' This may be medicine man hocus-pocus too, but I believed it worked and believing is often half of doing; and if Haynes didn't believe anything else, he believed that he wasn't alone, that his RANGERS were looking out for him and pulling for him.

Appalling? Maybe that is too strong a word. No, I looked it up in Webster's, and it just about fits the situation where one man lays by another and waits for him to shiver himself into a coma. I have thought about this instance often, trying to figure out why Haynes was "abandoned," as it were. RANGER Kilipia I can understand in that he was a Foreign Officer, with only a limited command of the English language and little understanding of "service ethics," for lack of a better term. But he did have enough concern to catch the first person, me, who came by and express his concern. What is most puzzling is that the buddy was from Haynes' own service and I would have thought service loyalty would have generated a more positive action, in the absence of "buddy loyalty." Perhaps he was simply too immature; tired; but I still can't excuse lack of loyalty. Perhaps this highlights a basic and subtle difference between "Regulars" and Guardsmen. To a Guardsman, each person is a 'personal charge' to a leader; one human being to another and not just a number, a replacement, or a transient who will not be here next year. In the Guard, we serve with each other for years; twenty or even thirty years. Each new man, we get to know in detail; learning his good and bad points, his strengths and weaknesses so that he can be developed into a member of the team. I think we learn to observe more carefully and to be more concerned in the Guard. Certainly this experience has strengthened that belief for me.

RANGERS EAT SNAKES?

Rumors persist about RANGER School that students eat snakes and bugs and anything else they can get their hands on; that RI's bite the heads off of rattle snakes, chickens and other creatures; and that there is one exercise in which students are given no food at all to survive a three day escape and evasion course. Most rumors have some basis in truth and all of the rumors may have been truth at one time, after all, the course has undergone some changes over the years. For instance I recall talking to the Marine Corps Liaison Officer who came out to Camp Darby to check on his Marines. He had been through the course in the late 50's and he described the bivouac area that they occupied.

"Yeah, we camped right there; same spot you all are in. But they would not give us pup tents and I was here in January. COLD! You talk about cold . . . Those old cheap sleeping bags would be frozen to the ground in the mornings. We had to dig sleeping pits - oh, about 4 feet by 6 or 8 feet by 4 feet deep; and we occupied those at night in a secure mode. It rained or showed about every third day or so, and everything in that hole was always either wet or muddy, or both. We slept in the open, we ate in the open, and we showered, if we showered, in the open."

In contrast to the conditions of the late 50's, I guess maybe we had it made. We had pup tents and we slept administrative in the bivouac site when we got to sleep. I can only recall crawling into that tent three times in ten days. We had CONEX boxes to store our gear in while off on patrol so it stayed dry. We had a group of picnic benches under a roof (no sides) in which to eat the few meals that we were served in Darby. The shower, though, was the real innovation. Picture an abandoned sheep shed that might have been picked up alongside Tobacco Road, painted green, and plucked down over a concrete trough in Camp Darby. The trough was crude, roughly 6 feet wide by 20 feet long and 6 inches deep - always filled with scummy water because of clogged drains. Showerheads on standpipes rose out of the gloom on each side of the trough. Un-dressing benches done up in Early American decor (straight out of the circle saw) adorned one side of the building. The area between the benches and the trough was inlaid with rocks carefully selected to provide maximum hostility to tender feet and blisters. The water supply? Plenty of it! All you could stand; and if it had been a degree colder it wouldn't have flowed through the showerheads.

"Everyone will get a shower DAILY!" It was SGT Rock promising a fate worse than death. "If anyone of you tarnish my fine reputation by offending the sensitivities of these fine RI's up here at this marvelous facility . . . . I got sum thin for ya RANGERS!"

He paced back and forth, waiting for the laughter and Uhh-Raahhh's to die down. "Now for you West Pointers, what I said wuz . . . if you don't wash your stinking XXX every day, I'm gonna kick your gonads up around your ear lobes. YOU GOT THAT?"

"Uhhh-Raahhh!"

"Now. . . for you Marines" and he smiled broadly as the company broke into catcalls, "You all see me after this formation for a lesson on what soap is. Tomorrow we'll discuss water. The next day, how they go together."

Although the shower is cold in the winter time, there is a warming shed, perhaps 10 feet by 10 feet, built off one side of the main structure. A blanket acts as a door between the shower hall and the warming room, lit by a single bulb that must have been at least 15 watts. The scene in there sparks visions of what a sauna in ancient China must have looked like.

Rough sawed slab board walls lined with shaved-head "warriors," for the most part not talking; just interested in getting dressed and out of the way to make room for others. The floor is slatted wood so that water would not stand; a pot bellied wood stove stood smoldering in the middle of the room to provide just enough warmth to break the chill.

"If I catch anyone sleeping in that warming room you can pack your #@**#! bags, RANGER!" warned SGT Rock.

So as far as facilities are concerned I can easily see how things could have been worse, but it is all relative. On eating snakes; No! We never ate a snake; nor did we clean or see a snake prepared for consumption. No bugs, no worms, no roots, no wild bird eggs; although we did have a full day of training and instruction on what could be eaten and how to find it, harvest it, trap it, kill it, prepare it, preserve it, and eat it. One lesson I can pass along is that if you should ever want to show off and bite the head off of a rattlesnake, don't do it right behind the head. You will get a mouthful of venom if you do. After a full day of detailed instructions and static displays, we were taken down by the lake and issued supper; live white bunny rabbits, live chickens, Raw vegetables, empty #10 cans, and empty .50 caliber ammunition cans. Each squad got two chickens, two rabbits, and a sack full of vegetables. There are a lot of people in this man's Army that don't know where Colonel Saunders gets his finger licking supplies. I say that based on the few people there who knew how or had ever cleaned a chicken before; or any other animal or bird for that matter. "YUCK!!" said one man when I started removing the intestines. There were some who looked on with ----- disapproval? as the rabbits were 'terminated.'

Ammunition cans make excellent field expedient pressure cookers. The rubber gasket in the lid must be removed and the water level must be maintained because if it gets too low, the fire will burn the paint inside the can and ruin the food. Over a good bed of coals, a chicken or rabbit will cook in about 15 minutes after the water comes up to temperature. The lid, without the gasket, fits just tight enough to generate some pressure but not enough to expand the vessel or blow up.

When the feast was cooked and divided up among the squad, one RANGER was sitting there on his haunches with a rabbit leg in his hand looking almost sad in the firelight. He looked across the fire and caught me looking at him.

"Pappy, do you know what tomorrow is?"

I had to think a minute, "Sunday, I think."

"Tomorrow," he said with deliberation, "tomorrow is Easter Sunday and we done killed all them bunny rabbits."

As far as foraging for food is concerned, we did not do it. We got hungry, but not hungry enough to eat a worm or bug or plant life raw; and during the whole 54 days we only had access to a fire three times exclusive of heat tabs; and it would take a lot of heat tabs to actually cook something.

They will barely boil coffee water. There was never any real time for foraging. On one occasion as we were moving across country in Florida, we made a security halt in a small glade. Apparently some regular troops had bivouacked there sometime in the past, and had buried their trash in a shallow hole. Animals, probably raccoons or armadillos, came along, smelled food, and dug the little dump up. Among this trash we discovered several tins of peanut butter and cheddar cheese. If this can be called foraging, then we did it. How old that stuff was, nobody knows; but it didn't get any older.

As my ace in the hole I always figured if things got bad enough that I could fashion myself a crude wooden bullet and fire it using a blank cartridge in the M-16, and kill a small bird or chipmunk or something. Things never got that desperate.

The final myth to comment on is the Escape and Evasion exercise. This is done during the Florida Phase and for us it was only a-dusk-till-dawn exercise. Shortly after dark we were released in groups of three along a control road. Our mission was to move to a rally point some 16 clicks away without getting caught. The area, about 4 or 5 clicks wide, between the start point and the rally point was crisscrossed with roads and trails and was supposedly heavily patrolled by both mounted and dismounted patrols. A lot of RANGERS got caught and were taken to a POW Camp. My three man team passed within hearing of the POW Camp and could hear the guards "torturing" the RANGERS that they had caught thus far. My team made the rally point about an hour later than we had planned on due to some mis-orientation, but we were well ahead of most of the teams.

So the E&E event is part rumor and part truth. Those who got captured had some unpleasant experiences in the POW Camp at the hands of SGT Brunswick; but if you evade capture, the whole event turns out to be a long walk in the woods with a few exciting moments as you lay in the shadows and watch a patrol go by, or you blunder upon a patrol and have to simply outrun them in the dark. When that happens you don't worry about anything but getting away. Direction, distance, briar patches, swamps, snakes; nothing bothers you. Run as hard as you can for about two minutes and drop down to listen. Chances are that they will not pursue you that far because they work primarily off of roads and trails and they don't have any desire to pursue you down into a swamp, overpower you and carry you bodily back to the road. They have easier targets to capture right on the roads.

BEAT THE MOON

The name of the game might be to beat the moon. Get to where you want to be before that old friend hides behind a hill. The average guy that goes to RANGER School simply cannot comprehend the extreme difference between moving cross country in the moonlight and in gouging cross country on a moonless night; night after miserable night. Some nights there simply is no moon and there is nothing to be done about that. Some nights the sky is overcast, and there is nothing to be done about that, either. But when the moon is up wolfman, you better move as fast and as far as you can. Be aware of the moon; most students are not. They ding around doing this and that; wasting valuable moonbeams until   it is too late. The moon is down and the patrol stumbles on. If wisely used, knowledge of the moon before hand could be an asset to RANGER students. Our light from the moon varied from nothing to all night illumination. It is important to note which end of the night you will have moonlight when there is only a few hours of it. Sometimes the moon is up when the sun goes down, and sometimes it comes up just before sunrise. Remember to allow the moon some time to gain some altitude because it is ineffective when low on the horizon.

SMALL THINGS

There are a lot of small things that one must get used to fast to make it through RANGER School in good form. The sooner you accept these things for what they are the better off you will be. First, you will never admit to anyone except your RANGER buddy that you are tired or hungry or sleepy to wet or cold or hot or hurt, or second best. Secondly, you will be tired and hungry and sleepy and wet and cold and hot and hurt; and in something, you will be second best. Next, do not argue with any RI. RI's do a lot of unexplainable things, but they do not set intellectual traps for you; they do not go out of their way to make a fool of you, that you'll do on your own. When they tell you to do something, do it. When they "strongly suggest" something, act upon it. If they give you an evaluation that you believe you can refute, don't! Take your contention to your TAC and let him settle it for you. If you think you can "snow" the RI, you're wrong. You'd probably stand a better chance getting sympathy from the Morgan Team.

If you think you will ever get to use all of the gear that you carry around in your rucksack all the time - forget it Jack! That gear is strictly carried to burn calories, but don't be caught without the entire load list in your ruck or on your body. Well, there are probably other reasons for carrying that gear around and given enough time to fabricate, I can probably list a few. It gives you practice in packing and unpacking so that you can learn to get to at what you are allowed to use in the minimum time in the dark, in the rain, in the cold, and while you are on the move. Techniques of keeping things dry are learned; or, failing that lesson, you can learn how to dry things out that are soaked. It stimulates the imagination and quickens the decision process. "OK, RANGERS, you may put on one piece of HAWK gear." Which piece? It teaches -responsibility. "You will not lose anything, RANGERS." It gives you something to tell your grandkids about. "What did you do in RANGER School Granddad?" "I carried a 90# pack kiddo". A full Ruck is easier to locate when you are recovering it after shedding it for action. It challenges your ingenuity to pack something additional when you are assigned to carry team equipment. "But I can't put a PRC77 in here with all this stuff. Now it weighs 118#!"

Finally, and seriously, in case of a real weather emergency, you can survive. But the most important reason for carrying all that gear is that it is part of the program. RANGER School is not a democratic institution, rather, it is a difficult program designed by professionals and it has over forty years of successful operational history.

Always carry a shaving brush and a dry rag so that you can get to them easily. At every opportunity, use these items to clean your weapon. A clean weapon at the right moment is worth a positive spot report; a slightly dirty one anytime is worth a lot of grief. If I had it to do over again, I would make me a long skinny sack out of O.D. tee shirts such that I could stuff my M-16 into it up to the rear of the receiver to protect it from dust during selected activities.

HAWK gear? What is HAWK gear anyway; and why is whatever it is, called that? HAWK gear is anything that is worn to keep the body warm and dry other than fatigues, boots, and patrol cap. HAWK gear is gloves, insulated underwear, wool shirts, field jackets or liners, wool scarf, rain parka or trousers, or the ear flaps of the patrol cap. The name comes from the wind; high altitude, cold, piercing, shrieking, spine tingling wind. The wind is called the "HAWK" in mountain lore, thus equipment that protects us from the cold (and rain) is called HAWK gear.

People vary greatly in their tolerance to temperature extremes. Class 6-81 had a Marine, for instance, that usually had on two to three layers of clothing more than everyone else during movement and during an extended halt or in a patrol base, he may have on six or eight layers of clothing on. Except during a rainstorm or in a strong wind, we normally removed all extra clothing for movement. I always carried a wool shirt with a field jacket' liner inside it so that I could get to it easily; usually on the top of my rucksack unless it was raining. At normal patrol movement rates in the mountains, in the winter, I would work up a mild sweat to the degree that the tee shirt would be damp; which was okay as long as we were on the move. If we made a halt that promised to be five minutes or more, depending on the weather, I would slip this shirt/liner on to prevent chilling. When the word came to move I would quickly shed the HAWK gear and stuff it back through the straps on top of the rucksack.

The GI wool scarf is one of the best pieces of clothing ever devised. There are a variety of ways you can wrap this around your head, face, mouth, neck, ears, or whatever part is cold. If you can keep your head and neck warm, you will find it gives you a tremendous feeling of well-being. When the back of my neck is cold the misery seems to be multiplied by three or four. I'll guarantee that you get more good out of a wool scarf per square foot of material or per ounce of material than any other piece of HAWK gear.

Another fine piece of gear is the poncho with liner. I carried my liner laced inside my poncho. On patrol base, often I would fold this into a pad just large enough to lie on and use it to insulate my body from the ground. Mother Earth is a tremendous heat sink, that is, it will suck all of the heat from your body so anything that you can do to insulate yourself is good. Some RI's would not allow us to use HAWK gear in that way; some would not let us use any HAWK gear at all . . . "When you see me putting on HAWK gear then you'll know it's time for you to do it" they would say. One RI like that wasn't so bad but when we hit three in a row like that once, I really thought someone would come down with lung rot or something. We survived it 3 to 5 days and nights in the elements of a North Georgia winter with never more than a tee shirt and fatigue shirt on. I learned that the body can stand more misery than can the mind. It was after this that I decided that I was going to wear my gloves - HAWK gear or not. It was during this time that I discovered that chapstick was a good treatment for cracked hands. Every finger was cracked in at least one place, and I think I was ready to go right up to the brink of disaster about glove wearing.

Another term that the RI's used often was "High Speed" gear. "None of that High Speed ---- RANGERS!" High Speed stuff was basically anything that wasn't O.D. in color; anything commercial; anything sold by "them God damn civilians." Knives, silva compasses, insulated clothing, climbing gear, watch, flashlight, etc.

There is a term called the "rucksack flop." The RI's absolutely hate it, that is, they hate to see RANGERS in the position referred to as the "rucksack flop." It is the easiest position to assume when carrying the ruck; it is the most comfortable position to be in with that monster on your back; it provides an unbelievably stable position from which to fire the M-16. It's no wonder the RI's don't want RANGERS using it! They would prefer us to try to assume the prone position with the ruck in place. PAIN! Pure pain! Absolutely contrary to the laws of nature and the geometric flexibility of the human body; and it's next to impossible to aim the M-16 laying prone, propped up on the elbows, belt buckle on the ground, and a 60+ pound load on your upper back. The rucksack flop is particularly comfortable in the mountains where you flop with the ruck on the upslope always on the up slope please, or you'll roll down hill in a flash of flailing arms and legs. Assuming the standing position from the flop is a trick in flatland. It can't be done (easily) directly. It's best to do a side roll coming into a position with both hands and both knees on the ground; then raise the upper body using the M-16 with the butt on the ground. Then placing the foot of the strongest leg flat on the ground, grunt hard, and stand erect. Nothing to it. You'll do it thousands of times.

The RI's at the various camps, i.e., Darby, Merrill, Florida, use different techniques. Don't ever say "But Sergeant, in the mountains we did it like . . . . ". DON'T do it. When in Rome do as the Romans do. In RANGER School, the RI's purposely use different techniques at the different locations so as to show students a variety of workable methods. In the mountains, the patrol base was always occupied on the stomach. In Florida, some RI's allowed us to maintain vigilance positions kneeling, or even standing. In the mountains, we never dug in a single time; in Georgia, every patrol base was dug in. In the mountains, everyone carried his weapon more or less like he wanted to; in Florida, everyone carried it at high port, ready. Methods of crossing danger areas, counter ambush techniques, lost RANGER policy, reconning the objective, occupying the patrol base, tying down equipment, and a long list of other things vary some with the training location. Listen to the RI. When he demonstrates a technique, use that technique and file all others for future use.

Gouging is a term that describes the movement of a RANGER patrol across country at night. It is a very appropriate word in that almost everyone gets gouged sooner or later; in the eye with a branch, in the shin by deadfall, in the groin by a cypress knee, in the hands by briars, or across frozen ears by a limb that the RANGER in front carelessly released as he passed. It could also appropriately be called groping because after 30 or 40 hours with no sleep and little rest, everyone begins to play follow the leader. I've seen 30 people stumble across the same log and it's only two feet long; I've seen 15 people become tangled in the same vine, and it's the only vine for two grid squares. Then exhaustion sets in; one tends to "plod" along blindly following tile soft luminous glow of the RANGER eyes ahead. You stare intently at them so as not to lose sight of them, groping with your hands into the darkness to fend off branches that seek your eyes, stumbling on two blistered, wet, cold, heavy, throbbing things that once looked like feet. Hour after hour the rucksack straps bind your shoulders and the metal frame digs into your hipbone until finally the vision begins to return, as the blackness of night turns to the soft gray of dawn. What an eerie feeling it is to greet the dawn after moving since sunset the day before. I always had the feeling that we were marching through a grave yard because everything was so quiet; so motionless. And we were zombies moving slowly, exhausted, through the swirl of early morning ground fog. There was also the feeling of relief because at least some rest could soon be had. Maybe not sleep but relief from that cursed rucksack and a cup of lukewarm coffee while waiting for the RI changeover to take place. We didn't say much to each other but we did communicate enough to let each other know that we were hanging in there.

"You look like HELL Gramps," said my RANGER buddy.

"Thanks, I thought for awhile I might have died and gone there," I replied.

Not a word has to be spoken, just eye contact and nods and gestures Sharing a cup of coffee or a lifesaver with a buddy quietly in the dawn is a memorable experience; binding; forging a memory that's revived many times over on an early morning when the fog is just so and the chill causes a gentle shudder of the shoulders. And all that really spoils the memory is the thought of that cursed rucksack and the endless grief that it inflicts.

Most people will doubt that RANGERS walk (or run or stumble) around for eight weeks with 90# or more on their backs. In fact, when I put it in those terms it does sound rather unbelievable; 90# of alien material on the back for most of the time for a period of 8 weeks. This deserves a calculation to verify it to myself

The following items were carried in the rucksack:

ITEM

	WEIGHT (#'s)
Rucksack	6.6
Bag, Waterproof	.75
Camouflage stick	.1
Canteen, 2 quart w/GP strap (filled)	4.2
Fatigues (1 set)	2.26
Foot Powder	.15
Gloves, leather, black w/inserts	.5
Gloves, leather, work	.5
Insect repellent	.2
Rain jacket and pants	1.7
Poncho	1.5
Poncho Liner	.25
Sleeping shirt or wool OG sweater	.3
Sling, 11-16 or M-6	.15
Socks, cushion sole (3 pair)	.54
Tape, black electrical	.1
Tool, entrenching (I per buddy team)	2.5
Cord, tie down	.05
Water purification tablets	.15
Weapons cleaning equipment	1.0
Toilet articles	1.2
Field jacket w/liner	4.8
Shirt, OG wool	1.5
Long Underwear	1.5
Spare flashlight batteries	.75
C-Rations (6 meals)	12.78
Overshoes, 10 buckle	5.0
Sleeping Bag (1 per buddy team)	9.0

Total 61.2 #

Add to the above the following items which are normally worn while on the move:

ITEM	Weight (#)
M-16 Rifle	6.5
Boots, combat	5.0
Belt, web	.1
Cap, field, patrolling	.2
Fatigues	2.26
Socks, cushion sole	.19
Underwear	.5
Notebook and pencils	.3
RANGER Handbook	.4
Compass, lensatic	.4
Pace cord, ID Tags	.1
Map with case	.4
Trousers, field w/suspenders	2.35

Optional	
Tobacco Products or candy	1.0
Handkerchief	.1
Extra socks	.19
Watch	.1
Pocket knife	.3

Total   20.39#

A RANGER Platoon of 30 men, a typical size, will be issued and carry the following items referred to as Battalion Equipment:

ITEM	Quantity	Weight (#)
Radio, PRC-77	2 each	50.0
Gun, Machine, 1-1-60	2 ea.	56.0
Wire, Field, EE-8	partial roll	8.0
Telephone, field	2 ea.	8.0
Binoculars,	1 ea.	2.0
Goggles, Night Vision, PVS-5	2 ea.	2.0
Radio, PRC-88	3ea.	12.0
Ammo for M-60	600 rounds	30.0
Grenades, smoke	6ea.	18.0
Claymore, 11-18	3ea.	9.0
Law, M-72	4ea.	6.0
Rope, climbing, 120 ft.	2ea.	25.0
Grenade launcher, M-203	2ea.	6.0
Batteries, spare for PRC-77	2ea.	4.

Total 236.0

236 divided by 30 equals 7.87# average/RANGER

The following items are carried on the Load Bearing Equipment (LBE);

Item	Weight
Pistol Belt and Suspenders 1 ea.	3.5
Ammo Pouches, 3 ea.	2.19
Canteen with cover and cup, 2 ea.	7.7
First Aid Pouch, 1 ea.	.1
Flashlight, 1 ea.	.82
M-16 Magazines and ammo, 5 ea.	3.5
Sheath Knife (optional)	1.2

The total average weight carried per Ranger from the skin out is then 61.27 + 20.22 + 7.87 + 17.81 = 107.17 #.

Even if I am 20% off, that is still about 86 pounds from the skin out when you are not burdened with something special like the radio or the M-60 machine gun.

But if you are lucky enough to carry the M-60 or the PRC-77, subtract the 7.87# which is your fair share of tire Battalion equipment and add back approximately 25 # to account for one of these special items. Your load is now in the 125# class range. This of course assumes that everything is dry, which it is not most of the time.

UNMARKED MAPS

One of the difficult parts of being a patrol leader is that <u>nothing</u> can be written on the map nor can grease pencil marks be left on the acetate map case. Along that same line, radio call signs, code words, nor frequencies can be written down and carried forward of friendly lines. The patrol start point, the general route, the general location of the ORP and the patrol base, and the location of the objective are not too difficult for the patrol leader to remember. Add to that though five or six check points enroute, five or six preplanned fire concentrations by four digit ID, alternate routes (with check points and concentrations), and azimuths and distances of the routes; and suddenly you have more than one man can handle. The secret, if there is one, is to assign various members of the patrol to memorize certain things. That sounds logical but don't laugh, such logic is not a naturally occurring phenomena in RANGER School.

There are certain key people who should be assigned to memorize certain data. For instance, the RTO should memorize call signs and frequencies; let the APL recall the operation codes; the compass man should know the sequence of azimuths and distances; let the lead squad leader keep up with fire support locations and ID; and the PL can have the ORP/Patrol Base/Objective. To be safe, assign these responsibilities to at least two people and make a list of <u>who</u> knows what. The importance of the list is so that when the leadership positions change in the middle of an operation, an orderly transition can be made.

Given more time for the planning and rehearsal phases, one could probably memorize all of the data required, but time is always a critical commodity. It is helpful, therefore, to use a minimum number of check points and fire support coordinates and try to limit the number of legs along the route of March. In Florida almost any move can be made with one azimuth and one distance, i.e., one leg; two at the most. In the mountains, <u>no</u> move can be made in one leg unless you are a mountain goat. Since RANGERS are mortal men they are constrained to the whims of mother nature and the crazy results of the ice age, use terrain features to your best advantage.

Terrain features are highly irregular and your route of march will be composed of many legs. A good terrain association man will not follow specific azimuths, rather, he will follow a general azimuth and rely on ground slope to channel him from point A to B.

The RI's will try to convince you not to follow ridgelines and not to walk mountain trails. Tactically unsound they say. The enemy watches trails and ridgelines they say. You have to pay some attention to that. But I would look at that map and it was almost brown there were so many contour lines on it. I would look at the enemy situation and I would say, there aren't enough troops in the whole world to guard all of those ridges. I've seen patrol leaders walk twenty yards from a trail; parallel a ridge stumbling and falling with one leg lower than the other for click after miserable click. I reasoned that a patrol walking a trail or a ridge could move faster, quieter, and incur less bodily damage than could a patrol walking off of the trail, so when I took my turn as patrol leader in the mountains, I did just that; and I justified walking trails and ridges to my RI.

I took over during consolidation of the objective with the mission to move and occupy a patrol base - twelve clicks and several mountains away. I can still see the -route in my mind; from the raid site it was nearly straight up 600 feet to the ridge crest. The ridge sloped up another 500 feet in elevation, colliding with other ridges enroute to a "gap" in the range. From the gap several fingers led down the other side and off in the distance and several hundred or thousand feet below the flickering lights of several villages scattered across a broad valley. The night was clear as a bell, dark, and cold in the brisk high altitude breeze.

I thought of the night before; we spent it on a neighboring mountain in a freezing rainstorm. I wished that SGT Rock had been there so I could have asked him if it was cold. This was one of those nights when the rain was barely liquid when it fell and the underbrush was coated with ice; the ground crunched with every step; ice formed in a thin sheet on the lower part of the parka jacket; and the wind was blowing unmercifully.

I estimate it was gusting to 40 or 50 mph. The air was literally filled with falling limbs and lightening exploded in eerie blue bolts all around. I remember most vividly following a small finger to the conjunction of the gap; and when we got into the throat of that gap, the wind was literally howling through. The roar was frightening and as the lightning flashed for as long as two or three seconds at a time, the file of men was like something out of a bad dream; men bent into the driving wind and rain, absolutely soaked to the bone and no hope of a fire to dry out by.

I thought of a description of Napoleon's retreat from Russia: "The cold was the abominable thing; the dreadful enemy against which man could not fight and which destroyed them."

It would be two more nights before we would be back into shelter. The hard thing about being in a miserable situation is to also know that the end of it all is a long way off. That's when leadership and discipline and training pay off. The leaders maintain discipline through their actions, their attitude, and their reaction to the performance of others. It's easy to recognize leaders during miserable situations; they are the ones who are trying to find solutions instead of compounding the problems; and they are usually the ones who are not complaining. (And it's amusing back in the "world" when a rainstorm comes up and people all around scurry for shelter.)

By contrast then, tonight was beautiful. I ordered a security halt and a rotation of equipment for the second time since leaving the low land below; and I got my map out for a check. The trick now was to move out of the gap and catch the correct finger, follow it the right distance, and drop down slope to catch a lower gap. If the lower gap was missed in the dark, we would be in "deep yogurt" so to speak, and probably would not realize it before walking several clicks out of the way. Mountains in the dark are somewhat like alligators - they all look alike. This is another reason I liked to "run the ridges." In walking a side slope it is easy to be diverted by an intersecting ridge and not realize it, after all, on a 1:50,000 scale map, every wrinkle in the ground does not appear on the map. You encounter some fairly large ground swells that simply do not appear on the map because of the large contour interval on the 1:50,000 map. Ridge running is by far more accurate as would be proven this night; and a dark night it was, too.

We had really been doing well; moving swiftly, easily by comparison to previous nights, and about as noiselessly as we had ever done day or night. I had been stopping after every major ascent to rest briefly and rotate loads among the platoon. With everything going so well the platoon was in very high spirits, as was I, so I decided I would take a few minutes to instruct the platoon in the logic of moving by the method that I was leading; after all, I was in charge. WRONG! The RI's let me go on for about five minutes before they lowered the boom. My mistake was that I thought I was in charge and I did not clear my action with them first. Right there on the top of a mountain in the middle of a movement phase, I called a rally and announced that we were going "admin" for a few minutes. Today, the Army would call this an After Action Review (AAR) and we would have been praised for stopping and conducting the AAR in accordance with FM 25-101. I was perhaps 10 years ahead of my time and the RI's were in no mood for my innovations. My logic was that we were all there to learn something and I wanted to simply tell the platoon why we were moving so smoothly; why everyone was in good spirits for a change; and what the tactical trade-off was in walking the ridges. And after all, RI's called admin halts all the time to critique us.

"What the hell do you think you are doing, RANGER Childers? You've been leading this platoon only about five hours now and already you think you're an RI or something. Knock off this crap and get back to reality."

Good initiative; poor judgment!

But that was only RI talk. If it had been a real negative, it would have come up in counseling later, which it did not; at least not negatively.

Things were going so good that at 0200 in the morning, the RI called me aside and told me to move about 200 yards further up the trail to a suitable location and go into a clandestine patrol base for sleep. "How much sleep?" I couldn't believe sleep!

"You figure that out, Old Man," drawled the RI, "You be at the coordinate that I gave you for your link up at 0700 in the morning. What you do between now and then and how you get there is your problem. But don't be late!!"
I was beginning to suspect an unusual patrol tour. Normally my tour would be over when we entered the patrol base. A new command would come on for occupation of the base, and still another command group for movement to and execution of link-up.

I did a quick recon to select a patrol base. Finding a perfect spot some 30 feet in diameter which was relatively clear of thick undergrowth in among a thick grove of pines and surrounded by heavy brush and briars, I led the platoon in and circled the RANGER file until the lead met the trail. We stood quietly in a circle approximately 20 feet in diameter. I started the headcount counterclockwise, "one;" it came back to me "36."

"Everybody lay down and face out. Go to sleep. " All accounted for. I take the first watch and wake Laster and Beckum in 30 minutes. They will stay up 30 minutes and pass it on clockwise around the circle. The situation must be reported by radio hourly; call sign and code-word will be on the radio tie down strap. Wake the circle if anyone approaches our position. Wake anyone who starts to snore. RI's are sleeping back on the trail; one guard must report to them hourly on radio check. Whoever is on duty at 0430, wake the circle. We have to move out as soon as possible after 0430 to make the link-up. Questions?"

None - only a snore from across the circle; "Hit it." In looking back over the course, that roughly two and a half hours sleep, was only one of three times during the entire course that my platoon got any sleep at night on a field problem. I mean real sleep; like as in lay down and forget-the-world kind of sleep.

0430 came quickly, and by 0440, we were filing out of the patrol base. No change of command had been made so I led on. I had carried an M-60 and a radio enough by now that I could gauge how fast we ought to move and not kill the people with the extra load. One of the best pieces of advice I ever received about RANGER School was given by my brigade Army advisor, Sergeant Major Ralph Beale. "You can't run up them mountains. Take em slow and steady so you are breathing deep and steady, but not huffing and puffing. When you're climbing up a rough side, take a few steps and halt a couple of seconds; a few more steps and halt."

We moved at a steady pace, climbing higher and higher in the pre-dawn chill. In twenty minutes I signaled a security halt and ordered the HAWK gear taken off, then on up toward the top of Fish Hook Mountain. We arrived just as the sun began to turn the low tufts of clouds a brilliant orange. It was 0550. Making a map check I figured we could stand a ten-minute break - early warning team fore and aft; relax. Our point man signaled for a halt just five minutes before 0700; link-up time. I went forward to find out why he stopped.

"Spotted someone about 100 yards ahead - see, there by that large boulder."

My "binos" made it out to be an RI. I left the platoon in security and took a contact team forward.

"Your platoon is the first one here, RANGER" the RI said to me. "The platoon that I'm walking with is wandering around on the next mountain lost" he pointed to the west. "I broke off from them on the last wrong turn and cut across over to here to let you know that your role is reversed - you will occupy the link-up site and receive them in. Did you get any sleep last night?"

"Yes Sergeant, we got a solid two and a half hours" I replied.

"They ain't got a wink!" he said dryly, "And neither did I."

About 0830, the other platoon came dragging up the Mountainside. They had been beating the brush all night without hardly a halt. They looked pitiful; haggard. I'll never forget RANGER Meridith's look-------- ZOMBIE!

"How did you get here so fast and get sleep too," the PL asked me.

"We moved on the ridges and game trails," I replied. He looked incredulous.

"No XXXX!" He exclaimed. "By God, I ain't walking on the sides of my feet another step!"

During the wait, my platoon had secured and organized the LZ on down the trail for the airlift out. We had heated water, shaved, drank coffee, and those who had any food left, had eaten. For food, I had one package of Campbell's Onion Soup mix (dry) left. It was either coffee or soup! I drank coffee - and ate the soup mix dry. What a picker-upper that is. Seriously, if you want to get yourself to attention, eat a package of onion soup mix; dry!

I figured I should have been graded for three or four patrols at least; a movement phase, patrol base phase, a second movement phase, a link-up operation, and an LZ security operation. WRONG!

"You get a go on your patrol, RANGER-OLD-MAN."

"Which one," I asked cautiously.

"You only had one, Gramps - they call you Gramps, don't they?"

"Yes Sergeant. Oh, I thought maybe you were letting me get two or three consecutively," I said getting a little bolder. He looked at me sort of curiously.

"No Gramps! You just had a long one. I wanted to see how deep you were. Now get out of here and send me your APL."

"Yes Sergeant," and I turned to double-time.

"RANGER Childers!"

"Yes Sergeant," I turned back. He spit a stream of juice and smiled out of the other corner of his mouth.

"You did an outstanding job RANGER. All of it!" he said; and I think if I could have read his mind, it would have said "and that includes the lecture on the mountain. "

In RANGER School, the most pleasant four words in the English language are "You got a go."

No task in RANGER School is simple. If it is simple then the RI will devise a way to make it difficult. Never mind if what or how you are doing a task makes sense to you or not. Don't argue; don't question; just do it. Hidden somewhere beneath the facade of urgency and confusion there is a principle, if not a practice, that they want you to learn. The one I recall most vividly is the Map Check under the poncho trick. Of course the principle involved is security, a condition that is maintained at all times.

Having spent all of my enlisted and junior officer career in the Armored Cavalry, there probably were a lot of infantry tricks that I did not know when I went to RANGER School. In a tank or personnel carrier if I wanted to read a map I simply closed the hatch and turned on a dome light. Not so simple on a RANGER operation. Want to read a map at night? Dig out a poncho and spread it out and crawl up under it with map, compass, and flashlight with a red filter installed. Sometimes there are one or two other RANGERS under there with you. Sometimes the wind is blowing and someone has to be detailed to stand by and hold the edges down against the gusting. Sometimes the RI will also join the party and suddenly it gets crowded. Sometimes it is raining fiercely to add to the complications.

I don't remember the red filter under the poncho trick being taught during a period of instruction; or maybe that was one of those instances when I dozed off and scribbled meaningless hieroglyphics across the notebook. But I remember the first time I observed it being practiced. It was in Camp Darby and my patrol had just occupied a patrol base. This particular base was an ideal location in terms of a place that no one would want to struggle through in the middle of the night looking for us. A thick, though not impenetrable tanglefoot of briars, honeysuckle, and deadfall about waist high made a complete protective barrier some 50 feet wide around our position. That sector that wasn't covered by the thicket was crossed by two narrow but deep streams. The area protected by these natural barriers was some 30 meters in diameter, fairly clean underneath, and generously spotted with towering trees, which provided excellent overhead concealment. Excellent, day or night. And DARK! You talk about dark! The darkness seemed to have substance, like it could be parted with the hand; like it touched my eyes as I strained to see into it. A typical RANGER School night as I would learn in the following weeks.

As the RANGER carrying the night vision goggles[5], it was my job to conduct an R&S (with a buddy of course) of our perimeter once local security had been established. Moving out of the perimeter at the 12 o'clock position we moved about 50 meters from the perimeter to circle the position clockwise and come back in at the 6 o'clock position

[5] We had AN/PVS-6 version goggles, not suitable for doing map reading

and report the status to the patrol leader. About 25 meters out, I turned to peer back toward the perimeter and of course could see nothing. I stood to listen for any sound beyond me such as an aggressor team trying to infiltrate us or track us. At this point in the school we were paranoid about being raided by the RI-led aggressors. Nothing heard, I pulled the night vision goggles straps over my head and adjusted them for fit. Flicking on the power switch I watched the field of view change from black to a glowing green. Turning back towards the perimeter I noticed a bright spot on MY goggles, an indication of a light source inside the perimeter.

"Some idiot has a flashlight on or is smoking inside the perimeter," I whispered to my buddy.

"I don't see a thing," he replied. He did not have a set of goggles.

"How about a red filter," I asked?

"Nothing," he replied, "there is no light source that I can see."

I did not know at the time what the answer was, but as we eased on around the outer perimeter on the R&S, I used those "lights" within the perimeter as a reference to guide our circular path. From one point I could see two and three individual spots in close proximity, all together creating an eerie ball of soft green light.

Upon returning to the perimeter and reporting to the patrol leader I learned the answer to the mystery. The patrol leader and two other RANGERS were under a poncho with red filtered flashlights planning the next phase of the operation. They probably felt very secure there thinking that the poncho was shielding what little visible light was generated by the red filters but the truth is, they were hiding from no one who might have a high technology gadget like a night vision device. The fact is that the exercise of trying to conceal light with a poncho is a futile counter against light amplification devices. Nevertheless, I do not advise telling the RI that it is a waste of time "cause he'll have sum thin for ya!"

THE DRIVE TO TODD FIELD

There are those who just want to make it there - any way will do. There are those who want to stand at the head of the line; sometimes no one does. And there is everyone else in between. My grandfather used to say he "can't understand anyone bothering himself to do anything that ain't the best he can do. I guess I inherited that attitude from Granddad; and my wife insists that I am a very poor loser. I do hate to be second best so I guess in that regard I am a poor loser. One advantage that I had in the course over the younger men is that I had observed winners and losers for twenty years longer than the rest of the class had. From thirty years of observation I know that the primary difference between number one and all the rest is usually effort. The old adage that "it just takes a few bucks more to go first class" applies equally here. A little extra effort can mean the difference between a go and a no go in RANGER School. Extrapolate that lesson to any other sector of life that pleases you; it will fit like machinery.

It would be interesting to know how many students go to the course with the hope of being number one. I know one other that did, an enlisted man in the third platoon. He confided to me that he hoped he would get the enlisted honor graduate award because it meant certain breaks for him. Maybe he had the wrong reasons. His failing was that when he was in a leadership role, he was a tyrant and expected everyone to perform flawlessly or he ranted and raved. When he was in a "follower" role, he was not overly cooperative; he was not a volunteer. Well, quite simply, people recognized his style and they reciprocated in kind, causing him to fail some patrols.

I went there to be number one though I admitted it to no one; no proclamation to the class, no hopeful confessions even to my RANGER buddy. My only confidant was my wife and she was right, I do not like to lose. To quote General Patton, "I wouldn't give a hoot in hell for a man who lost and laughed." For a person who does not lose well, his greatest fear may be that people will know that he wanted to be number one and didn't make it. So I never share my personal goals with peers. My strategy is to simply work harder and longer than the rest and never look back to see if someone is passing.

One of the "old salt" stories in the Army is "don't volunteer for nothing." I'd like to refute that as a magnificently ill-advised piece of trite. Volunteer for everything! I don't mean just when the RI or TAC is around; that is spotlighting. I mean all of the time: in the privacy of the barracks when the squad leader needs a volunteer to serve in the mess hall; in the bush when a recon is required; when fire watch is required; when an extra load is to be carried; when part of a patrol order needs to be written; when coordination is required. Volunteering is the essence of cooperation and teamwork, which are ultimately the secrets to a successful platoon.

The road to Todd Field is strewn with a multitude of obstacles any one of which can be your undoing. To be forewarned is to be forearmed, but just being armed is not enough. As a student you must also be constantly alert that some of these things don't sneak up on you ONLY when you are tired and vulnerable. Basically there are two periods of time that a RANGER is vulnerable to being sent home; during the first nine days, and anytime thereafter. I describe it like that because during the first nine days there are several things that you only get to fail once:

> PT Test
> RANGER Runs
> Land Navigation
> Performance Tests

Of course during this first nine days you could also fall prey to things beyond your control such as injury, sickness, or personal problems at home. Class 6-81 lost people due to injury and personal problems. You may also discover that you simply don't have the heart for it; a little shortage of determination and desire. Those we call "quitters." My most profound advice is to not be a "quitter." The staff will not allow "quitters" to leave graciously. It is conceivable also that you could accumulate enough Major Minus spot reports to be boarded out, but that did not happen in Class 6-81. If it had, I would have been suspicious that such a RANGER was deliberately trying to get kicked out so he wouldn't have to go through the quitter routine. Negative spot reports (Major or Minor) could be given for such things as attitude, repeated correction in almost anything, loss or negligent damage to equipment, safety infraction, unauthorized sleeping, smart-mouthing, failure to follow instructions, violation of creed, poor performance in a leadership role, poor performance in general, failure to have your pace cord, compass, or RANGER handbook on your body, dropping your rifle, having a dirty rifle, rifle selector switch not on safe, or an endless list of do's and don'ts which they will acquaint you with day after day.

Actually there are four categories of so-called Critical Incident Reports (CIR) that can reflect either good or bad on the RANGER: major satisfactory, minor satisfactory, major unsatisfactory, and minor unsatisfactory. In RI terminology these would be called a "Major (or Minor) Plus (or Minus) Spot."

Three Minor CIRs equal one Major; any Major or Minor Plus Spot cancels any Major or Minor Minus Spot respectively, and vice versa; and three Major Minus Spots is cause enough to drop you from the course. Honor graduates can have no unsatisfactory CIRs or Minus Spots on the books.

Beyond the first nine days, any of the above can still ambush you and in addition, you have to face patrolling, peer ratings, confidence courses, mountaineering performance testing, and that all-encompassing condition of just being tough enough. These things have all been discussed in detail in other sections except for the last item. How does one describe the condition of being tough enough? Well the dictionary gives the definition as follows:

Capable of sustaining great tension or strain without breaking. Firm and resilient in substance. Not easily separated. Possessing moral or intellectual endurance; steadfast; persistent. Unmanageably rough, unruly, or vicious. Disreputable; vulgar. Severe, rigorous. A rowdy; ruffian.

And since endurance is used several times, the dictionary defines it as:

The act or capacity of bearing up under hardship or prolonged stress. The state or power of lasting. Continued existence.

More I cannot add without being verbose.

WHY PEOPLE FAIL

It's going to hurt me to say this, but all RANGER course graduates are not real RANGERS. They, like Engineering School graduates with their diplomas and no experience, simply have the credentials to gain employment. Some RANGER graduates hang in there and get the Tab because someone told them it will be good for upward mobility, and that is the only reason they endured the course. These graduates will never develop their basic knowledge into an art, rather, they will use their diploma as a lever to go into another field entirely. Engineers may go into management, sales, or personnel and never design anything. RANGERS may go into artillery, armor, aviation, etc., and never use those acquired military skills, but wherever they go, they will carry with them the leadership principles learned, the pride of accomplishment, the confidence born of hardship, and perhaps, the memory of those who did not make Todd Field. Those who dropped out during the first few days survive in your mind as vague, nameless forms, but those who shared the hardship of patrols with you will live vividly for many years.

There are so many ways to fail that it is really amazing that the attrition rate is only 30-40 percent in a normal class. Failure modes can be organized in two basic categories: those beyond your complete control and those within your control. Those beyond your control include injury, sickness, family problems, personal unsuitability, and peer ratings.

Drop out by reason of sickness and injury need little explanation except to say that RANGERS are exposed to conditions that are conducive to producing sickness and injury more in eight weeks than the average person will be exposed to in his entire lifetime. With the body in a run-down condition due to limited food, lack of sleep and rest, and physical exhaustion; exposure to the elements on a 3 to 5 day winter patrol in the mountains of Northern Georgia is a prescription for sickness. At the other end of the spectrum is a long, hard patrol in the searing heat of the Florida swamps resulting in heat stroke or head exhaustion. Seventy-two hours of training is all that can be missed before being mandatory dropped or set aside for recycle.

There are things that one can do to stave off sickness, particularly the weather related variety. Pace yourself; graduation, not capitulation, is the goal. Keep watch on your body and your buddy; and have him reciprocate. Keep critical HAWK gear readily accessible and use it wisely. More is not always better. Unless it is raining, snowing, or blowing, a standard fatigue uniform and gloves (if allowed) is all you need when on the move (in the winter). Too many layers will cause sweating, then, when you halt, those clammy underclothes will cause a chill that even additional layers will not satisfy. Chills lead to colds and colds run the body down more so that you can't perform mentally or physically.

Drink plenty of water, winter or summer. Eight to ten quarts per day is not an extraordinary consumption rate for the Florida phase in a winter cycle while three or four quarts in a winter mountain phase is common. The body runs on water. Don't get the often expressed but mistaken idea that "well, it's winter; the sun isn't shining, sweat is not dripping off my brow or running down my back, I don't need water." You can sit around the office all day in the winter and get by with an occasional glass of water or a couple of gulps from the water fountain as you pass by it coming from coffee break. When you carry 90 pounds and more from the skin out all day, making elevation changes of 300 to maybe 800 feet three or four times as you cross and re-cross the famed Tennessee Valley Divide; you are expending a lot of horsepower. Human-generated horsepower, like the old fashioned steam locomotive of by-gone days, requires water. The body chemical plant will try its best to do what it can with the raw material it is supplied. If you do not give it enough water, it will try to manufacture it from what you do give it, but that process is inefficient so that the ill effects become exponential. Do your body a favor. Give it water directly and let it turn every other precious bit you give it into other products that it also needs desperately.

As we know from the starvation protests in Ireland, a man can go about 69 days without food but lack of water will kill you much faster. What really happens is that after about three days without water, your brain tells your kidney to shut down because the brain mistakenly calculates that by shutting down the kidney and saving the meager reservoir of water that is in the body, perhaps the body will ultimately survive. The problem is that once the kidney shuts down, it is very hard to get it kick started again. The real answer is to keep pumping in the water. A simple way to check if you are dehydrating is to check your water; your urine. If it is very yellow you are probably not consuming enough liquids.

In Florida, many people literally cannot carry enough water out of base camp to keep from dehydrating. The answer, refill your four-quart capacity from various field sources as you move along. The RI's will not always give a lot of time for watering so every time a stream is crossed, we would remove the lid from one or more canteens and allow water to flow in as we crossed. Then of course we had to add the little gray water purification tablets. There are other technologies now to substitute for the tablets.

Sometimes, we would be allowed to secure an area around a stream while everyone got his canteens refilled. In almost every patrol base, a watering team was organized to re-supply the platoon with water. Now the critical element in all of this field watering is the water purification tablets and the proper use thereof. RANGERS are supposed to be "certified" in certain soldier tasks before being admitted to the course, among these tasks are the ones on water treatment. Several people obviously "fudged" that certification, as they did not know how to treat water. Several were using tablets that were reddish in color - not steel gray like they are supposed to be. Some drank their water directly after shaking it up a little, rather than wait the prescribed 25 minutes. I cautioned probably half the platoon on these points.

On one occasion the water supply at the Florida RANGER Camp became contaminated, or so they said. We were lined up alongside Field #6 awaiting the arrival of our helo's when the word came down.

"Dump all of your canteens RANGERS. The base water supply is contaminated," shouted an RI.

"All of them, Sergeant," we asked?

"All of them! by the numbers. I want to see every canteen empty, and I <u>will</u> check!" he promised.

I felt like I was pouring my blood on the ground because it took a lot of water to run my machine.

"Don't look so sad, Pappy," said RANGER Smith, "it's only water. Florida has plenty of it.,, "Check your map," I replied, "There's none shown anywhere near where we are going."

I was still thinking about the water problem when the helo's started to arrive, first two, then others began to filter in. The first two both had red doors which I noted with some curiosity, but shifted back to thoughts of water. When the third and fourth arrived also with red doors, my curiosity got the best of me.

"What do the red doors mean Sergeant?" I asked the RI.

"Those red doors are why you may not have to worry about water, Old Man" he said dryly, "Those are student pilot ships. You may never need water again."

Ever watch a small group of wood ducks come sailing in about dusk looking for a place to light among old moss covered trees and cypress knees? They're all generally following the leader, that is, they are all going to land on the same body of water, but each has his own flight profile, speed, approach angle, and splash down. That's the way these guys flew; too much pitch, too much yaw. We bobbed up and down as we frantically pursued the ship ahead of us and tried to elude the one to our left rear - no, right rear. Skids in the trees, whop, whop, whop; the blades gasp for air as we make a turn that defied description. Our trail ship is passing us on the inside curve and the RANGER passengers sitting in the door way (on the floor) grin at their coup and unanimously give us the finger. We display the candy bars that our crew had given us and smile. They display the candy bars their crew had given them - and the 32 OZ Pepsi Cola they were passing around. We unanimously gave them the finger and veered off to the right in a turn that put us back in march order.

Injury is an event that is largely beyond your control - but not completely. Most injury can be avoided by staying alert, by thinking before acting, by being in good physical shape to begin with, and by following instructions. Consider the RANGER who is stumbling through the mountains simply following the RANGER eyes in front of him and causes the RANGER behind him to wrench a knee because he did not pass back the warning of a stump hole in the trail. And talk about not thinking; how about the RANGER who decided to stick 3 M-60 rounds (live blank) into the ground as little legs to support his C-Rats Can while heat tabs burning in the triangle heated his meal. And to take maximum advantage of this field expedient, he decided he would sit very close to this clever arrangement, wrap his legs snugly around it and absorb the escaping heat. You guessed it! BOOM! Brass fragments in the family jewel box. Then there is the RANGER who was trampled in the asphalt when he fell out (literally) on a RANGER run because he wasn't in shape, or those who fall off of obstacles because of lack of strength. And there is a broad range of injuries, large and small, that are the result of failure to follow instructions from blistered feet to frost bite; mountaineering related accidents to rubber boat accidents; and hand to hand bone crunching to Victory Pond madness.

Family problems present a unique crisis decision and this is why one should be truly committed to completion before attending the course. This commitment must extend to everyone that touches your life and causes you to make decisions. Class 6-81 had the basis for a real soap opera in this regard, and a real dichotomy of decision situations. On one hand was the RANGER whose unstable wife was taking great advantage of his absence back home. His attitude was "I've got too much invested in RANGER School right not. When I graduate I'll go back and solve that problem." On the other hand was the RANGER who, halfway through, fell in love with one of the female medics and quit. SGT Rock had some choice comments about that situation.

Personal unsuitability fits in the category of "things beyond your control" in that people who fail for this reason do not realize that they are unsuited for such a course until they get involved and find it out. I suspect that many people who fail in this category have entered the course without the full realization of what they have gotten in to. Perhaps they have been told how tough it is going to be but regarded the advice with some detachment; perhaps they have been given false encouragement; perhaps they entered on the basis of "I'm as good as Joe and he did it." However they got there, the end result is the same. Enduring the strain is simply more than they wish to put up with. Some people are not suited to being cold, hungry, tired, dirty, sleepy, hurt, humbled, and hassled for the privilege of wearing six gold letters on a background of black. So one morning they drag themselves out of the rack and decide, "today is my last day." And they drop out of a run or they fake an injury or they gather their pride up into a tiny bundle and lay it on the TAC's desk and say, "I want to quit."

Battle is an orgy of disorder. No level lawn nor marker flags exist to aid us in strutting ourselves in vain display, but rather groups of weary, wandering men seeking gropingly for means to kill their foes. The sudden change from accustomed order to utter disorder, to chaos, but emphasizes the folly of schooling to precision and obedience where only fierceness and habituated disorder are useful.

Gneisenau

As the last item in the category "beyond your control," I have saved the discussion on "peer ratings" until last because it could be swung into the category "within your control." Peer ratings are extremely important and I think more important than the average RANGER realizes. The RI's and TAC's cannot possibly watch over a hundred RANGERS all of the time. Many events occur in the privacy of the squad, platoon, or company that would never come to the attention of the TAC's except for peer rating. The RANGER who tries to avoid doing his share of the unit work by lingering in his locker rather than grab a mop; the RANGER who is always last to square away his bunk, to draw or turn in his weapon, to get out of the bed or the head; the RANGER who never volunteers for duty and who does a sluggish job when he is appointed; who rarely contributes his vocal cords to the unit's howling and growling; who won't keep himself camouflaged without constant monitoring; who gives in so often and so easily to the albatross of sleep at the sacrifice of the perimeter; who would prefer to avoid carrying his share of extra equipment; who gripes continuously when in a subordinate role and questions each order or direction; who dips his paddle rather than stroking hard; these are the people who should be "written up" at peer rating time. Perhaps it is a sign of the times that they are not identified properly at peer rating time so that they could be counseled and either corrected or dropped.

This, of course, is only my perception of and opinion of how it was in a single class, 6-81. I believe that the RANGER Department can rightfully lay claim to being the best trainers in the US Army; but I also believe that some people are "getting by" because all students do not do their part at peer rating time in identifying those RANGERS who, by RANGER standards, are of marginal quality. RANGERS should be made to understand their responsibility; their duty, to hold the standards high by rating very objectively, even callously. Perhaps by subjecting each person they rate to the acid test question "If I-had a choice would I, as a PFC, follow that man on a deep reconnaissance mission into enemy held territory at this point in time?" A very different peer rating system would surface. This is not to imply that any RANGER student is capable of leading such a mission at the end of the first peer rating, rather, it is the attitude or mindset that I think should be encouraged; the School intended approach of correction through counseling rather than compassion through cover-up. The real compassion is due when a marginal RANGER gets a lot of people in trouble, and it belongs to the survivors of those who are lost.

Reasons for failure, which are largely within the control of the individual, are those already discussed in previous paragraphs that discussed how RANGERS are evaluated. Ft Benning publishes a pamphlet describing the RANGER Course, ST 21-75-1. It is highly recommended.

Is there a "secret" to getting through RANGER School? NO, not A secret, but several secrets. Unfortunately, I cannot list them one, two, three, so they can be memorized and practiced, because most of them are locked within each RANGER. They are part of the reservoir that must be tapped during the long hours of hardship and stress. They will be dredged up one by one in the heat of Ft. Benning, the cold of the mountains, and the damp of the swamp. They will keep you awake when sleep is as precious as blood; they will drive you forward when rest would be the answer to a prayer; they will feed you when hunger is devouring your will to stay. And when it's over; when the tab is on the shoulder and time has healed the hurt, dulled the memory of hardship and suffering, and left only the fondly remembered that makes good stories, each RANGER knows the secrets. Secrets vary in number and form with each RANGER, but there must always be a common denominator and I think it is PROMPT OBEDIENCE and SELF-DISCIPLINE.

Other secrets are based on what soldiers believe in. Some of what they believe in is what they have read, or heard, or been a part of. They read and react to different stimuli but soldiers are prone to respond to things that are said, or supposedly said, by warriors and statesmen and famous people. Some of these sayings become their model and the fuel to power their engine of determination. **Appendix F** presents a collection of quotations that have powered my engine.

Techniques are different from secrets for techniques can be practiced and mastered. One key technique is planning and issuing a patrol order. It comes under the planning phase of the RANGER evaluation. In Class 6-81, the planning phase was, except in one instance, always assigned to an officer, i.e., he was an officer before he got his head shaved and became a RANGER. The exception was when the staff boo-booed and gave the planning phase to a Marine Corporal thinking he was a Second Lieutenant. The error did not exonerate the Corporal however, and he took a no-go on the job. "Well," he said afterwards, "it was a natural mistake. Everybody knows that a Marine Corporal is as good as an Army Second Lieutenant any day."

This planning phase is particularly important during the Darby portion of the Benning cycle because a great deal of detail is required in a patrol order. The patrol order planning bays are very nice; equipped with park bench type seating, large planning boards, sand tables, wall size operation maps, and multiple chalk boards are available. What the RI's are looking for is a "school solution" type presentation. At this point in time the platoon or squad will have no SOP's established or practiced so every maneuver, every action on contact, and every battle drill that involves orchestrated movement must be drawn on a chalkboard for explanation. For example, when the patrol leader is giving the order and he is covering actions on contact and he says "If we are ambushed in a near ambush . . . " he has to have an illustration on the chalk board showing the position and action of each patrol member and what that member does in the scenario being described. Typically, an illustration had to be put on a chalkboard for:

- Ambush (near and far)

- Air attack

- Trucking and detrucking plan

- Air movement plan

- Crossing danger areas (3 methods)

- Movement techniques

- Entry and exit friendly forward units

- ORP and patrol base recon and occupation

- Actions at the objective

In addition, we had to cover but not illustrate hand and arm signals, a detailed fire support overlay had to be made in duplicate, a realistic terrain model had to be created in the sand table, and detailed coordination had to be accomplished in the areas of:

- Fire support

- Friendly forward units

- Adjacent units

- S2/S3

- Aerial Re-supply

- Transportation

- Rehearsal area

- Test fire area

- Logistics (food, ammo, camo, heat tabs, etc.)

With this detail as a basis to describe the complexity of the planning phase, let's run lightly through how the patrol leader must orchestrate this affair if he is to get a "GO" on his task. Typically the patrol leader and one or two other RANGERS (to help take notes) would receive the patrol mission around 1800-1900 in the evening. Class 6-81 had 10 squad-sized patrols which meant that the oral order down to the patrol leaders was accompanied by a number of matrix charts showing a variety of data for each patrol.

The data included for each patrol:

Block of numbers to identify pre-planned fires

Checkpoints/routes

OP's

Adjacent units

CEOI data

Supporting units such as artillery, aviation, etc.

Objective locations

Departure/-return times

Times to coordinate specific items

All of this data is dumped on the patrol leader very hurriedly, as part of the mission. The S-3 reads through the five paragraph operation order very hurriedly - once. He refers to the matrix charts at the appropriate time as he zips through the paragraphs in a very crisp, military monologue. Questions when it is over? "Don't be silly! This is RANGER School, not Kindergarten. What were you; sleeping?! I'll know tomorrow when I grade you RANGER!"

Eight out of ten patrol leaders failed that first planning phase because they were unprepared to handle that volume of data with absolutely no warning. As time went on at Darby, pass rates became much better because we learned the tricks of the trade so to speak. We learned from previous mistakes, and we learned how to handle that mass of information; how to segregate it, and how to divide the workload and coordinate a team effort to accomplish the mission. This is easy to say now but at the time it did not seem so simple. I know; I was one of those first patrol leaders. I felt deluged with data and naked of direction but I sat down and quickly examined what I had available, what had to be accomplished, and what else was required. I looked at the critical times for coordination and worked them into my own warning order time schedule. Suddenly the whole thing looked like just another fire drill. Fire drills are easy if you don't get excited; don't forget to separate the wheat from the chaff. Identify tasks and prioritize them based on time (they are all important); assign people to a job who can do the job; and most important, don't try to do the whole thing by yourself. This is a team effort and as team captain, patrol leader, your job is to develop a time schedule using the backwards planning technique, organize the men and equipment to match the mission, and divide the work and assign tasks with deadlines.

This would result in the issuance of a patrol warning order in the planning bay. The warning order is brief but its manner of presentation is important. It must be presented boldly and with a show of confidence. Stand up like a man in charge and reel off the data on the chart boards with military precision. The kind of data to be presented is illustrated as follows:

Warning Order for a Recon Patrol

1. Situation: a. Elements of the 32d Motorized Rifle Division and the 2d SAM Brigade are presently defending High ground south along Highway 26 and south and west along Orion Road. The enemy thrust has been stalled/. B. Friendly: 1st Brigade, 21st Infantry Division is occupying the high ground south of Highway 137 and west of Highway 355 to Hollis Creek. -_____ Company, 75th Infantry will be operating in 1st Brigade sector.

2. Mission: Patrol ____will conduct a recon NLT _____ of a suspected enemy position at GL _____, to determine enemy activity and gather SIR.

3. General Instructions:

Chain Of command Name	Planning Guidance	Special Equipment	Ammo	Uniform & equipment Common to all	Time Schedule What when where who
Jones 1	PL/Sqd Ldr	List of stuff	Type qty	Stuff in detail	
Smith	RATELO				
King	Compass man				
Johnson Moore Brown Freeman	Fireteam A				
Willis Brock Graves	Fireteam B				

4. Specific Instructions: B team leader, you are second COC and therefore in charge all time during my absence. I want you to insure the time schedule is adhered to, oversee the drawing of all equipment and ammunition and insure weapons are test fired. Additionally, I want you to insure all canteens are full, magazines are loaded, and equipment is packed and tied down prior to the OPORD. Alpha Team Leader, see me at the completion of this WO for instructions regarding coordination. Your fireteam will prepare the sketches and terrain model for the OOPORD. Ranger Wilis, you will prepare two copies of the fire support overlay. The uniform for OPORD is same as this WO, everyone must e seated in the bay NLT 0655. Fireteam leaders, designate your own COC within your fireteam prior to the OPORD. Time now is _____. What are your questions?

With this done, the whole patrol knew the time schedule and who was responsible for what and when and where. For the patrol leader, the next big event is the operation order or patrol order, usually given around mid morning of the following day. His primary job until then is to work on writing paragraph three of the patrol order and to supervise the activities of the other people who are assigned tasks such as constructing the terrain model, developing the fire support plan, making sketches to support the briefing of the warning order, and coordinating with various other players both internal and external to the Patrol.

There never seems to be enough time. Patrol Order time is on you before you know it; the time of truth. The school provides blank formats based on the RANGER Handbook. Follow it precisely. Speak loud and clear; confidently; precisely. Since someone else has written most of the Patrol Order for you, but for paragraph three, be sure that you at least read each part once before you get up in front of the squad and the RI to give the order. You've got to read it like you wrote it yourself without stumbling and bumbling through it; without "uh" and "ahh" and "you knows. "

Sleep will have been of poor quality the night before; cold, cramped in a pup tent, and only about four hours of it which was probably broken by a tour of duty on local security. Wake up will be long before dawn, cold and damp. You don't want to leave that sleeping bag, or unbutton that tent. Dress and lace the boots in the cramped pup tent with your RANGER buddy because outside it's really cold. Everything you own has to be packed up and stored in the conex box before first formation so ask your buddy if he's ready, take a deep breath, and break out of the tent. The area is a mad house, orders being barked here and there by student commanders and RI's, flashlights bobbing everywhere as RANGERS pack and curse and pack. Someone gives the countdown time for first formation.

"If I don't make it go ahead without me," quips someone.

"Wake me up for lunch," wisecracks another.

"I'll wake you up for lunch with the Colonel," roars a familiar voice out of the darkness, "You better get your funky smelling sorry no-good out of shape bodies on them cables on time today STUDDS!"

At Darby, there was a small clear area near the bivouac site that we would form up in for instruction, harassment, roll call, or any other reason where they wanted the class in a single formation. There were ½ cables stretched taunt along the ground to mark where they wanted the rows of students to line up. Toes on the cable line.

Patrol order time! Be confident. Roll call. Instruct the APL to stand by and keep everyone awake. Recite paragraph one while one of the squad leaders points to appropriate areas of the large map that depicts the situation.

Paragraph two, mission; read it twice. The format is important; who, what, where, when and why. Period!

Paragraph three, Execution, is given using the terrain model to explain the concept of operation and subordinate tasks. Start from the end of the final inspection and go step-by-step through completion of mission and return to friendly lines. The terrain model is always introduced by orienting the observers in direction and identifying major features and "decorations" on it. The last part of paragraph three, coordinating instructions, is where all of the sketches are used. And on through paragraphs four and five.

I don't have any statistics to prove this, but I think a larger percentage of people failed this planning phase than they did any other phase or task. I was lucky for my several years experience both as a staff officer in the Guard and as a program manager in civilian life, because I could organize and present the data professionally. I had a total of three turns as the patrol leader during the planning phase, including the one as Company Commander in Florida, and passed them all.

As the class moved on to the Mountain Phase, the planning bays were not as nice and more innovation was required. We used LRRP ration cardboard boxes and felt tip pencils in lieu of chalkboards for part of our sketches because of the shortage of chalkboards. Finally, as we moved on to the Florida phase, there were no planning bays whatsoever, and we did it real-world style, depending primarily on the terrain model and what we could now legitimately call SOP.

WHEN IT'S OVER

There are times when it seems that it will never be over. Like a bad dream that one dreams over and over, the patrols all seem the same somehow. Gouging along click after miserable click; fill your pace cord with knots, and then start to untie them. Why doesn't some bright young man invent some kind of counter that will fit in the hollow handgrip of the M-16 and eliminate that silly pace cord? (Actually, I did that. It works like a charm. But why bother now with Global Positioning Systems (GPS) available so inexpensively?) One thinks about all of the silly things as he stumbles along in the night; and he thinks about it a lot after it is all over. I found myself back in the bush several times after graduation only to be awakened by my wife and discover it was another bad dream. And things back in the world seem to be so simple; so clean and meaningless; so without challenge, without fear, without pride.

RANGER School is a "high" as strong as any drug because it releases man to encounter his most basic drives - fear, aggression, courage. Unlike other animals who seek merely to dominate, man is an aggressive animal to the point of killing. Though we do not actually kill each other, the drive to kill is there; only the reason is absent. This drive manifests itself in courage and courage is the force that maintains the process of putting one foot in front of the other; or is it the fear of someone thinking you have no courage. Perhaps Field Marshall Slim put it best in his memoirs: "I do not believe that there is any man who would not rather be called brave than have any other virtue attributed to him." But when it's over, one has the opportunity, if he will, to sit and sanely examine himself and his performance both as seen by others and by himself.

Because RANGER School is such a high, it is difficult to get over; at least I find it so. I don't think one ever gets over it. It is a memory that you are always willing to recall and recount. It is a metric by which you always tend to compare other life events

Watching the TV show "World at War" one evening, an Englishman, former Royal Naval Officer, was being interviewed on how he adjusted to "normal life" after the war. He expressed my sentiments exactly regarding the adjustment process although I realize the vast difference between war and RANGER School; still the sentiment principles are the same.

He said, "Coming back from the war where decisions and death were so indelicately entwined on a daily basis; where the promise of eternity welled up with each wave, I could NOT be at all concerned about a (peacetime) decision as to what silver should be placed out for Lord and Lady Whoever. These people; these strangers back here who had not shared the same hardships as we on the line shared for literally years; these people with whom I had no bond forged by desperation, meant nothing to me. What they thought important was to me simply not. It took me two years to reconcile this. And even now, thirty-six years after the fact, I find myself sitting with a group of friends, perhaps having a drink and making small talk, and my mind will drift back to the battle and I'll think, MY GOD these people don't know what we went through! They have never tasted life so close to death."

Much like the anonymous remark scribbled on a C-Ration carton discovered in the aftermath of Khe Sahn, Viet Nam: "To those who have never fought for it, freedom has a taste the protected will never know."

Similarly I found the same kind of adjustment story in talking to a Viet Nam Veteran. A comrade in arms in the Virginia Guard related his adjustment to a civilian life after being at war: "I bounced around from job to job, unable to find anything that I really wanted to do. I don't guess I stayed anywhere for more than six months. My final job before coming to full time employment with the Guard was with SEARS. I had what is considered to be a good job - in management. One day I was sitting in a merchandising class and the instructor was droning on about displaying merchandise – "there are three kinds of space: linear space, vertical space, and cubic space ." And I thought to myself, boy this is really exciting!! Last year I was on the ground in Viet Nam making decisions on who was going to get the next medivac out; who was going to live or die and now I'm going to learn how to decide whether to stack light bulbs high, wide or deep! So I quit! I said, this is not for me; I just could not get excited about stacking merchandise. Then I got this job with the Guard and I'm happy as a pig in a mud hole, because I'm making real decisions again. Not life and death decisions, but meaningful decisions relating to training and readiness. And how I train my people now may mean life or death at some time in the future; and that is important to me. I'm contributing."

The good, the bad, and the ugly; I thought it was a movie but it turned out to be a school in Georgia. "Give me your cold, your tired, your hungry and hopeless masses',,," Whoever said that must have been the Chaplain at RANGER School. Probably everyone comes away from there with some favorite phrase in mind; with some special lessons learned; certainly with a new outlook on what hardship is, a new lease on life. Distance, obstacles, pain, fear, doubt, uncertainty, warmth, cold, hunger, rest, sleep, comfort, responsibility, failure, triumph, teamwork, friendship; all have a new meaning to a RANGER.

That new meaning, that new context in which they have true meaning, is time. A RANGER can do anything in time.

After all these pages of trying to describe the experience, I read back over it still with a void. I simply cannot describe it to my own satisfaction. Hopefully I have alerted the reader as to what to expect and how to perform but RANGER school is something that cannot be experienced in the library. It is like playing a car race machine in an electronic arcade in lieu of driving a grand prix racer; the thrill is simply not there. It has to be lived by each student.

I can easily divide my life into two distinct phases: before RANGER School and after RANGER School. Or, I could add a third phase – RANGER School itself. It is unlike any other life experience. I talked to several graduates before I went; people from a broad cross section of life's experience.

A Lieutenant Colonel in the Virginia Guard who went while he was on active duty, although he never subsequently served in a RANGER Battalion, got out of the Army after a regular tour, joined the Guard, and is now a very successful businessman. A Major in the Virginia Guard who graduated RANGER School while on active duty in 1959, went on to become a Special Forces officer with multiple tours in Viet Nam. Finally a Lieutenant Colonel who served as the 116TH Brigade Senior Army Advisor, a career officer in the Army, was an Airborne Ranger and Special Forces in Viet Nam with multiple tours, and later commanded the lst Battalion, 75th RANGERS at Fort Stewart, Georgia. Though they all went through their RANGER training years apart and had varied backgrounds both before and after RANGER School, it's more than mere coincidence that they all expressed precisely the same sentiments about the experience. "It's the best School in the Army system." It's a total experience; one which will never be surpassed by anything else you may ever do in life." Just words? Maybe, but how does one express experience? Poets spend their lives trying to express themselves and probably die unsatisfied with how well they have expressed themselves.

NOTHING! Not money nor power nor influence nor position; possessions, prestige (real or imagined); even the love of a good dog; nothing can compete with self-confidence which has been proven under the severe test conditions of The Army RANGER School. For me, the singular distinction of my graduation status makes all of the tangible things in life that I never took the time to pursue seem mundane.

Perhaps General Patton expressed it best as he reflected upon the most complex human experience of recorded history - World War II.

"Compared to war, all other forms of human endeavor are reduced to insignificance."

It took about ten days of R&R for me to begin to actually miss RANGER School. But I do miss it; perhaps that is why I decided to write about it. And would I do it again? In a heartbeat! Yes! In fact, I would like very much to do it again in ten years (a number I gave when I first wrote this account), because it has been the greatest personal challenge in my life, and my greatest professional triumph. Now after even more years in the Guard and being promoted to Major General and given command of a Division; after being in two more war zones as a advisor to combat commanders; I still feel the same. No experience in my military career or my parallel civilian career surpasses that of RANGER School. No experience has been more valuable to me nor so universally useful.

I recall vividly an incident in the fall of 1981. I had been on a worldwide tour of many military bases conducting CBR defense assessments in my civilian job. Flying from Japan to Hawaii on a wide body passenger plane, a L1011, I had set my wrist alarm to wake me about an hour from the airport so that I could shave and freshen up in preparation for debriefing the staff at CINCPACFLT.

I awoke, looked back to check the signs on the lavatories, and was fumbling to get my ditty bag out of my carry-on bag. Suddenly a loud explosion erupted to my rear. Oxygen masks dropped down for several rows fore and aft of me. The air was filled with a acrid smell of black powder. The plane was only about 25-30 percent filled with passengers, but they were all up and screaming and struggling with life vests, praying, crying, screaming, and blocking the passageways. I knew immediately that it was some kind of a bomb. I also knew that we were at 33,000 ft altitude and an hour from terra-firma. I knew immediately that it was too far to swim even if we could somehow land in one piece and I doubted very much that a water landing could be made. I also could see that there may be a fire back there wherever the bomb had been. I could see stewardesses trying to get down the aisle and calm the passengers, but they were really having none of her encouragement.

So in my best RANGER voice I yelled "Sit Down." It got the attention of several men near me and one of them responded "We are going down." I glared him down and yelled back "We are not going down until the Captain says we are going down. So sit the #@&@^% down and shut up." They did.

The stewardesses came through grabbed fire extinguishers and put the fire out. One even climbed down through the hole blown in the floor that separated the passenger cabin from the cargo area in the belly of the airplane and checked fire down there. About 4 minutes after the explosion, the Captain came on the intercom to announce that there had been a malfunction in the oxygen system. We passengers had a good laugh out of that.

Then after a few more minutes he came over the intercom again to ask if there was a doctor on board. Ten seats behind me a 16-year-old Japanese boy had committed suicide by cranking off a home made briefcase bomb beneath his seat. Though it was sufficient to blow him in half and create a seat-sized hole in the floor, it was not powerful enough to rupture the fuselage and de-pressurize or otherwise dangerously damage the airframe. I could speculate how I may have reacted prior to RANGER School. I like to think that RANGER School, only a few months behind me then, gave me the basis for a cool head in that instance.

I often have breakfast on my patio very early in the morning when the East is just beginning to redden; I like to go stand in the snow on a cold night and study the crisp shadows cast by a full moon. These private moments and nature's creations, especially the chill in the air, takes me back to a patrol somewhere in time. I wonder how many RANGER patrols are in their patrol base sleeping and how many are still struggling under heavy load, cold, hungry, sleepy, tired, and wishing it would just end. Yes, I miss it out there. It was an experience that I don't think will ever be reduced to insignificance by time or events. Part of me will always be out there, in spirit at least - DRIVING ON.

EPILOGUE

With a very special and deep feeling of a loss, I learned of the death of one of my class. After retiring from the National Guard (44 years) and the Civil Service (38 Years), I accepted employment with a Defense Contractor. Working on a project, I went to the Pentagon to keep and appointment with the Assistant Secretary of Army for Manpower and Reserve Affairs. Getting there early (RANGER School lesson), I did a recon of his office (RANGER School lesson), and then went to the snack bar (never pass up an opportunity for caloric intake) for a cup of coffee. As I got my coffee and was scanning the room for a place to enjoy it, I noted a LTC who just looked so very familiar. I looked at his nametag. Laster. That name was so familiar. That face is in my memory bank somewhere. Who is this? Where do I know this soldier from. Airborne badge above the left breast pocket, no other ribbons or badges or tabs. Couldn't place him. He was busily engaged in conversation with two other people. Finished my coffee and paced back to the office where I had the appointment. Who is this guy??

After the appointment, in the outer office, there he sat. Military Aide to the ASA. Well I had to stop and ask. "Where do I know you from?"

"I don't know, but you sure look familiar to me too."

"Maybe I know you from the 82nd ABN; I retired from the National Guard and we used to have a lot of interface with them."

"National Guard! Hold it. Hold it", he said as he pointed a finger at me and struggled to get his monitor lit up.

As his monitor lit up from screen saver and his wallpaper popped on the picture, it was a picture of RANGER Class 6-81.

"This is it! That's you," pointing at the bald head (very close haircut) just beneath the Ranger Tab, "RANGER Childers."

So it was a brief, good, totally unexpected reunion. He had served with a number of the class in the immediate years after graduation and certainly knew more than I did about any of them. And here he gave me the very sad news of the untimely death of one of our class from cancer; my very own RANGER Buddy, Campana.

Rangers Lead The Way.

APPENDIX A

Ranger History

The history of U.S. Rangers dates back to pre-revolutionary times when units specifically designated as Rangers and using Ranger tactics were employed on the American frontier; this as early as 1670. Among these were the Rangers of Captain Benjamin Church who brought the Indian Conflict known as "King Phillip's War" to a successful conclusion in 1675.

Rangers were organized in 1756 by Major Robert Rogers, a native of New Hampshire, who recruited nine companies of American colonists to fight for the British during the French and Indian War. Ranger techniques and methods of operation were an inherent characteristic of the American frontiersmen; however, Major Rogers was the first to capitalize on them and incorporate them into the fighting doctrine of a permanently organized fighting force.

In the French and Indian War (1754-1763), Robert Rogers developed the Ranger concept to an extent never known before. A soldier from boyhood, Rogers published a list of 28 common sense rules, and a set of standing orders stressing operational readiness, security, and tactics.

Rogers established a training program in which he personally supervised the application of his rules. In June 1754, Robert Rogers was conducting live-fire training exercises. His operations were characterized by solid preparation and bold movements. When other units were bivouacked in winter quarters, Rangers moved against the French and Indians by the use of snowshoes, sleds, and even ice skates. In a time when the English colonists were struggling, Roger's Rangers carried the war to the enemy by scouting parties and raids. His most famous expedition was a daring raid against the fierce Abenaki Indians. With a force of 200 Rangers, traveling by boat and over land, Rogers covered 400 miles in about 60 days. Penetrating deep into enemy territory, and despite losses en route, the Rangers attacked and destroyed the Indian settlement and killed several hundred Indians; the Abenaki were no longer a threat. Rangers continued to patrol the border and defend the colonists against sporadic Indian attacks for the next decade.

On June 14, 1775, with war on the horizon, the Continental Congress resolved that "six companies of expert riflemen be immediately raised in Pennsylvania, two in Maryland, and two in Virginia." In 1777, this force of hardy frontiersmen provided the leadership and experiences necessary to form, under Dan Morgan, the organization George Washington called "The Corps of Rangers". Also active during the Revolutionary War were Thomas Knowlton's Connecticut Rangers. This force of less than 150 hand-picked men was used primarily for reconnaissance. Knowlton was killed leading his men in action at Harlem Heights.

Also during the American Revolution was Francis Marion who terrorized the entire British Army in South Carolina, striking with swiftness, and then vanishing ghost-like into the swamps. Born near Georgetown, South Carolina, Marion was for years a peaceful farmer. When the Cherokees began their massacres he began his fighting career, learning the Indian techniques of surprise attack and sudden disappearance, how to use swamps and forests as cover. Thus when England sent a vast fleet to capture Charleston, Marion was already an accomplished strategist. From a tiny, unfinished island fort he defied a total of fifty warships. He and his men crippled the entire British fleet and saved the city, though they lacked adequate ammunition, achieving the first important victory of the American Revolution. When Charleston fell to the enemy, Marion escaped and formed Marion's Brigade, one hundred fifty tattered, penniless patriots. None received pay, food or even ammunition from the Continental Army.

The best-known Rangers of the Civil War period were commanded by the Confederate Colonel John S. Mosby. Mosby's Rangers operated behind Union limes south of the Potomac. From a three-man scout unit in 1862, Mosby's force grew to an operation of eight companies of Rangers by 1865. He believed that by the use of aggressive action and surprise assaults, he would compel the Union forces to guard a hundred points at one time. Then, by skillful reconnaissance, he could locate one of the weakest points and attack it, assured of victory. On his raids, Mosby employed small members, usually 20 to 50 men. With nine men, he once attacked and routed an entire Union regiment in its bivouac. Equally skillful were the Rangers under the command of Colonel Turner Ashby, a Virginian widely known for his daring. The Rangers of Ashby and Mosby did great service for the Confederacy. Specialists in scouting, harassing, and raiding, they were a constant threat and kept large numbers of Union troops occupied. Rangers who fought for the United States during the Civil War should also be mentioned. Mean's Rangers captured Confederate General Longstreet's ammunition train, and even succeeded in engaging and capturing a portion of Colonel Mosby's force.

With America's entry into the Second World War, Rangers came forth to add to the pages of history. Major General Lucian K. Truscott, U.S. Army Liaison with the British General Staff, submitted proposals to General George Marshal that "we undertake immediately an American unit along the lines of the British Commandos" on May 26, 1942. A cable from the War Department quickly followed to Truscott and Major General Russell P. Hartle, commanding all Army Forces in Northern Ireland, authorizing the activation of the First U. S. Army Ranger Battalion. The name RANGER was selected by General Truscott "because the name Commandos rightfully belonged to the British, and we sought a name more typically American".

Captain William Orlando Darby, a graduate of West Point with amphibious training, was promoted to major, and organized the unit within a few weeks after receiving his assignment. Thousands of applicants from the 1st Armored Division and the 34th Infantry Division and other units in N. Ireland were interviewed by his hand-picked officers, and after a strenuous weeding out program at Carrickfergus, the First Ranger Battalion was officially activated there on 19 June, 1942.

More rugged and realistic training with live ammunition was in store for the Rangers at the famed Commando Training Center at Achnacarry, Scotland. Coached, prodded and challenged by the battle-seasoned Commando instructors, commanded by Colonel Charles Vaughan, the Rangers learned the rudiments of Commando warfare. Five hundred of the six hundred volunteers that Darby brought with him to Achnacarry survived the Commando training with flying colors, although one Ranger was killed and several wounded by live fire.

Meanwhile forty-four enlisted men and five officers took part in the Dieppe Raid sprinkled among the Canadians and the British Commandos-the first American ground soldiers to see action against the Germans in occupied Europe. Three Rangers were killed, several captured and all won the commendation and esteem of the Commandos. Under the leadership of Darby, promoted to Lt. Colonel, the 1st Ranger Battalion spearheaded the North African Invasion at the Port of Arzew, Algeria by a silent night landing, silenced two gun batteries and opened the way for the First Infantry Division to capture Oran. Later in Tunisia the 1st Battalion executed the first Ranger behind-the-lines night raid at Sened, killing a large number of defenders and taking ten prisoners with only one Ranger killed and ten wounded. On March 31, 1943 the 1st Ranger Battalion led General Patton's drive to capture the heights of El Guettar with a twelve mile night march across mountainous terrain, surprising the enemy positions from the rear. By dawn the Rangers swooped down on the surprised Italians, cleared the El Guettar Pass and captured two hundred prisoners. For this action the Battalion won its first Presidential Citation and Darby won his first DSC.

After Tunisia, the 3rd and 4th Ranger Battalions with the 1st Battalion as cadre were activated and trained by Darby for the invasion of Sicily at Nemours, Algeria in April 1943. Major Herman Dammer assumed command of the 3rd, Major Roy Murray the 4th, and Darby remained CO of the 1st but in effect was in command of what became known as the Darby Rangers force. The three Ranger units spearheaded the Seventh Army landing at Gela and Licata and played a key role in the Sicilian campaign that culminated in the capture of Messina.

The three Battalions were the first Fifth Army troops to land during the Italian Invasion near Salerno. They quickly seized the strategic heights on both sides of Chinuzi Pass and fought off eight German counterattacks, winning two Distinguished Unit Citations. It was here that Colonel Darby commanded a force of over ten thousand troops, elements of the 36th Division, several companies of the 82nd Airborne Division and artillery elements, and it was here that the Fifth Army advance against Naples was launched with the British 10th Corps.

All three Ranger units later fought in the bitter winter mountain fighting near San Pietro, Venafro and Cassino. Then after a short period of rest, reorganizing and recruiting new volunteers, the three Ranger Battalions, reinforced with the 509 Parachute Battalion, the 83rd Chemical Warfare, 4.2 Mortar Battalion and 36th Combat Engineers, were designated as the 6615 Ranger Force under the command of Darby who was finally promoted to Colonel. This Force spearheaded the surprise night landings at the Port of Anzio, captured two gun batteries, seized the city and struck out to enlarge the beachhead before dawn-a classic Ranger operation.

On the night of January 30, 1944, the 1st and 3rd Battalions infiltrated 5 miles behind the German Lines while the 4th Battalion fought to clear the road toward Cisterna, a key 5th Army objective. But preparing for a massive counterattack, the Germans had reinforced their lines the night before, and both the

1st and 3rd were surrounded and greatly outnumbered. The Rangers inflicted many casualties but ammunition and time ran out, and all along the beachhead front supporting troops could not break through the strong German positions. The loss of the 1st and 3rd Battalions combined with the heavy casualties the 4th Battalion sustained, however, was not entirely in vain, for later intelligence revealed that the Ranger-led attack on Cisterna had helped spike the planned German counterattack.

The 2nd Ranger Battalion, activated on April 1st, 1943, at Camp Forrest, Tennessee trained and led by Lt. Colonel James Earl Rudder, carried out the most dangerous mission of the entire Omaha Beach landings - in Normandy, June 6th, 1944. Three companies, D, E, and F assaulted the perpendicular cliffs of Point Du Hoc under intense machine-gun, mortar and artillery fire and destroyed a large gun battery that would have wreaked havoc on the Allied fleets offshore. For two days and nights they fought without relief until the 5th Ranger Battalion linked up with them. Later with the 5th Battalion, the 2nd played a key role in the attacks against the German fortifications around Brest in the La Coquet Peninsular. This unit fought through the Central Europe campaign and won commendations for its heroic actions in the battle of Hill 400. The 2nd Ranger Battalion earned the Distinguished Unit Citation and the Croix de Guerre and was inactivated at Camp Patrick Henry October 23rd, 1945.

The Fifth Ranger Battalion activated September 1, 1943 at Camp Forrest, commanded by Lt. Colonel Max Schneider, former exec officer of the 4th Ranger Battalion, was part of the provisional Ranger Assault Force commanded by Colonel Rudder. It landed on Omaha Beach with three companies of the 2nd Bn., A, B and C, where elements of the 116th Regiment of the 29th Inf. Division were pinned down by murderous cross fire and mortars from the heights above. It was there that the situation was so critical that General Omar Bradley was seriously considering redirecting reinforcements to other areas of the beachhead. And it was then and there that General Norman D. Cota, Assistant

Division Commander of the 29th Division, gave the now famous order that has become the Motto of the 75th Ranger Regiment: "Rangers, Lead The Way!" The Fifth Battalion Rangers broke across the sea wall and barbed wire entanglements, and up the pillbox-rimmed heights under intense enemy machine-gun and mortar fire and with A and B Companies of the 2nd Battalion and some elements of the 116th Infantry Regiment, advanced four miles to the key town of Vierville, thus opening the breach for supporting troops to follow-up and expand the beachhead. Meanwhile C Company of the 2nd Battalion, due to rough seas, landed west of the Vierville draw and suffered 50% casualties during the landing, but still scaled a 90 foot cliff using ropes and bayonets to knock out a formidable enemy position that was sweeping the beach with deadly fire.

The Fifth Battalion with elements of the 116th Regiment finally linked up with the beleaguered 2nd Battalion on D+3, although Lt. Charles Parker of A Company, 5th Battalion, had penetrated deep behind enemy lines on D Day and reached the 2nd Battalion with 20 prisoners. Later, with the 2nd Battalion the unit distinguished itself in the hard-fought battle of Brest. Under the leadership of Lt. Colonel Richard Sullivan the Fifth Ranger Battalion took part in the Battle of the Bulge, Huertgen Forest and other tough battles throughout central Europe, winning two Distinguished Unit Citations and the French Croix de Guerre. The outfit was deactivated October 2 at Camp Miles Standish, Massachusetts.

The Sixth Ranger Battalion, commanded by Colonel Henry (Hank) Mucci, was the first American force to return to the Philippines with the mission of destroying coastal defense guns, radio and radar stations on the islands of Dinegat, Suluan offshore Leyte. This was the first mission for the 6th Battalion that was activated at Port Moresby, New Guinea in September 1944. Landing three days in advance of the main Sixth Army Invasion Force on October 17-18, 1944, they swiftly killed and captured some of the Japanese defenders and destroyed all enemy communications.

The unit took part in the landings of US forces in Luzon, and several behind the lines patrols, penetrations and small unit raids, that served to prime the Rangers for what to become universally known as the greatest and most daring raid in American military history. On January 30th, 1944, C Company, supported by a platoon from F. Company, struck 30 miles behind enemy lines and rescued five hundred emaciated and sickly POWs, survivors of the Bataan Death March. Carrying many of the prisoners on their backs, the Rangers, aided by Filipino guerrillas, killed over two hundred of the garrison, evaded two Japanese regiments, and reached the safety of American lines the following day. Intelligence reports had indicated the Japanese were planning to kill the prisoners as they withdrew toward Manila. Good recon work by the Alamo Scouts also contributed to the success of the Cabanatuan Raid led by Colonel Mucci.

The unit later commanded by Colonel Robert Garrett played and important role in the capture of Manila and Appari, and was preparing to spearhead the invasion of Japan when news flashed the war with that nation was ended. It received the Presidential Unit Citation and the Philippine Presidential Citation. It was inactivated December 30th, 1945 in the Philippines.

Little is known by the public at large about the Ranger Battalion that was formed December 20th, 1942, with volunteers from the 29th Infantry Division then stationed in England commanded by Major Randolph Milholland, this unit also was trained by the British Commandos at Achnacarry, Scotland, and its highly motivated Rangers, eager for action, had high hopes of operating independently on Commando type missions. After graduating with honors, the unit was attached to Lord Lovat's Number 4 Commando Troop for tactical training and cliff climbing, winning the respect of Lord Lovat and the approval of Brig. Gen.

Norman Cota who was then chief liaison for Maj. Gen. Russell Hartle.

The battalion was formed on the 20th of December 1942, at Tideworth Barracks, Salsbury Plain, England. At that time, the 1st Ranger Battalion, was the only US Ranger battalion in the ETO; it departed in October with the 1st Division for the North Africa Campaign. The directive that the battalion authorized three officer4s and fifteen enlisted soldiers from the 1st Ranger Battalion to form the nucleus, the remaining members of the 29th Provisional Ranger Battalion were volunteers from the division. Major Milholland, from the 115th Infantry Regiment was given command of this battalion. By the end of the war Major Milholland would be promoted to LTC and command 3rd Battalion 115 Infantry.

The 29th Provisional Ranger Battalion participated with British commandos in three raids of the coast of Norway. The first raid was to destroy a bridge. men did go on a raid with the Commandos on an island off the coast of France and acquitted themselves well, killing three Germans, and on the 20th of September, 1943, a company moved to Dover to take part in a raid on the Continent. The raid was ultimately canceled and later, Headquarters, 29th Infantry Division issued General Orders disbanding the unit on October 18, 1943. Many of the Rangers went back to their former companies in the 29th Infantry Division and fought from D Day to the day the Germans were defeated.

Merrill's Marauders, a Ranger type outfit, came into existence as a result of the Quebec Conference of August, 1943. During this conference, President Franklin D. Roosevelt, Prime Minister Winston Churchill of England, and other allied leaders conceived the idea of having an American ground unit spearhead the Chinese Army with a Long Range Penetration Mission behind enemy lines in Burma. Its goal would be the destruction of Japanese communications and supply lines and generally to play havoc with enemy forces while an attempt was made to reopen the Burma Road.

A Presidential call for volunteers for "A Dangerous and Hazardous Mission" was issued, and approximately 2,900 American soldiers responded to the call. Officially designated as the 5307th Composite Unit (Provisional) code name "GALAHAD" the unit later became popularly known as MERRILL'S MARAUDERS, named after its leader, Brigadier General Frank Merrill. Organized into combat teams, two to each battalion, the Marauder volunteers came from a variety of theatres of operation. Some came from Stateside cadres; some from the jungles of Panama and Trinidad; and the remainder were battle-scarred veterans of Guadalcanal, New Georgia, and New Guinea campaigns. In India some Signal Corps and Air Corps personnel were added, as well as pack troops with mules.

After preliminary training operations undertaken in great secrecy in the jungles of India, about 600 men were detached as a rear echelon HQ to remain in India to handle the soon-to-be vital air-drop link between the six Marauder combat teams (400 to a team) and the Air Transport Command. Color-coded Red, White, Blue, Green, Orange and Khaki, the remaining 2400 Marauders began their March up the Ledo Road and over the outlying ranges of the Himalayan Mountains into Burma. The Marauders, with no tanks or heavy artillery to support them, walked over 1,000 miles throughout extremely dense and almost impenetrable jungles and came out with glory. In five major and thirty minor engagements, they defeated the veteran soldiers of the Japanese 18th Division (conquerors of Singapore and Malaya) who vastly outnumbered them. Always moving to the rear of the main forces of the Japanese, they completely disrupted enemy supply and communication lines, and climaxed their behind-the-lines operations with the capture of Myitkina Airfield, the only all-weather airfield in Burma.

For their accomplishments in Burma, the Marauders were awarded the Distinguished Unit Citation in July, 1944. However, in November, 1966, this was redesignated as the PRESIDENTIAL UNIT CITATION which is awarded by the President in the name of Congress. The unit was consolidated with the 475th Infantry on August 10, 1944. On June 21, 1968, the 475th was redesignated the 75th Infantry. It is from the redesignation of Merrill's Marauders into the 75th Infantry Regiment that the modern-day 75th Ranger Regiment traces its current unit designation.

The outbreak of hostilities in Korea in June of 1950 again signaled the need for Rangers. Colonel John Gibson Van Houten was selected by the Army Chief of Staff to head the Ranger training program at Ft. Benning, Georgia. On September 15, 1950, Colonel Van Houten reported to the Chief of Staff, Office of the Chief of Army Field Forces, Fort Monroe, Virginia. He was informed that training of Ranger-type units was to begin at Ft. Benning at the earliest possible date. The target date was October 1, 1950 with a tentative training period of 6 weeks.

The implementing orders called for formation of a headquarters detachment and four Ranger infantry companies (airborne). Requests went out for volunteers who were willing to accept "extremely Hazardous" duty in the combat zone in the Far East. In the 82nd Airborne Division, it is estimated that as many as 5,000 men (experienced Regular Army Paratroopers) volunteered. Orders were issued and those selected shipped to Ft. Benning. The First group arrived on September 20. Training began on Monday, October 9, 1950, with three companies of airborne qualified personnel. On October 9, 1950 another company began training. These were former members of the 505th Airborne Infantry Regiment and the 80th Anti-aircraft Artillery Battalion of the 82nd Airborne Division. Initially designated the 4th Ranger Company, they would soon be redesigned the 2nd Ranger Infantry Company (Airborne), the only Department of the Army authorized, all-black Ranger Unit in the history of the United States.

All volunteers were professional soldiers with many skills who often taught each other. Some of the men had fought with the original Ranger Battalions, The First Special Service Force, or the Office of Strategic Services during World War II. Many of the instructors were drawn from this same group. The faces of this select group may have appeared youthful, but these were men highly trained and experienced in Ranger operations during World War II. Training consisted of amphibious and airborne (including low-level night jumps) operations, demolitions, sabotage, close combat, and the use of foreign maps. All American small arms, as well as those used by the enemy, were mastered. Communications, as well as the control of artillery, naval, and aerial fires, were stressed. Much of the training was at night.

The 1st Ranger Infantry Company (Airborne) departed from Ft. Benning, Georgia on November 15, 1950, and arrived in Korea on December 17, 1950, where it was attached to the 2nd Infantry Division. It was soon followed by the 2nd and 4th Ranger Companies, who arrived on December 29. The 2nd Ranger Company was attached to the 7th Infantry Division. The 4th Ranger company served both Headquarters, Eighth US Army, and the 1st Cavalry Division.

Throughout the Winter of 1950 and the Spring of 1951, the Rangers went into battle. They were nomadic warriors, attached first to one regiment and then another. They performed "out-front" work: scouting, patrolling, raids, ambushes, spearheading assaults, and as counterattack forces to regain lost positions. They were attached on the basis of one 112-man company per 18,000-man infantry division.

The Rangers went into battle by air, land and water. The 1st Ranger Infantry Company (Airborne) opened with an extraordinary example of land navigation, then executed a daring night raid 9 miles behind enemy lines destroying an enemy complex. The enemy installation was later identified by a prisoner as the Headquarters of the 12th North Korean Division. Caught by surprise and unaware of the size of the American force, two North Korean Regiments hastily withdrew from the area. The 1st Company as in the middle of the major battle of Chipyong-Ni and the "May Massacre." It was awarded two Distinguished Unit Citations. The 2nd and 4th Ranger Companies made a combat jump at Munsan-Ni where Life magazine reported patrols operating North of the 38th parallel. The 2nd Ranger Company plugged a critical gap left by a retreating allied force. The 4th Ranger Company executed a daring over-water raid at the Hwachon Dam. The 3rd Ranger Company (attached to the 3rd Infantry Division) had the motto "Die Bastard, Die!" The 5th Ranger Company, fighting as an attachment to the 25th Infantry Division, performed brilliantly during the Chinese "5th Phase Offensive." Gathering up every soldier he could find, the Ranger company commander held the line with Ranger Sergeants commanding line infantry units. In the Eastern sector, the Rangers were the first unit to cross the 38th parallel on the second drive North.

The 8th Ranger Infantry Company (Airborne) was attached to the 24th Infantry Division. They were known as the "Devils." A 33-man platoon from the 8th Ranger Company fought a between-the-lines battle with two Chinese reconnaissance companies. Seventy Chinese were killed. The Rangers suffered two dead and three wounded, all of whom were brought back to friendly lines.

The 75th Ranger Regiment is linked directly and historically to the 13 Infantry Companies of the 75th that were active in Vietnam from February 1, 1969 until August 15, 1972.

The 75th Infantry Regiment was activated in Okinawa during 1968 and traced its lineage to the 475th Infantry Regiment, thence to the 5307th Composite Provisional Unit, popularly known as Merrill's Marauders. Historically, company I (Ranger) 75th Infantry, 1st Infantry Division and Company G, (Ranger) 75th Infantry, 23rd Infantry Division (Americal) produced the first two US Army Rangers to be awarded the Medal of Honor as a member of and while serving in combat Ranger company. Specialist Four Robert D. Law was awarded the first Medal of Honor with I\75 while on long range patrol in Tinh Phoc Province RVN. He was from Texas. Staff Sergeant Robert J. Pruden was awarded the second Medal of Honor with G\75 while on reconnaissance mission in Quang Ni Province RVN. He was from Minnesota. In addition to the two Medal of Honor recipients above, Staff Sergeant Lazlo Rabel was awarded the Medal of Honor while serving with the 74th Infantry Detachment (LRP), a predecessor to Company N, (Ranger) 75th Infantry, 173rd Airborne Brigade while on a long-range patrol Binh Dinh Province, RVN. He was from Pennsylvania.

Conversion of the Long Range Patrol Companies of the 20th, 50th, 51st, 52nd, 54th, 71st, 78th, and 79th Infantry Detachment and Company D, 151st Infantry Long Range Patrol of the Indiana National Guard, to Ranger Companies of the 75th Infantry began on 1 February, 1969. Only Company D, 151st retained their unit identity and did not become a 75th Ranger Company, however, they did become a Ranger Company and continued the mission in Vietnam. Companies C, D, E, F, G, H, I, K, L, M, N, O and P (Ranger) 75th Infantry conducted Ranger missions for three years and seven months every day of the year while in Vietnam. Like the original unit from whence their lineage as Neo Marauders was drawn, 75th Rangers came from Infantry, Artillery, Engineers, Signal, Medical, Military Police, Food Service, Parachute Riggers and other Army units. They were joined by former adversaries, the Viet Cong and North Vietnamese Army soldiers who became "Kit Carson Scouts", and fought alongside the Rangers against their former units and comrades. Unlike Rangers of other eras in the 20th Century who trained in the United States or in friendly nations overseas, LRP and Rangers in Vietnam were activated, trained and fought in the same geographical areas in Vietnam.

Training was a combat mission for volunteers. Volunteers were assigned, not accepted in the various Ranger Companies, until, after a series of patrols, the volunteer had passed the acid test of a Ranger, Combat, and was accepted by his peers. Following the peer acceptance, the volunteer was allowed to wear the black beret and wear the Red, White and Black scroll shoulder sleeve insignia bearing his Ranger Company identity. All Long Range Patrol Companies and 75th Ranger Companies were authorized Parachute pay. Modus Operandi for patrol insertion varied, however, the helicopter was the primary means for insertion and exfiltration of enemy rear areas. Other methods included foot, wheeled, tracked vehicle, airboats, Navy Swift Boats, and stay behind missions where the Rangers remained in place as a larger tactical unit withdrew. False insertions by helicopter was a means of security from ever-present enemy trail watchers. General missions consisted of locating the enemy bases and lines of communication. Special missions included wiretap, prisoner snatch, Platoon and Company size Raid Missions and Bomb Damage Assessment (BDA) following B-52 Arc-Light missions. Staffed initially by graduates of the US Army Ranger School (at the outset of the war, later by volunteers, some of whom were graduates of the in-country Ranger School, the Recondo School and, line company cadres), Paratroopers, and Special Forces trained men, the bulk of the Ranger volunteers came from the soldiers who had no chance to attend the schools, but carried the fight to the enemy. These Rangers remained with their units through some of the most difficult patrolling action(s) in Army history, and frequently fought much larger enemy forces when compromised on their reconnaissance missions.

Army Chief of Staff Creighton Abrams, who observed the 75th Ranger operations in Vietnam as Commander of all US Forces there, selected the 75th Rangers as the role model for the first US

Army Ranger units formed during peacetime in the history of the United States Army.

The outbreak of the 1973 Middle East War prompted the Department of the Army to be concerned about the need for a light mobile force that could be moved quickly to any trouble spot in the world. In the Fall of 1973, General Creighton Abrams, Army Chief of Staff formulated the idea of the reformation of the first battalion-sized Ranger units since World War IL In January, 1974, he sent a message to the field directing formation of a Ranger Battalion. He selected its missions and picked the first officers. He felt a tough, disciplined and elite Ranger unit would set a standard for the rest of the United States Army and that, as Rangers "graduated " from Ranger units to Regular Army units, their influence would improve the entire Army.

On January 25, 1974, Headquarters, United States Army Forces Command, published General Orders 127, directing the activation of the 1st Battalion, 75th Infantry (Ranger), with an effective date of January 31, 1974. In February, the worldwide selection was begun and personnel assembled at Fort Benning, Georgia, to undergo the cadre training from March through June 1974. On July 1, 1974, the 1st Battalion, 75th Infantry (Ranger), parachuted into Fort Stewart, Georgia.

The modern Ranger Battalions were first called upon in 1980 as elements of 1st Battalion, 75th Infantry (Ranger) to participate in the Iranian hostage rescue attempts. The ground work of today's Special Operations capability was laid during training and preparation for this operation. Rangers and other Special Operations Forces from throughout the Department of Defense developed tactics, techniques, and equipment from scratch, as no doctrine existed anywhere in the world.

The 2d Battalion, 75th Infantry (Ranger) soon followed with activation on October 1, 1974. These elite units eventually established headquarters at Hunter Army Airfield, Georgia, and Fort Lewis, Washington, respectively.

During the United States' deployment on October 25, 1983, to Grenada, the mission of the Rangers was to protect the lives of American citizens and restore democracy to the island. During this operation, code-named "URGENT FURY, " the 1st and 2d Ranger Battalions conducted a daring low-level parachute assault (500 feet), seized the airfield at Point Salines, rescued American citizens at the True Blue Medical Campus, and conducted air assault operations to eliminate pockets of resistance.

As a result of the demonstrated effectiveness of the Ranger Battalions, the Department of the Army announced in 1984, that if was increasing the size of the active duty Ranger force to its highest level in forty years, by activating another Ranger Battalion and a Ranger Regimental Headquarters These new units, the Id Battalion, 75th Infantry (Ranger), and Headquarters and Headquarters Company, 75th Infantry (Ranger), received their colors on October 3, 1984, at Fort Benning, Georgia. On February 3, 1986, World War II Battalions and Korean War Lineage and Honors were consolidated and assigned by tradition to the 75th Ranger Regiment. This marked the first time that an organization of that size had been officially recognized as the parent headquarters of the Ranger Battalions.

The entire Ranger Regiment participated in OPERATION "JUST CAUSE", in which U.S. forces restored democracy to Panama. Rangers spearheaded the action by conducting two important operations. The 1st Battalion, reinforced by Company C, 3d Battalion, and a Regimental Command and Control Team, conducted an early morning parachute assault onto Omar Torrijos International Airport and Tocumen Military Airfield, to neutralize the Panamanian Defense Forces PDF 2d Rifle Company, and secure airfields for the arrival of the 82d Airborne Division. The 2d and 3d Ranger Battalions and a Regimental Command and Control Team, conducted a parachute assault onto the airfield at

Rio Hato, to neutralize the PDF 6th and! Oh Rifle Companies and seize General Manuel Noriega's beach house. Following the successful completion of these assaults, Rangers conducted follow-on operations in support of Joint Task Force (JTF)-South. The Rangers captured 1,014 Enemy Prisoners of War (EPW), and over 18,000 arms of various types. The Rangers sustained 5 killed and 42 wounded.

Elements of Company B and 1st Platoon, Company A, 1st Battalion, 75th Ranger Regiment deployed to Saudi Arabia from February 12, 1991 to April 15, 1991, in support of OPERAITION DESERT STORM. The Rangers conducted raids and provided a quick reaction force in cooperation with Allied forces; there were no Ranger casualties.

From just 1993, to October 21, 1993, Company B and a Command and Control Element of 3d Battalion, the 75th Ranger Regiment deployed to Somalia to assist United Nations forces in bringing order to a desperately chaotic and starving nation. Their mission was to capture key leaders in order to end clan fighting in and around the City of Mogadishu. On October 3, 1993, the Rangers conducted a daring daylight raid in which several special operations helicopters were shot down. For nearly 18 hours, the Rangers delivered devastating firepower, killing an estimated 300 Somali's in what many have called the fiercest ground combat since Vietnam. Six Rangers died.

APPENDIX B

RANGER CLASS 6-81
BENNING PHASE PUBLISHED TRAINING SCHEDULE

DAY 1, WEDNESDAY, 25 FEB 81

0300 – 0530	Ranger Run (2-mile run) and PT Test
0600 – 0700	Chow
0700 – 1000	Draw Equipment (includes travel time)
1030 – 1230	Victory Pond Ranger's in action demo
1230 – 1300	Sack Lunch on site
1300 – 1430	In processing/Admin
1430 – 1730	Airborne Refresher
1730 –1800	Return to Harmony Church site
1800 – 1900	Chow
1900 – 2100	Inspections

DAY 2, THURSDAY, 26 FEB 81

0400 – 0600	Hand-To-Hand Combat
0600 – 0630	Recover from above
0630 – 0730	Commo Security Techniques
0730 –1030	Demo Training (includes movement/chow)
1730 –1830	Evening Chow
1830 – 2030	Inspections (and other pain)

DAY 3, FRIDAY, 27 FEB 81

0500 – 0600	RANGER Run (3 miles) plus Worm Pit (Actually, wake up time was 0300 by the Morgan Team, who entertained us until the scheduled wake up time)
0600 – 0630	Recovery time
0630 - 0730	Chow
0730 - 0930	Medical Considerations for RANGERS
0930 – 1400	Advanced Airborne Procedures
1400 – 1730	Distance Determination
1730 – 1830	Chow
1830 – 2030	Terrain Comparison and route selection
2030 – 2200	Fundamentals of Patrolling
2200 – 2300	Inspections (and other pain)

DAY 4, SATURDAY, 28 FEB 81

0400 – 0600	Hand-To-Hand Combat
0600 – 0630	Recovery Time
0630 – 0730	Chow
0730 – 2000	Terrain Association, Land Navigation Test
20000 – 2100	Sack Lunch back at Harmony Church site

DAY 5, SUNDAY, 1 MAR 81
(Today was my Wife's Birthday)

0400 – 0500	RANGER Run (3.5 Miles) + Worm Pit
0500 – 0530	Recovery time
0530 – 1730	Fundamentals of Patrolling
1730 – 1800	Church
1800 – 1900	Inspections

DAY 6, MONDAY, 2 MAR 81

0430 – 0630	Hand-To-Hand Combat
0630 –0700	Recovery Time
0700 –1830	Fundamentals of Patrolling
1830 –1930	Chow

DAY 7, TUESDAY, 3 MAR 81

0430 – 0600	RANGER Run (3.5 miles) + Worm Pit
0600 –0630	Recovery time
0630 –0730	Chow
0730 –0930	Fundamentals of Patrolling
0930 –1130	Hand-To-Hand Combat
1130 –1200	Recovery Time
1200 – 1300	Chow
1300 –1700	Fundamentals of Patrolling
17 00 –1800	Chow
1800 –1900	Mission Briefing
1900 -	Inspection

DAY 8, WEDNESDAY, 4 MAR 81

0400 – 0600	Hand-To-Hand Combat
0600 – 0630	Recovery time
0630 – 0730	Chow
0730 – 1200	Move to and set up in Camp Darby
1200 – 1600	Air Operations
1600 – 1700	Bivouac details
1700 – 1900	STANO
1900 – 2100	Briefings
2300 –2400	Bivouac

DAY 9, THURSDAY, 5 MAR 81

0001 – 0600	Bivouac
0600 – 1800	Cadre-Led Recon Patrols
1800 – 1900	Chow
1900 – 2030	Recon Patrol Mission Briefing
2030 – 2300	Prep for Patrol
2300 – 2400	Bivouac

DAY 10, FRIDAY, 6 MAR 81

0000 – 0700	Bivouac
0700 – 1300	Artillery support for patrols

(This was one of those little mentioned, "must pass" tests)

1300 – 1700	Air Re-supply and field expedients
1700 – 2300	Preparation for Patrol

DAY 11, SATURDAY, 7 MAR 81

0001 – 0400	Bivouac
0400 – 2400	Reconnaissance Patrol

DAY 12, SUNDAY, 8 MAR 81

0001 – 1100	Reconnaissance Patrol continues
1100 – 1300	Assault the Darby Queen
1300 – 1400	Chow
1400 – 1630	Cadre-Led Combat Patrol
1630 – 1730	Church
1730 – 1830	Chow
1830 – 2330	Cadre-Led Combat Patrol
2330 – 2400	Bivouac

DAY 13, MONDAY, 9 MAR 81

0001 – 0500	Bivouac
0500 – 0600	Chow
0600 – 1700	Cadre-Led Combat Patrol
1700 – 1800	Chow
1800 – 2300	Combat Patrol Mission Briefing/Prep
2300 – 2400	Bivouac

DAY 14, TUESDAY, 10 MAR 81

0001 – 0400	Bivouac
0400 – 0500	Chow
0500 – 2400	Combat Patrol

DAY 15, WEDNESDAY, 11 MAR 81

0001 – 1200	Combat Patrol
1200 – 1300	Chow
1300 – 1600	Training Summary by RIs
1600 – 1900	Chow and Bivouac activities
1900 – 2030	Recon Patrol Mission Brief
2030 – 2400	Bivouac

DAY 16, THURSDAY, 12 MAR 81

0001 – 0400	Bivouac
0400 – 2400	Recon Patrol

DAY 17, FRIDAY, 13 MAR 81
(NOTE: No one noted that this was Friday the 13th)

0001 – 1100	Recon Patrol continues
1100 – 1200	Clear Bivouac, i.e. break camp
1200 – 2100	Return to Harmony Church Site , conduct retests for

those who needed to, conduct peer evaluations, get another haircut (as if we needed one), had a good supper and hot shower)

DAY 18, SATURDAY, 14 MAR 81

0430 – 0530	RANGER Run (5 miles) + Worm pit
0530 – 0600	Recovery
0600 – 0700	Chow
0700 – 1200	Victory Pond confidence events

1200 – 1400	Hand-To-Hand Combat
	King-Of-The-Pit madness
1400 – 1500	Chow
1500 –1800	RI Time

DAY 19, SUNDAY, 15 MAR 81

0600 – 1700	A day of madness, filled with much activity and preparing to move out to Camp Merrill for the Mountain Phase the next day.
1700 – 2300	First break of the course

Notes: 1: Morning start times shown were the training times. Wakeup or getup time was always at least an hour earlier.

2: The remaining two phases of the course, Mountain Phase and Florida Phase, were not conducted on a published schedule; rather, they were more mission oriented than time dependent. Although I am sure that the RIs knew what they were going to do to us, we did not have a very long picture in front of us.

(This is all of the schedule that survived Ranger School; the misery went on for another 49 days, but who is counting,)

APPENDIX C

The 1995 Training Incident that Killed 4 Ranger Students

Ranger School, like many other aspects of military life, has a definite and real element of risk. Students, and everyone that cares for the student, should be aware of that risk and they should also be aware that the Army has gone to great lengths to minimize the risk and to aggressively monitor risk assessment and risk management.

I submit that the reaction to the death of 4 students in 1995 is the most vivid example of how the Army seeks to provide realistic and challenging training while being sensitive to and responsive to risk.

Since 1952, 23 soldiers have died in RANGER training and numerous others have been injured to various degrees including falls, pulled muscles and twisted joints, concussion, pyrotechnic injury, rope burn, abrasion, infection, broken bones, gouged eyes, frostbite, hypothermia, heat stroke and stress, drowning, electrocution, lightning strikes, and automobile accidents. Between May 1985 and February 1995, no one died in training. Then in a single night, four students died and four others were hospitalized in hypothermia incidents in the Swamps of Florida. The September 1995 issue of Esquire Magazine presented a story by Philip Caputo entitled "The Black Badge Of Courage" that was an excellent account of how this tragedy unfolded. I highly recommend that students go to their local library and get this account and read it.

A brief summary of the tragedy is as follows. It was a normal tactical mission, which required the unit to move down the Yellow River via LRB (Little Rubber Boat), land at a pre planned point, and conduct a cross-country move to an assigned objective on dry ground. As often happens (it certainly happened to my class), the landing was at a site other than that which they planned. Because of the unusually high water levels encountered once at the planned site, the RI's decided to continue downriver to more suitable sites. In spite of a dry landing, they soon found themselves in much more water than they had planned on; knee deep, waist deep, and sometimes over their heads. Five inches of rainfall in Georgia and Southern Alabama combined with unusually high tide in Pensacola Bay that would prevent the Yellow River from draining the swamp caused this most unusual flooding condition that set the stage for the tragedy. By late evening, some of them had been immersed for over 8 hours. Their body heat, energy, and mental acuity draining from them with each step. Eventually, the RI declared the tactical move terminated and reverted to essentially an administrative move in an attempt to get the Rangers to high and dry ground. They then encountered a deep slough, which required a deliberate water obstacle crossing via rope.

This crossing began about 1730, darkness in February. The sun is down. Everyone has been wet for hours. They are not moving while the rope bridge is installed. Hypothermia begins to set in on all of them to varying degrees depending on various factors relating to body type and energy conversion. One Ranger went down with second-stage hypo-thermia. Medivac was called and lifted out the stricken ranger using a jungle penetrator. Shortly afterwards, two more rangers went down and required medivac that took another 45 minutes to execute due to darkness, confused signals, and the sheer complexity of doing this under the conditions. Rangers are by now beginning to climb trees to get out of the miserable water. They are shivering and cramped and don't want to continue the move but are motivated by the RI's to continue.

Another ranger goes down with severe hypothermia around 1900. The single medivac helicopter that had pulled three casualties from the swamp had to divert and land at Camp Rudder due to insufficient fuel to make it to Eglin Air Force Base. Unfortunately there was no refuel capability at Rudder so now the chopper had to wait for a fuel tanker to be sent from Eglin. The rangers in the swamp realized that no other chopper would be back on station for over an hour. In fact, it was about two hours before the chopper was again overhead of the stricken rangers. Again it had difficulty in getting the jungle penetrator through the canopy of trees and safely extracting those who were determined to be critical and in desperate need of extraction by the most expedient means. It finally made an extraction; meanwhile the determined rangers were continuing to struggle across the swamp toward higher ground and to an ambulance that had been moved down to rendezvous with them.

The first ambulance departed carrying the most critical, including Sansoucie, about midnight. The second ambulance left for Fort Whalton Beach shortly afterwards with Palmer. It was at this time that the group discovered that Ranger Dodge was missing. And an immediate search began by those who could muster the energy to assist. The search was to no avail. Dodge was found the next day face down in the water only yards from high ground. Four Ranger Students died of hypothermia/drowning on this mission: Sergeant Norman Tillman, Second Lieutenant Curtis Sansoucie, Second Lieutenant Spencer Dodge, and Captain Milton Palmer.

There is nothing more tragic than the loss of young soldiers in this way. What they might have become, we will never know.

After an extensive investigation of the events surrounding this tragedy, the Army took numerous positive steps to ensure that the conditions that contributed to these deaths will not occur again. Some $2.5 million dollars was spent on safety related improvements to include:

Motorola "whisper" radios for nontactical communications
Satellite-mapped training routes for each day of training
Microwave towers to give full radio coverage of training areas
without relays
Remote weather sensors to report conditions to headquarters
and hand held units.
Box Lights mounted in treetops to mark landing zones for rescue
aircraft
Dive teams on call in the vicinity of training
Precisely marked drop sites for LRBs
2000-gallon fuel tank at field 6 for medevac helicopters
Black Hawk helos in place of Hueys
Tactical operations Center in headquarters building
One-man rafts in emergency kits
Hypothermia bags in emergency kits
Hand-held GPS devices to help instructors navigate
Measuring staffs for RI's
Revised training standards
Improved river level forecasting and Redesign of swamp training
lanes
Standardized daily instructor briefings
Revised immersion guidelines
Mass casualty rehearsals and procedures
Increased student meals to two a day and required sleep to 2
hours
Increased student training in stream crossings
Officials screen student medical records and flag those with
previous weather injuries and Identify weak swimmers
Reinforced Ranger Buddy system
Revised winter rucksack packing list
Additional staffing

APPENDIX D

Observation Report (OR)

The Observation Report (OR) is a small pocket book that the Ranger Instructor carries for each RANGER on patrol. It contains a series of tasks that the RANGER is expected to perform to standard. The standard is often a multiplicity of events associated with preciseness and/or time. The RANGER(s) in the leadership position(s) will be given a "GO" or "NO GO" on each action. Occasionally a "not applicable" grade will be made, but I think that is rare. Very early in the course, these ORs were handed out to the class for study. Most of us did not realize the importance of these documents at the time, nor did we really have time to study them. We carried them around for several days and then turned them back in. Anyone who had lost it, was in a heap of trouble. The tasks, actions, and standards are described in the following paragraphs.

Phase I - Planning for and preparation of the patrol.

I. Task: Take charge of a patrol in garrison
1. Action: establish chain of command (Standard: 5 minutes)
Insure that all members of the patrol are aware of the chain of command

2. Action: Operate through chain of command
Standard: Utilize the chain of command; require a status report within 10 minutes accounting for all men and equipment. Issue all instructions and orders to the immediate subordinate leaders

3. Action: issue orders and instructions.
Standard: Within 20 minutes issue initial orders and instructions to subordinates required to begin preparation for the mission

4. Action: Organize to accomplish the mission.
Standard: Distribute heavy equipment evenly throughout the patrol (i.e. machine guns, radios, wire, ammo, etc)

II. Task: Take Charge of a Patrol in the field (Actions 5, 6, and 7 must be accomplished within 15 minutes for BRD, 20 minutes for MRD, and 30 minutes for FRD)

1. Action: Insure security is established/maintained.
Standard: Establish/maintain all-around security with emphasis on most dangerous avenues of approach
Check or confirm location of all elements and automatic weapons.
Take action to correct all noise and light discipline violations observed.

2. Action: Exchange information and equipment.
Standards: Make a map check. Determine location to within 200 meters.
Exchange necessary equipment with previous PL.
Inform all immediate subordinate leaders of new chain of command within 5
minutes of receiving guidance of cadre.
Require immediate subordinates to account for all men and equipment prior to
continuing the task at hand.

3. Action: Issue initial orders and instructions:
Standards: Issue preparatory instructions to immediate subordinate leaders
required to continue or change the task at hand.

4. Action: Reorganize to accomplish the task at hand.
Standard: reorganize personnel and equipment to accomplish the task at hand.
Issue Frag order when change of mission occurs. Must include situation, which
causes the change, new mission of the subordinates, and coordinating
instructions or state "no coordinating instructions".
Correct weak or unsatisfactory actions.

III. Task: Communicate with immediate subordinates.

5. Action: keep subordinates informed
Standard: inform subordinates of any changes in the situation.

6. Action: Insure task is understood.
Standard: Give specific instructions e.g. time to start and complete tasks,
number of items, etc.
Be available to answer questions when work is being accomplished.
Use feedback to verify understanding.

7. Action: Use the chain of command.
Standard: Stay within span of control (3-5 men)
Hold immediate subordinates responsible for tasks assigned.

IV. Task: Motivate a Patrol.

1. Action: Set the example.
Standard: Personally adheres to established standards and procedures, e.g. light and noise discipline, camouflage, etc.
Shares hardships, dangers, and deprivations.
Eats, sleeps, only after the welfare of the men is provided for.

2. Action: Provide command presence.
Standard: adjust plans as soon as changes in METTS dictate.
Corrects subordinates when required.
Display initiative.
Maintains a positive can do attitude

3. Action: Look out for subordinates' welfare.
Standard: adjusts rate of march and techniques of movement to the terrain and enemy situation.
Rotates heavy equipment and difficult duties.
Makes rest halts and replenishes water as required.
Allows sufficient time for meals/personal hygiene and monitors patrol's condition.

V. Task: Supervise subordinates.

1. Action: Assign subordinates responsibility for completing tasks.
Standards: Clearly state what is to be done.
Delegate authority to accomplish the task.
Establish the priority of the task.

2. Action: Establish Standards.
Standard: State how well task is to be accomplished.

3. Action: Allocate available resources.
Standard: Designate which personnel and materials necessary for the task.

4. Action: Follow Up.
Standard: Determine that tasks are being accomplished as directed (Spot check).
Question Subordinates to determine if they understood the concept of your op order.

5. Action: Recognize performance.
Standard: Recognize and encourage good actions.

VI. Task: Issue a warning order.

1. Action: Insure designated personnel are present.
Standard: As a minimum, all immediate subordinate leaders must be present.

2. Action: Issue a brief statement of the situation.
Standard: State the current friendly locations and enemy locations and the designation of major units.
State intentions/activities of all forces when known.

3. Action: Issue the mission of the patrol.
Standard: A clear concise statement to include who, what, when, where, and why.

4. Action: Issue general instructions.
Standard: Include the following:
        Organization IAW METT.
        Chain of Command
        Subunit missions
        Special equipment
        Ammunition
        Uniform and equipment common to all
        Time Schedule

5. Action: Issue special instructions.
Standard: Task subordinates to accomplish tasks, i.e. draw and distribute ammo and equipment, prepare target list, obtain water, etc.
State time, place, uniform and who will attend operation order.

VII. Task: Effect Coordination.

1. Action: Follow the time schedule.
Standard: Adhere to the time schedule issued in the orders.

2. Action: Conduct forward unit coordination.
Standard: Correctly utilize chapter 3 of the Ranger Handbook.

3. Action: Conduct adjacent unit coordination.
Standard: Correctly utilize Chapter 3 of the Ranger Handbook.

4. Action: Conduct aerial resupply coordination
Standard: Correctly utilize Chapter 3 of the Ranger Handbook.

5. Action: Conduct aerial movement coordination.
Standard: Correctly utilize Chapter 3 of the Ranger Handbook.

6. Action: Conduct rehearsal area coordination.
Standard: Correctly utilize Chapter 3 of the Ranger Handbook.

VIII. Task: Insure designated personnel are present.

1. Action: Conduct a role call or use other appropriate means to insure that designated personnel are present.
Standard: As a minimum, all immediate subordinate leaders must be present.

IX. Task: Issue paragraph I of the Operation Order.

1. Action: State the enemy situation.
Standard: A weather forecast and its probable effect on the operation.
A description of the terrain to be crossed.
The strength, known locations, recent activities and identification of enemy units in the area and his probable course of action.

2. Action: State the friendly Situation.
Standard: The mission of the next higher unit.
The locations and planned actions of units on the right and left, the objectives and planned routes of adjacent patrols.

3. Action: State attachments and detachments.
Standard: List all attachments and detachments.
List effective times of all attachments and detachments.

X. Task: Issue Paragraph 2 of the Operation Order.

1. Action: State the Mission.
Standard: Must include who, what, where, when, and why the action is to be accomplished.

XI. Task: Issue paragraph 3a of the operation order.

1. Action: State the concept of the operation.
Standard: State in general terms the scheme of maneuver.
General direction the patrol will travel, method of travel, i.e. foot, vehicle, etc
What the patrol will do at the objective i.e. recon, raid, ambush
State in general terms the external fire support available to the patrol.

XII. Task: Issue paragraph 3b, subunit mission of the operations order.

1. Action: State missions to subordinate units.
Standard: Include who, what, where, when, and why.

2. Action: State instructions to select key individuals.
Standard: Detailed instructions to key individuals and leaders. Must state:
What, when, where, and why.

XIII. Task: Issue paragraph 3c of the operations order.

1. Action: State times of departure and return.
Standard: Must be in accordance with those given in the next higher
Operations Order.

2. Action: State action during halts.
Standard: State how the patrol will be arranged during halts (i.e. movement,
formation, security halt). Illustrate by diagram each of these.
State if contingency plans will be issues.

3. Action: Select the movement technique to be outlined.
Standard: describe the movement technique to be used based on a need for
control, terrain and possibility of enemy contact.

4. Action: State the routes to be taken. Movement fire support may be stated
here or in action 49.
Standard: Illustrate routes to and from the objective.
State alternate routes.
If more than one insertion point is planned, must include routes from each of
these.
Routes selected will avoid known or suspected enemy location.
Box in patrol with identifiable terrain.
State fore support available and preplanned targets to support the movement
concept.

5. Action: State a plan for departure from and reentry of friendly front lines.
Standard: Friendly unit coordination. (Must state sequence, where, and who
will do what).

6. Actions in IRP or detrucking point. (Must state security actions and
contingency plan).
Actions at departure/reentry points. (must have sketch or sand table and
explain actions).

XIV. Task: Issue paragraph 3c of the operation order.

1. Action: State location of planned rallying points.
Standard: as a minimum must list and describe the IRP and RRP.

2. Action: Describe actions at rallying points.
Standard: Must include occupation, reorganization, when to leave and actions to be taken prior to aborting the mission.

3. Action: State action to be taken on enemy contact.
Standard: Must address both the far ambush, the near ambush, and sniper fire.
Chance contact.
Indirect fire and aerial attack.

4. Action: State actions to be taken at danger areas.
Standards: Issue specific plan for any known danger areas the patrol will encounter.
Issue a general plan for negotiating linear, small open and large open danger areas.

XV. Task: Issue paragraph 3c, action at the objective, of the operation order.

1. Action: State a plan for selection and occupation of the ORP.
Standard: must include a plan to locate, clear, secure, and occupy the ORP.

2. Action: State a plan for the leader's recon.
Standard: Must include a plan to pinpoint the objective, to emplace security, and actions on enemy contact.

3. Action: State a plan for actions at the objective.
Standard: Combat--State a plan for assaulting the objective using all supporting weapons and emplacing security elements.
Recon-- State a plan for the reconnaissance of the objective and the security measures to be taken. Security, surveillance and confirmation of SIR.

4. Action: State alternative plans in a case of compromise.
Standard: Combat -- State the plan for assaulting the objective (combat, and use of all supporting weapons. What to do in case compromise prior to assaulting the objective)
Recon--State the plan for reconnaissance of the objective. What to do in case of compromise prior to completion of the mission.

5. Action: State a plan for withdrawal.
Standard: A signal for withdrawal.
Where the patrol will assemble
Routes for separate elements such as security.
Account for personnel and equipment, and redistribution of ammo.

6. Action: State a plan for dissemination of information.
Standard: Must state where, who, when, what dissemination is to occur (ORP for a recon patrol, a safe distance away for a combat patrol)

XVI. Task: Issue paragraph 3c of the operation order.

1. Action: State fire support plan. (May be covered when discussing actions at the objective)
Standard: As a minimum, fire support plan would include on call fires of those targets that are capable of preventing the patrol from accomplishing its mission.

2. Action: State plan for rehearsal.
Standard: Must state time place uniform equipment priority and type of rehearsal.
Include as a minimum actions at the objective.

3. Action: State plan for inspections.
Standard: Must include times, places, uniform, equipment, and type of inspections.
If subordinate leaders are to inspect the patrol, they must be designated.

4. Action: State plan for debriefing.
Standard: Place and method of debriefing, who will debrief the patrol.
A statement of the specific information requirements.

XVII. Task: Develop and issue paragraph 4 of the Operation Order.

5. Action: Issue a complete service support plan.
Standard: Include rations, arms, ammunition, uniform, and equipment if not stated in warning order.
A method of handling KIA and MIA, friendly and enemy personnel, POW, and captured equipment enroute and at the objective and in accordance with Geneva convention.

XVIII. Task: Issue paragraph 5 of the Operation Order.

1. Action: State a signal plan and the running password.
Standard: State frequencies, codes, and call signs with higher headquarters, adjacent units, and within the unit.
State the challenge and password.
State hand and arm signals to be used.

2. Action: State the chain of command.
Standard: All patrol members know the chain of command.

3. Action: State leader Location.
Standard: State the location of leader during movement and during actions on the objective.

XIX. Task: Issue appropriate annexes.

1. Action: Issue annexes to support the mission.
Standard: Supports the concept of operation.
Format IAW the Ranger Handbook.
Comply with the information issued in the next higher operation order.

XX. Task: Issue the Operation Order.

1. Action: Issue the operation order in the correct manner.
Standard: Action must be taken to insure that all personnel remain awake.
A time check must be given at the end of the order.
Effectively used training aide and sketches.
Spot check subordinates to insure that order was understood.

XXI. Task: Conduct an initial inspection.

1. Action: Conduct the inspection.
Standard: The inspection must be systematically organized and must be executed by the leader or his designated subordinates (if by subordinates, PL must spot check)
Make on-the-spot corrections, make or have made a list of discrepancies.
Form the unit in garrison to allow all personnel being inspected to observe the inspection of each individual to facilitate rapid correction of common discrepancies (i.e. horseshoe, circle, semicircle)

2. Action: Inspect equipment.
Standard: Check to see that ammo is well distributed and loaded.
Commo, equipment, weapons, uniforms, and all special equipment are present, clean, and operable.

3. Action: Inspect personnel.
Standard: Ask mission oriented questions.
          Correct all erroneous responses.

XXII. Task: Direct and supervise a rehearsal.

1. Action: Conduct the rehearsal.
Standard: The unit must arrive at the assigned rehearsal area at the time specified and with the uniform and equipment specified in the OPORD.

On-the-spot corrections must be made of any deviation from the procedures outlined in the OPORD.

The terrain available in the rehearsal area must be used to gain realism.

Rehearsals must be conducted in the sequence stated in the OPORD unless changed by the PL.

2. Action: Select the most appropriate form of rehearsal.
Standard: The type of rehearsal selected (full force, reduced force or brief-back) must be appropriate to the time available, enemy situation, and light conditions.

3. Action: Rehearse essential aspects of the operation.
Standard: As a minimum, actions on the objective, actions on enemy contact, and actions at danger areas must be rehearsed.

XXIII. Task: Organize and conduct final inspection.

1. Action: Organize the unit for inspection.
Standard: The inspection must be systematically organized and must be executed by the leader or his designated subordinates (if by subordinates, he must spot check.)

On-the-spot corrections must be made and use must be made of the list of discrepancies from the initial inspection.

Form the unit in garrison to allow all personnel being inspected to observe the inspection of each individual to facilitate rapid correction of common discrepancies (i.e. horse shoe, circle, semicircle)

Form the unit in the field by sub-unit while maintaining security or by inspecting on position.

2. Action: Conduct the inspection.
Standard: Check to see that ammo is distributed and loaded.

Commo equipment, weapons, uniforms, and all special equipment are present, clean, operable and tied down in accordance with Ranger SOP.

Spot check to insure tasks are understood.

Insure that no marked maps or notes of military information are present.

That camouflage is present and IAW soldier's manual infantry skill level 1 manual.

Correct deficiencies noted.

XXIV. Task: Direct and supervise an airborne/air assault insertion.

1. Action: Supervise loading of helicopter and monitor flight route.
Standard: Must follow the loading plan as presented in the OPORD.

Must remain oriented in the aircraft and notify personnel on his aircraft of each check point.

2. Action: Supervise assembly.
Standard: Conduct a security/assembly/listening halt out of sight of the LZ/LD.
Request and receive a status report of personnel and equipment from his subordinate leaders.
Checks and determines location within 200 meters.

XXV. Task: Direct and supervise an air assault extraction.

1. Action: Supervise ex-filtration by helicopter
Standard: Recon PZ to insure no enemy, present, conditions safe for helicopters to land.
Establish rally points near PZ, establish and maintain security.
Mark PZ, (mirror, VS-17 panel, smoke. Etc.)
Control air traffic IAW Ranger Handbook Chapter 7
Formulate and follow a loading plan
Remain oriented during flight, announces checkpoints.

XXVI. Task: Direct and supervise departure of a friendly unit.

1. Action: Move to and occupy detrucking point.
Standard: Must link up with the guide at a predesignated point.

2. Action: Effect final coordination.
Standard: Must issue a contingency plan prior to departing for the CP.
Take the guide, compass man, and communications.
If there has been previous coordination, the leader must determine if there are any changes. If there has been no previous coordination, he must coordinate completely in accordance with the Ranger Handbook.
Information obtained must be disseminated prior to departure of FFU.

3. Action: Depart Friendly Forward Unit.
Standard: Depart quickly and silently
Execute a security/listening halt out of sight and sound of friendly lines.

XXVII. Task: Move a small unit cross-country.

1. Action: Control Navigation.
Standard: Make a map study of the route before beginning movement.
Be able to pinpoint location within 200 meters when asked.
Check with the compass man's azimuth on the leader's own compass and corrects deviations.
Follow the planned route or modify it based on the enemy's situation and/or terrain.

2. Action: Move tactically.
Standard: Use movement technique appropriate to the likelihood of enemy contact.
Avoid known or suspected danger areas.
Maintain security when crossing danger areas.
Maintain light and noise discipline and establish and maintain security at halts.
Arrive at destination in time to accomplish mission.

3. Action: Establish rally points.
Standard: Designate rally points enroute as appropriate.
Rally points must be easily identifiable and should provide natural cover and/or concealment

4. Action: Maintain personnel accountability.
Standard: Account for all personnel as minimum after all halts and after crossing danger areas and obstacles.
Maintain rate of movement based on METT
Take actions to prevent breaks in contact.

5. Action: React to chance contact with an enemy force.
Standard: Direct patrol to take cover and make an estimate of the situation
Issue specific orders consistent with the situation. (orders must be tactically sound i.e. attack, defend, or withdraw.)
Effectively employ automatic weapons, indirect fire, and special weapons as applicable.
Establish security and call in spot report after action is complete.
Maintain positive control throughout the encounter.

6. Action: Move in a timely fashion consistent with the tactical situation.
Standard: Complete the move within the designated time.

XXIX. Task: Select, direct, and supervise the occupation of an ORP.

1. Action: Recon the ORP.
Standard: Halt the unit and establish security prior to reaching the tentative ORP.
Issue a complete contingency plan before departing to recon the tentative ORP.
Take appropriate personnel to recon the tentative ORP (i.e. compass man, security, and communications)
Select and ORP based on METT
Secure and maintain surveillance on the site prior to occupying it.

2. Action: Occupy the ORP.
Standard: Maintain security, light, and noise discipline during occupation.
Occupy the ORP in a planned controlled manner.

Inspect to see if final preparations were completed in the ORP before conducting actions at the objective (i.e. all equipment present, personnel re-camouflaged.)

XXX. Task: Conduct a leaders recon

1. Action: Prepare for Leader's recon
Standard: Must issue a contingency plan prior to departing on the recon
Take appropriate subordinates

2. Action: Establish a release point.
Standard: Establish a release point between the ORP and the objective in a position that is concealed from the objective OR state that the ORP will be the release point.

3. Action: Pinpoint the objective/ambush site.
Standard: Identify the objective and leave surveillance personnel at the Objective.

4. Action: Conduct the recon.
Standard: Selected positions must be pointed out to subordinate leaders. Leader's Recon team must not be compromised to the point of aborting the mission.

5. Action: Confirm the plan.
Standard: Ensure the plan, as stated in the OPORD, will work; or make adjustments as necessary to meet the actual situation by issuing a FRAGO

XXXI. Task. Conduct actions at the objective.

1. Action: Prepare for the reconnaissance.
Standard: The leader must check with surveillance personnel for changes before moving into position.
Establish and maintain security during actions at the objective.

2. Action: Execute the reconnaissance.
Standard: Must be executed in accordance with the OPORD or FRAGO
Available equipment must be used (i.e. NVG, Binoculars, etc.)
Stealth must be maintained.
If detected, must take appropriate action (i.e. withdraw to a predesignated position, reorganized if required and, if all information has not been gathered, return and complete the reconnaissance.)
Make a detailed sketch or take a picture of the objective.

XXXII. Task. Conduct actions on the objective.

1. Action: Begin actions at the objective.
Standard: Depart the ORP in an order or movement that facilitated occupation of positions.
The leader must check with surveillance prior to or upon moving into the PLD.
Security must be established prior to moving into positions and maintained throughout actions at the objective.
If compromised while moving into position, initiate the assault.
Automatic and special weapons must be positioned and used in accordance with METT.

2. Action: Conduct the Assault.
Standard: Assault must be initiated upon signal and with mass casualty producing fires.
Fire and maneuver using individual rushes must be used until fire superiority has been established.
The leader must control the fighting with subordinate leaders responding to his orders.
When resistance is overcome, the objective must be secured.

3. Action: Accomplish the mission after the objective is secured.
Standard: A search of the area and enemy must be carried out and recorded.
Casualties (enemy and friendly) must be identified, treated, per Geneva convention.
All PW's must be handled in accordance with OPORD
Ammo must be redistributed
The unit must withdraw from the objective within three minutes after all special teams have completed their mission.

XXXIII. Task: Conduct an ambush

1. Action: Begin actions at ambush site.
Standard: Security elements employed to cover avenues of approach into site to preclude enemy detection.
Type of ambush selected consistent with the expected target.
Type and formation of ambush suitable for the terrain.
Do not cross/enter the kill zone.

2. Action: Emplace the ambush.
Standard: Emplace automatic and special weapons to provide coverage of entire kill zone
Place individuals and sectors of fire to completely cover the kill zone.
Enforce noise and light discipline to preclude detection by enemy.
Establish/maintain communications with all subordinate leaders

3. Action: Conduct the ambush.
Standard: Initiate ambush with mass casualty-producing weapon.
Initiate when bulk of enemy force is in the kill zone.
Search all enemy and equipment if applicable
Capture all living enemy at the ambush site and then destroy or capture all enemy equipment.
Blindfold and gab all captured who cannot be secured/properly controlled.

XXXIV. Task: Direct and supervise withdrawal from an objective and dissemination of information.

1. Action: Move to the ORP of rendezvous point.
Standard: Must maintain security at the ORP or clear rendezvous point prior to occupation.
Account for all personnel and equipment at the ORP rendezvous point.

2. Action: Disseminate information.
Standard: Conduct dissemination at a safe location (ORP for a recon, at least one terrain feature or a safe distance away for combat or a compromised recon.)
Maintain security during dissemination (at least 75% of personnel on alert)
All SIR which was gathered and verified must be disseminated to subordinate leaders.
Must allow for subordinate leaders to disseminate information.
Information must be recorded and sketches of the objective must be made.
Light and noise discipline must be enforced.

XXXV. Task: Conduct reentry of friendly unit lines.

1. Action: Occupy the RRP.
Standard: The RRP must be located out of sight and sound of friendly lines.
Security must be established and maintained in the RRP.
Must make required reports to higher headquarters and wait for confirmation prior to departing
Issue a contingency plan prior to departing.
Take the compass man, two security men, and communications.

2. Action: Reenter a friendly unit.
Standard: Locate the reentry point.
If reentry point is not located after initial probe, return to RRP. Per OPORD?SOP, contact higher headquarters or wait until daylight before attempting further probing.
Respond to the challenge with the correct password.
Each member of the unit must be counted and recognized as he passes through the wire.

3. Action: Accomplish actions for, in, and around the entrucking/departure point
Standard: The unit must occupy a location in proximity of the entrucking/departure point.
The leader must take the guide, compass man, and communications with him whenever he departs the patrol.
He must issue a contingency plan prior to departing the patrol.
The spot report should provide only information of immediate tactical value to the forward unit.
XXXVI. Task: Debrief a patrol upon completion of an operation.

1. Action: Conduct the debriefing.
Standard: All members of the unit must participate.
All information gathered must be collected and recorded in the correct format (i.e. Patrol report).
Detailed sketches or pictures must be prepared o any enemy positions encountered to include dimensions of any fortifications and/or crew-served weapons, distances between items on the objective, north-oriented arrow, locations of enemy personnel, direction and evaluation of crew-served weapons, and paths walked by sentries. Etc.

2. Action: Turn in information to debriefing officer/NCO (RI)
Standard: The report, any supporting documents (maps, sketches, etc), all captured enemy equipment and/or documents and Dog Tags of KIA must be turned in.

XXXVII. Task: Occupy a Patrol Base.

1. Action: Begin actions to occupy a patrol base.
Standard: PL must halt the patrol away from the tentative patrol base.
Establish all around security.
Issue a complete contingency plan to the APL.

3. Action: Recon the tentative patrol base.
Standard: PL must take only the necessary personnel for navigation, communications, and security.
Patrol base is away from danger areas and likely areas of enemy activity.
PL must personally inspect the tentative patrol base.

3. Action: Occupy the Patrol Base.
Standard: Occupy the patrol base in accordance with one of the techniques described in the Ranger Handbook.
Utilizing the natural cover and concealment, light and noise violations must be corrected.
The PL must direct/supervise the final adjustment of the perimeter.

R and S Team(s) must be dispatched to reconnoiter the area around the patrol base.

4. Action: Emplace LP/Ops
Standard: As a minimum, LP/OP must immediately be established and on the route of the patrol leading into the patrol base.
OP/LPs must be briefed on duties, what to do if contact is made, and what to do if the patrol base comes under attack.
Communications must be established with the LP/Ops.

XXVIII. Task: Conduct patrol base activities.

1. Action: Assign priorities
Standard: PL must designate which activities are to take place, the sequence they will take place, personnel to accomplish specific actions, an alert plan, probable move out time, and a time for stand-to.
Work priority will include as a minimum: commo with higher headquarters, weapons maintenance, personal hygiene, rest, and medical evacuation/care.
Designate an alternate patrol base.
Issue an evacuation plan.

2. Action: Continue patrol base activities.
Standard: At a minimum, 20-25% of personnel must be awake and on security.
Automatic weapons must be placed on the most likely avenue of approach or where the leader feels they will offer the best protection for the perimeter and increase his control and flexibility of their use. (PL must explain his decisions to the RI)
Develop a fire plan.
Supervise established tasks.

XXXIX. Task: To move Patrol utilizing trucks.

1. Action: Brief Truck Drivers.
Standard: Brief drivers on routes, actions on enemy contact, truck interval, and speed.

2. Action: Inspect trucks.
Standard: Inspect the following: fuel, oil, water, battery, tires, windshield wiper, brakes, and turn signals. Insure that canvas and bows are off, troop seats up, sandbags on floor, tailgate down, troop safety strap off. Inspect drivers' physical condition.

3. Action: Position patrol leader and key individuals.
Standard: Position IAW OPORD

4. Action: Cross load the patrol on trucks.
Standard: Personnel and equipment loaded IAW truck annex of OPORD.

5. Action: Maintain orientation/location.
Standard: Locate all checkpoints; be able to give location when asked within 200 meters; arrive at correct detrucking point.

6. Action: Depart on time.
Standard: Patrol departs on trucks within 5 minutes of time schedule.

7. Action: Communicate between trucks/NES
Standard: Follow paragraph 5 of OPORD.

XXXX. Task: Link-up with adjacent unit.

1. Action: Preparation for linkup.
Standard: Call in correct phase line or spare, prior to link-up.
Occupy a rally point near the link-up point.
Issue a detail contingency plan to the APL or PSG before reconning for link-up site

2. Action: Conduct of Link-Up
Standard: Navigate to the actual link-up site.
Maintain communications with the patrol.
Secure the link-up site.
Use near and far recognition signals.

3. Action: Movement of unit through link-up site.
Standard: Patrol leader moved quickly and easily back to patrol or have it brought forward.
Passage into the friendly unit area controlled and expedited.
Task: Select and occupy a patrol base for a small unit.

4. Action: Select and occupy a false patrol base.
Standard: PL must recon and secure the false patrol base using an appropriate number of personnel.
PL must insure that security is established and maintained.
PL must supervise the accomplishment of the following priorities of work:
    Security
    Maintenance of weapons
    Personal Hygiene
    Eating

Release, plan etc., for use of actual PB, where appropriate.

5. Action: Select and occupy a clandestine Patrol Base for a small unit.
Standard: The actual patrol base must afford maximum cover and concealment and multiple routes of withdrawal.
The patrol should use maximum stealth.
Security must be established and maintained. Claymore mines and STANO devices must be properly emplaced.
Disseminate plan for quick evacuation.

XXXI. Task: Establish a defensive position.

1. Action: Issue instructions to subordinates.
Standard: Instructions must be clear, tactically sound, and understood by all. Instructions must include changes to organization, if needed, defensive sectors, and priority of work as a minimum.

2. Action: Maintain security.
Standard: Establish early warning (i.e. security patrols, LP/OP, STANO devices)
Supervise subordinates in maintaining security at all times.
Emplace noise and light discipline.
Position automatic and special weapons to cover avenues of approach and to mutually support each other if possible.
Detect enemy movement through early warning system.

3. Action: Maintain communications.
Standard: Maintain communications with higher headquarters and with subordinates units at all times.

XXXII. Task: Conduct a defense.

1. Action: React to enemy movement.
Standard: React IAW Pare 4-17, 4-18, and 4-23 FM 7-10.
Display initiative and determination.
Supervise subordinates.
Maintain positive control.
Maintain control of rates and direction of fires.
Inform higher Headquarters of situation at earliest opportunity.

XXXXII. Task: Move a small unit by boat

1. Action: Prepare boats, equipment, and personnel for movement.
Standard: Establish security at the preparation site.
Insure boats are properly inflated and serviceable/.
Insure equipment is properly waterproofed and secured within the boat as necessary.

Insure that personnel are wearing life preservers correctly and weapons are properly secured.
Assign personnel and equipment to boats so as to disperse key assets. (leaders, radios, automatic weapons, etc)

2. Action: Control Navigation.
Standard: Make a map study of the route before beginning movement.
Embark on time.
Be able to pinpoint location within 200 meters when asked.
Employ proper techniques of water navigation.
Follow the planned route.
Debark at the correct drop site.

3. Action: Move tactically.
Standard: Maintain proper dispersion between boats.
Maintain light and noise discipline.
Maintain positive control throughout the boat move.
Maintain communications with higher headquarters.

4. Action: Debark and continue mission.
Standard: Establish security at the drop site/.
Debark personnel in a orderly manner.
Prepare boats properly for recovery
Reorganize the patrol quickly.
Account for all personnel and equipment.
Clear the drop site quickly.
Maintain noise and light discipline.

XXXXIII. Task: Select a crossing site.

1. Action: Establish security.
Standard: Halt the patrol out of sight of the stream.
Emplace security up and down stream on the near shore.
Maintain light and noise discipline.

2. Action: Recon crossing site.
Standard: Locate near and far shore anchor points.
Avoid obstacles in stream/.
Brief bridge team commander on crossing site.

XXXXIV. Task: Direct, prepare, and control a patrol during stream crossing.

1. Action: Supervise preparation for crossing.
Standard: Insure that personnel and equipment are properly prepared for stream crossing.

Insure that the one rope bridge is constructed correctly.
Insure that the near and far shore lifeguards are in position prior to patrol members crossing stream.

2. Action: Control stream crossing
Standard: Insure personnel cross in the designated order of movement.
Insure that light and noise discipline is maintained during crossing.
Insure a continuous smooth flow of personnel during crossing.

3. Action: Maintain security.
Standard: Insure that security is established on the far shore and adjusted as personnel cross the stream.

XXXXV. Task: Reorganize and continue mission.

1. Action: Account for personnel and equipment.
Standard: Insure that all personnel except the near shore lifeguard and equipment have crossed the stream prior to disassembly of the bridge.
Insure that all components of the bridge kit are accounted for and secured.
Account for all special equipment (radios, binoculars, starlight scopes, etc.)

2. Action: Depart stream-crossing site in a timely manner.
Standard: Issue necessary instructions to continue mission and depart bridge site in 30 minutes.

(END)

APPENDIX E

Physical Fitness Training

General William T. Sherman in a speech to his troops near the end of the American Civil War said, "Young men think that war is all glory, but boys, war is all hell." Over the years that portion of the speech has been shortened to the simple phrase "WAR IS HELL," and few people even know who said it. Many things make war a hell, but perhaps the physical strain takes as great a toll as any other factor. I make no attempt to be profound when I say that war is inevitable. History is profound! History extrapolated predicts war. This coupled with the published force structure says very plainly that anyone in the National Guard should be prepared in every way that they can to survive the inevitable.

Total physical readiness, then, is very important to me. Total readiness includes mental and physical readiness. Without mental readiness, you lack the incentive and confidence and without physical readiness, you lack the stamina. I think this philosophy applies equally in war and in peace; to a military person as well as to a civilian who faces a stressful life. The army has had its ups and downs over the years in a lot of areas, but it's physical training program has always been of the highest quality. Certainly there can be no doubt that they have trained more people than any other organization or corporation in the world. Their database and experience factor is solid for over 40 years and millions of trained personnel and that is hard to argue with.

FM 21-20 is the Army's "bible" of physical training and includes programs for individuals as well as teams. Because I think that military style physical training is so easily adapted to hectic modern-day schedule of busy people; I have extracted those portions of FM 21-20 that could be of benefit to individuals who want to stay fit and don't know where to start. The millions of people who have been conditioned using these techniques should be proof enough that the techniques work; only I did not get through RANGER School using a paperback, get-fit-quick-program written by some pure competitive, athlete, coach, or sports physician.

Physical readiness includes a healthy body, the capacity for skillful and sustained performance, the ability to recover from exertion rapidly, the desire to complete a designated task, and the confidence to face any situation. Physical readiness training must be carefully planned and executed. To do this you must understand the many considerations involved in the development of an effective program.

People vary in their physical makeup. The body reacts differently to varying degrees of stress, and no two bodies react the same to the same stress. To attain the maximum benefit from training, each person must know these basic physical differences between people in general and between males and females.

The average 18-year old male is 70.2 inches tall and weighs 144.8 pounds. The average female of the same age is 64.4 inches tall and weighs 126.6 pounds. The male's greater height gives him greater lung volume speed, and power. Since he is 20 to 25 percent heavier, the male has more explosive and throw power. The percentage of muscle mass compared to total body weight is 50 percent greater in the male. Even if the female is the same size as her male counterpart, she will be only 30 percent as strong as the male, due in part to this physical difference. This means the male usually has an advantage in speed and power over the female.

Females have 20 to 30 percent more body fat than do males. The location of this body fat is another important factor to know. Men accumulate body fat primarily on the back, chest, and abdomen. Women accumulate fat on the waist, arms, and thighs. Thus, the center of gravity is lower in the female than in the male. This makes the female more buoyant and stable, but she has to overcome more resistance in activities requiring lower body movement.

Females have less bone mass than males, but their pelvic structure is wider. This gives the male an advantage while running, because he does not sway as much from side to side. When the arms are extended in front of the body, hands touching and palms upward, most females' arms form an X, but most males' arms form straight lines extending from the shoulders. The angle of the female forearm in relation to the upper arm causes reduced leverage. This is a distinct disadvantage for most females when doing an exercise such as a pushup.

The female's heart is 25 percent smaller than the male's. The male's heart can thus move more blood with each heartbeat. The larger heart size is related to the slower heart beat (five to eight beats a minute slower) in males. This slower heartbeat is evident while at rest and at all levels of exercise. Most females become fatigued sooner at all levels of exercise. The male has 8 percent more red blood cells than the female. Since red blood cells carry oxygen in the body, and since oxygen is the primary ingredient in energy production, the male has a definite advantage. Most females tire quicker than males because women usually work closer to their maximum capacity than men.

The lung capacity of the male is 25 to 30 percent greater than that of the female. This gives the male another advantage in the processing of oxygen.

There are two types of body heat. The first type consists of higher internal body temperature and is caused by physical activity. The other is the outside temperatures that act with humidity to produce heat stress on the body. Women have higher body temperatures and fewer sweat glands than do men. Women, therefore, do not begin to sweat until higher body temperatures are reached. Since women have more fatty tissue, which acts as an insulator, it is harder for them to release their excess body heat. As a result, they are more susceptible to heat injury during physical activity than men.

Two important conclusions should be evident from the discussion above. First, most females must work harder to accomplish the same tasks as males. Second, most males can sustain a greater work rate than their female counterparts.

Understanding the physical differences between males and females is but the first step in planning physical training. The American Medical Association's Committee on Sports believes there is no reason for women to be more susceptible to athletic injury than men. However, adequate physical readiness should be developed before extensive physical stress is undertaken. The legs are particularly susceptible to injuries and discomforts. Shin splints and stress fracture injuries can occur, if conditioning is not achieved before demands become too great.,
An exercise program should not begin unless one is in good health. It would be advisable to have a doctor check you over and concur in the level of activity that you plan to engage in if you have not engaged in physical activity for a long period of time. If you are over 35, the importance of a physical exam prior to beginning is even more important. Individuals who have high risk factors should exercise only under the supervision of trained medical personnel.

Extensive research has documented the relationship between the eventual development of heart disease and the risk factors of high blood fat content (Cholesterol), high blood pressure, smoking, family heart disease, fatness, and abnormal electrocardiogram. Exercise can play an important role in reducing these risk factors. I have been keeping in shape with military-style exercises since 1963 and I think my score in RANGER school against a class average age of 23 is testimony that exercise is good for you.

However, improper exercise in a high-risk population could be dangerous. It is unwarranted to assume that an individual is not a high risk just because he works hard all day or because he was a high school football hero. Antedates about the "picture of health" person dropping dead during a sandlot soccer game are commonplace. In a study designed to evaluate these risk factors in subjects over 35, an increased amount of risk factors was noted among the sample.

Anyone who is about to begin an exercise program should be made aware of these risk factors. If you have two or more of the following characteristics, consult a physician before beginning an exercise program:

- HYPERTENSION (blood pressure above 140/90)

- Family history of heart disease (one parent with heart disease)

- Excessive smoking

- High fat levels in the blood

- Diabetes

- Obesity (more than 20 percent overweight)
  Inactive lifestyle

No one who has disease of the arteries, a history of heart attacks, or any other serious medical problem should begin an exercise program except under the supervision of trained medical personnel.

The most serious problem encountered as a result of an exercise program is the possibility of heart attack. Therefore, if an individual develops chest pain or any other abnormal signs (for example, unusual sweating or breathlessness, dizziness, faintness), exercising should stop and medical attention should be sought.

Heat Exhaustion or heat stroke can result from exercise and may become serious. Exercise on hot days should take place either early in the morning or late in the afternoon so as to avoid the hottest parts of the day. Exercise programs should be canceled or curtailed on very hot, humid days in order to avoid heat injury.

The most common problems in running will be foot, ankle, knee, and leg injuries. Although it is very difficult to totally eliminate such injuries, a great deal can be done to keep them to a minimum. First of all, many such injuries can be prevented by using proper footwear. Running shoes must fit properly, and they should have multi-layered, flexible soles with adequate arch and heel support. Nylon uppers are usually the most comfortable. The type running surface will determine the injury rate. Soft surfaces are best for injury prevention. Running should be conducted on grassy areas, parade fields, dirt paths, or park trails whenever possible.

Clothing should be comfortable and loose fitting. A T-shirt and gym shorts are best in favorable weather. In cold weather, clothing may be added according to preference, such as a sweat suit, a jogging suit, or even long underwear. In very cold weather, gloves and ear-protecting caps may be necessary. Plastic or rubberized suits are not advisable because they cause excessive sweating and because they prevent evaporation and can lead to dehydration and a dangerous rise in body temperature.

Proper warm-up and cool-down periods with stretching exercises will also help prevent injuries. Warm-up exercises are an especially important part of, any injury prevention program. During moderately cold weather you can run in a T-shirt and long trousers but you should have a long-sleeved, hooded garment to put on while you do your cool-down exercises.

People who have problems with their knees may wish to add leg exercises that specifically strengthen the thigh muscles (quadriceps). Strengthening these muscles will help prevent knee injuries. Examples of such exercises are leg lifts, knee bends with weights (squats), and many of the grass drills.

Physical readiness can be defined as those factors that determine ones ability to perform heavy, physical work and those that help maintain good health and appearance. Factors or components of readiness are:

· Muscle Strength

· Muscular Endurance

Cardio respiratory Endurance

Other factors, such as speed, agility, coordination, and balance, are more properly classified as components of "motor" fitness. The components of physical readiness are based on the sources from which energy is derived for muscular activity. The first source, the one most immediately available, is the family of phosphate chemical compounds stored in the muscle fibers. The supply of these compounds, however, is very limited; it is lost quickly by even brief muscular work. Non-repetitive pushing or lifting actions are examples of stored energy being used. This aspect of readiness is commonly referred to as muscular strength.

One improves muscular strength by increasing the amount of muscle tissue and its stored energy content. The next source of energy, in order of availability, is energy derived from chemical processes, which require no oxygen (anaerobic). This energy-producing pathway is characterized by a partial breakdown of food stores (primarily carbohydrates), which requires no oxygen in the chemical action. It is a source of muscular energy in circumstances where oxygen delivery has not yet met the demands, as at the beginning of intense exercise or when the need for energy exceeds that made available by oxygen. A 100-yard sprint is an example of anaerobic activity. The third source of energy is from processes, which require oxygen (aerobic). In contrast to the non-oxygen component, carbohydrates and fats are completely broken down by chemical reactions that require oxygen. This pathway is slower to yield energy since the oxygen has to be delivered from the outside air through the lungs and blood. However, it is much more efficient; it produces more usable energy for the same amount of food-stores burned. Walking and cross-country running are typical aerobic activities.

Other terms commonly used and which have the same meaning as aerobic fitness are stamina and Cardio respiratory endurance. The term aerobic fitness is used here since it represents specifically the energy-producing component involved. The physiology of aerobic fitness is well known.

Aerobic energy production is composed of the following steps;

> Ventilation of the lungs with air

> Movement of oxygen from the lungs into the blood stream

> Delivery of oxygen-laden blood to all tissues of the body by the heart

> Regulation of blood vessel size to distribute blood, e.g. away from inactive tissue and toward active muscle

> Movement of oxygen from blood to the muscle cells

> Breakdown of food-stores with oxygen to produce energy in the form of phosphate compounds

> Breakdown of food stores with oxygen to produce energy in the form of phosphate compounds

An individual's aerobic fitness is determined by the sum of the size or capacity and the efficiency of all of these components of the aerobic cycle. Use (training) of the cycle will expand one or more of these components and thus increase the aerobic power and capacity. In contrast, disease may reduce some components and thus decrease the aerobic fitness.

Aerobic fitness is a function of four types of factors:

Genetic

Activity or training

Environment

Health

It is generally believed that approximately 80% of one's aerobic potential is genetically determined, leaving about 20% that can be modified by training. To achieve exceptionally high levels of aerobic fitness, as seen in national or Olympic-caliber athletes, a person must virtually inherit a high potential for aerobic fitness in addition to training hard to fully develop it. Beyond the inherited level, the usual way to expand aerobic level is by continually performing physical readiness training. By repetitively tasking the body beyond its previous level, one can achieve a higher level of physical readiness.

The genetic factor is expressed in the size and quality of the aerobic cycle components listed above. Thus, some individuals inherit a larger heart, greater blood flow capacity, and a particular makeup of muscle fibers in the large skeletal muscles. A number of factors may decrease aerobic fitness.

These include:
Age

Anemia (red corpuscles of the blow are reduced in number, or their content is deficient).

Carbon monoxide from tobacco smoking or pollution

High altitude exposure (oxygen deficient)

Illness or disease
Much of the decrease in physical readiness typically seen with increasing age is due to inactivity, but this need not be so. An hour a

day may seem like a big investment of time but then the return on investment is so great. My continued good health is worth the investment. There is a great deal of satisfaction and pure pleasure to know that even at over 40 (when I first wrote this; now 61), I can still keep up with and even outdo most soldiers in their 20's. I am simply not ashamed to say there is a sense of accomplishment and pride when presented with the bulging waistlines of the non-exercise crowd and listen to their labored breathing as they struggle up a few flights of stairs. And yes, there is some amusement as I listen to them promise themselves and others that they are going to have to get back on a program of exercise or diet and lose a few pounds. Only they can do it. Talking about it will not do it!

Any condition which reduces the ability of blood to carry oxygen will also reduce the person's aerobic fitness. Anemia is a condition of reduced oxygen-carrying blood cells, while carbon monoxide blocks blood cells from carrying oxygen. Medical conditions that impair oxygen transport and therefore reduce aerobic fitness include diseases of the lungs, which interfere with breathing; disabling heart conditions; and severe blocking of arteries and veins, which interferes with blood flow.

In summary, a healthy individuals aerobic fitness is determined by a complex formula that includes genetic factors and a long list of unknowns and wild guesses, modified by training and environmental conditions. Most people, though, I am convinced can control their physical destinies if they have the will to do so. Like getting through RANGER school, will power is a very strong factor. It is not easy. For most people, it is very difficult to keep up the kind of training program necessary to maintain the balance of good health, good fitness, and good feelings about themselves to the extent that they are satisfied with the return on the investment of time and effort and sacrifice.

The purpose of an aerobic training program is to improve the capacity of the aerobic-cycle components to deliver oxygen to the working muscle. Improvement is achieved by subjecting the body to a stress (e.g. running) and allowing it to recover. This stress should not be so severe that it takes 3 or 4 days to recover. It is not necessary to become excessively fatigued and develop sore, aching muscles in order to train. A good thought to keep in mind is: TRAIN DON'T STRAIN. A major problem with beginners in a training program is that they try to do too much, too soon. They become excessively fatigued, develop muscle soreness, become discouraged, and drop out; or, in the case of people who are doing it solely due to some kind of peer pressure rather than because they want to, develop negative attitudes. To avoid these pitfalls, it is important for beginners who have not been exercising regularly, to start slowly. Improvement can be achieved without placing excessive stress on the body. It must be kept in mind that many individuals, especially those in sedentary jobs, may not have exercised regularly for many years. The effects of years of inactivity will not be reversed by a few days or weeks of exercise. Remember, it took years to create those extra cells filled with pounds of fat; it cannot be reversed safely in days or weeks. The training program should start with a workload that is easily handled. The workload should be gradually increased in order to achieve a proper training effect. The reason for the slow start is to give the muscles and circulatory system a chance to adapt to the new routine. In the beginning, workouts should be at least three tines per week, with a day or two of rest between workouts. After the first two or three weeks, the load and frequency per week may be increased.

Whatever you do, consult with your healthcare giver before starting any exercise or diet program.

Cycling, swimming, and cross-country skiing are all good aerobic exercises, but they require special equipment or facilities. An easily administered, inexpensive, and efficient aerobic exercise is running. Because of the popularity and year-round availability of running, the major focus is on the initiation and maintenance of a running program. However, alternative forms of exercise will also be discussed for those who may be unable to participate in a running program.

Every exercise session should begin with a warm-up period of 5 to 10 minutes. The purpose of the warm-up is to loosen and stretch the muscles. This should be done slowly and gently, not with quick, jerky movements. The tendency of many exercisers is to get it over with quickly so they can get on to other things they really want to do more so they rush through the warm-up or simply skip it altogether. A particular effort should be made to stretch the muscles in the back of the thighs and the calf. A word of caution is in order here. If you have a history of lower back pain, sciatic, lumbago, etc., exercises that stretch the leg muscles must be chosen carefully so that the back muscles are not over stretched. A standard, flatfooted, feet together toe touch is especially not good for people with back trouble, nor for anyone for that matter.

There are two exercises that are very good for warm-up. The first involves placing the feet shoulder-width or further apart and alternating the touching of toes with the opposite Hand, i.e., right hand to touch left foot and vice versa. This exercise stretches the back thigh muscles (hamstrings) but is not as hard on the back as the standard toe touch. This is not an endurance or speed event. Move slowly and deliberately, perhaps not even touching the toes for the first few cycles but eventually touching the toe, and even spreading the feet further apart to increase the reach required. The second exercise that can be used is to stand slightly more than an arm's length away from a wall, or other vertical support, with feet apart and toes pointed slightly in. Extend the arms forward and press the palms against the support, leaning against it while keeping the heels on the ground. Gradually lean closer and closer to the support. Repeat this about 10 times, each repetition lasting 5 to 10 seconds. This is good for stretching tile calf muscles and for treating and preventing shin splints (muscle pulled away, the bone). These exercises should be supplemented with other events such as bent-leg sit-ups, pushups, side straddle hops, and bend and reach. Another good calf stretcher is to stand on the bottom tread of a stair, facing up the stairs. Balance on the leading edge of the tread with your toes (lead part of the foot). Lift yourself up on the toes slowly, and then allow yourself to go down until the heels are lower than the toes, then back up. This exercise will fool you so just do a few the first time and work into it slowly.

A physical readiness training program should be divided into three phases: PREPARATORY, CONDITIONING, and MAINTENANCE. Each phase represents a step toward a high level of physical readiness. The phase at which a person begins should vary, depending upon physical condition, activity history, and in most cases, age. A young, healthy person may be able to start with the conditioning phase. One who has been exercising regularly may already be in the maintenance phase. However, those who have been sedentary, especially if they are over 35, overweight, or both, should begin with the preparatory phase.

The purpose of the preparatory phase is to develop the Cardio respiratory system and the muscles of the legs so that they are accustomed to exercise. In other words, to build muscles to handle the stress of the conditioning phase. To achieve this, begin by walking 14 to 20 minutes, three times per week. Walk at a comfortable pate, but do not overdo it. Continue at this level until there is no undue fatigue or muscle soreness a day or up to three days after the event. The onset of soreness after strain varies with levels of strain and with and among individuals. Once this point has been reached, increase the time to 20 to 25 minutes and walk at a faster pace. When a brisk walk for 20 to 25 minutes can be successfully handled, begin by alternating walking and jogging for 20 to 25 minutes. Begin each session by walking and gradually increase the amount of time spent jogging. If you feel uncomfortable (breathless), while jogging, slow down and walk. Continue to alternate until jogging can be maintained for 10 minutes. When this can be done the preparatory phase is completed. Don't be condemned about what the general public thinks or does as you walk and jog along. As popular as jogging is, there are still those motorists who get some sort of charge out of jeering, horn honking, and wisecracking when they meet or pass exercisers. Then I often see runners who seem to think there is some sort of embarrassment or stigma to be felt if they have to slow to a shuffle or walk. They quickly return to a run when a car or another runner suddenly appears over the hill or around the curve, and back down again when the intruder is past. Don't worry about them. It's your body. Do what is good for it.

The purpose of the conditioning phase is to begin the expansion of the physical capacity of the Cardio respiratory system. This is done by increasing the amount of time spent running. Starting with the 10 minutes running time that was achieved during the preparatory phase, gradually increase running time by 1 or 2 minutes each workout until running is continuous for 20 to 25 minutes. This should be done at least three times a week. During the conditioning phase, the frequency of exercise, i.e., the number of times per week may be increased. However, it is not essential because a frequency of three times per week is an adequate training stimulus. During this phase, running speeds will probably become faster. By the end of this phase, a distance of about 2.5 miles in 25 or 30 minutes is a realistic goal. Remember that, during this phase, a physical readiness capacity is increased by increasing running time (duration) and running speed (intensity). Follow the same guidelines given in the preparatory phase. Breathlessness is a sign of training too hard, so slow down. If fatigue and sore muscles occur in the days following the exercise, it indicates that the intensity is too great, and the running should be adjusted accordingly.

Once the preparatory and conditioning phases have been completed, it is desirable to keep physical readiness at the level achieved in those phases. This is the purpose of the maintenance program. Most exercise experts agree that a workout of 20 to 25 minutes, three times per week, will maintain good physical readiness. Workouts should always be preceded by warm-up exercises and followed by cool-down periods. During the maintenance phase, it may be desirable to continue increasing the running time and frequency. A realistic goal, initially, would be 30 to 45 minutes of exercise 5 days a week. Anything beyond this should be gradual. Increasing the workout slowly will avoid injury due to excessive stress. Individuals who have the desire and the capability should be encouraged to go beyond the minimum level. The maintenance phase should become part of your lifestyle. The benefits of an exercise program wear off rapidly once the program is discontinued. For that reason, the maintenance phase should become an indefinite phase.

There are factors, which prohibit an individual from participating in a running program. Therefore, certain activities may be used as supplements or alternatives to running. Swimming, cycling, and cross-country skiing are excellent endurance exercises and are adequate substitute for a running program but they require more than a pair of shoes and trunks. Rope skipping is another good exercise for large muscle mass. However, it is of such high intensity that it is difficult to continue for more than a few minutes. Some runners use it as a substitute for running during bad weather. Handball and the racquet sports (tennis, squash, and racquetball) involve bursts of intensive activity for short duration. Activities of this type do not provide the same degree of aerobic training as exercises of longer duration at lower intensities. However, these sports do provide some aerobic benefits and are excellent supplements to an aerobic training program. If played on a daily basis, they could even be an adequate substitute for minimal aerobic training. Because it increases endurance, running would probably help improve the performance in these sports, but the reverse is not necessarily true.

A discussion on the benefits of running can spark a controversy about as quickly as politics, particularly from the people who dismiss running as a passing fad or an irrational response to subconscious anxiety. The benefits of running go far beyond simple Adidas sport togs, electronic pulse counters, and devices to keep pesky dogs from chasing you at O5OO in the morning. It affects the personality and attitude. The ability or capacity for running has been shown capable of predicting success in one field and I suspect that it could be reliably linked to success and drive in many other areas. Running is after all one of the most natural things that man does. He has been bounding around chasing food and fame probably since he first stood erect and made a fist.

From August to November 1978, a research team from the Army Research Institute Field Unit at Fort Beginning, Georgia, collected data on strength and cardiovascular fitness (stamina) from all entering airborne trainees. Among other questions, the project sought to answer the question, " which physical fitness test events are the best predictors of success?" Individual success was defined as "successful if he finished his airborne training with the same group with which he started." The major reasons why people were disqualified were "low motivation, poor physical fitness, medical problems, administrative problems, and failing either the mock tower or the swing-landing trainer phase of training." As an interesting note, most of the medical problems which caused people to be turned back were injuries incurred during the morning runs. The conclusion was that "upper body strength, trunk strength, and stamina are all important contributors to Airborne training success, with stamina being the most important." Also, as reported by Frederick Dyer and William Burke in the INFANTRY Magazine, "the two mile run also proved the best predictor of Airborne training success." To show that running is more than running, the study showed that those who failed due to low motivation had run the two miles a full minute slower, on the average, than the successful soldier." Those who failed because of confidence-related events (the mock tower and swing-landing trainer) "had run the 2-miles half a minute slower, on the average, than the successful soldiers."

There are five principles of physical readiness; Progression, Overload, Balance, Variety, and Regularity. To allow for adjustments in body functioning as the-program progresses, and to insure attainment of objectives, the principles of physical readiness must be applied.

PROGRESSION: In the beginning stages, the load must be moderate. Gradual progression from this low state of physical readiness to a higher state is possible through application of a progression program.

OVERLOAD: To reach the desired level of physical readiness; the physical load must be increased as strength and endurance increase.

BALANCE: An effective program utilizes various types of activities and provides for development of strength, endurance, flexibility and coordination, as well as basic physical skills.

VARIETY: Some programs fail because the routine becomes boring. The most successful programs include conditioning activities as well as some competitive events.

REGULARITY: There is no easy or occasional way to develop physical readiness. Regularity of exercise is a must. Daily exercise is best, but every other day is the recommended minimum routine. You can crash diet and lose enough to get into that special outfit for a weekend affair, but you cannot "crash exercise" without possible injury. If you want to be in shape and stay in shape, then it simply must become a way of life, and I think it is certainly a way TO life .... longer life that is.

The end objective of military physical readiness, to survive on the battlefield, is of course different from the civilian's objective in physical readiness; but some of the intermediate objectives of military physical readiness are interesting to contemplate and I think challenging. They are to;

· Develop sufficient strength and endurance to sustain activity over a long period.

· Develop muscle tone adequate to maintain good posture and reasonable weight.

Develop proficiency in physical skills essential to personal safety and survival to include:

      X   Running- Distance and sprint running on roads and cross-country

      X   Jumping- Broad jumping and jumping down from a height

      X   Dodging- Changing direction rapidly while running

      X Climbing and Traversing - Climbing ropes, poles, walls, and cargo nets; traversing horizontal objects such as ropes, pipes, and ladders.

      X Crawling - High and low crawling for speed and quietness

      X Throwing - Propelling objects such as grenades for distance and accuracy.

      X Vaulting - Crossing over low objects such as fences and barriers by use of hand assists

      X Carrying - Carrying objects and employing man-carry's.

      X Balancing Maintaining body balance on narrow walkways and at heights

      X Falling - Dropping to the ground from standing, running, and jumping positions.

In acquiring the above skills, a number of benefits are generated which are equally applicable to military or civilian. These benefits are:

      ➢   Improves muscular tone and develops muscular strength and endurance. Improves Cardio respiratory endurance, or wind, by increasing lung capacity to absorb more oxygen.

      ➢   Speeds up circulation of the blood and forces it to serve all parts of the body, and improves the efficiency of the heart, lungs, and blood vessels.

      ➢   Maintains flexibility and develops the ability to rapidly accomplish a greater number of physical tasks.

➤ Regulates and assists elimination of body waste through the bending and twisting of the body and the speedup of body pressures.

➤ Relieves tension through working off of excess energy.

➤ Often improves sleep because of the natural relaxation that follows exercise. A by-product of sound sleep is often relief of tension.

➤ Helps control fat (obesity) by using up excessive fat-producing food elements.

➤ Reduces susceptibility to injury. Muscles, tendons, and joints are strengthened and injuries such as hernia, back strain, and joint sprains are less likely to occur if muscles are maintained in proper order and tone.

The Human Body

Everyone who undergoes physical conditioning should possess a practical understanding of the nature of physical readiness. To intelligently condition the human body, one must understand the way exercise affects the body organs and systems, and they should also be aware of the disadvantages of being unconditioned. The human body must be understood before the proper techniques can be employed to condition it. If you do not understand how the body functions, you may fail to properly condition yourself. With a basic understanding of how the body functions, one can develop an effective physical readiness training program. With knowledge, a solid program can be developed and fads, which are often projected as shortcuts to physical readiness, can be avoided.. To be effective one must understand the relationship of physical and mental readiness. Physical and mental health cannot be separated. Poor physical readiness can be caused by mental as well as physical disorders. A sound mind is characterized by cheerfulness, confidence, and interest. An unhealthy state of mind is characterized by indifference, discouragement, worry, or a feeling of inferiority. The physical readiness training program can improve the mind as well as the body.

Attaining physical readiness is not an overnight process; the body must go through three phases. During the preparatory phase, the body goes through a soreness and recovery period. When a muscle with a poor blood supply (such as a little-used muscle) is exercised, the waste products produced by exercise collect faster than the blood can remove them. This acid waste builds up in the muscle tissue and irritates the nerves in the muscle fiber, causing soreness. As the exercise program continues, the body is able to circulate the blood more rapidly through the muscles and remove the waste materials, which causes the soreness to disappear. As the body passes through the preparatory phase and into the second, or conditioning phase, the volume of blood circulating in the muscles increases, and the body functions more efficiently, In the first few weeks, the Improvements are rapid, but as a higher level of skill and conditioning is reached, the improvement becomes less noticeable. During these first two phases, the body has reached a level of physical readiness near to or at peak condition. In some cases, it may be a plateau beyond which the individual can progress only through a continued rigorous training program. During the final, or continuing, or maintenance phase it is necessary to continue exercising at approximately the same intensity to retain the condition developed. For example, a person who has been trained until he is in excellent condition will lose his readiness on a 20-day break if he does nothing to maintain it. For the human mechanism to remain conditioned, a maintenance program should be instituted.

Through strenuous exercise, it is possible to maintain readiness in 20 - 25 minutes a day, three times a week.

When the individual reaches their highest level of readiness, they are at their "crest load" If he increases the amount of exercise, "oxygen debt" may develop (that is, his muscles may develop more lactic acid than the blood can carry away), and they may be forced to stop their exercise. Continued training can raise the crest-load level. This is an important consideration in physical readiness training.

Use of muscles improves strength and endurance; disuse results in wasting away or lack of growth. Stated another way, muscles are developed through exercise in proportion to the intensity of the exercise. With a certain amount of exercise, muscles develop only enough to perform that amount of exercise with ease. Only the number of muscle fibers needed to move a given load are brought into play. If there is no further increase in the demand, there is no improvement in muscle function or in strength or endurance. To improve the amount of work a muscle can do, the demand must be increased. For example, it is assumed that an individual is able to lift a weight of 40 pounds with the right arm. If this individual were to exercise with a weight of only 3 or 4 pounds, they could exercise until the muscle was practically exhausted, and still such exercise would not markedly increase the strength of the muscle, as they already have more than enough strength to handle that much weight. On the other hand if this individual were to exercise with a 40-pound weight, they would tire rapidly, perhaps in five or six movements. If they were to continue to exercise with this load until they could raise it 15 or 20 times, and then increase the weight to 45 pounds, then to 50 pounds, adding additional weight as the strength increased, the muscle would develop in size and strength very rapidly. Another example may be found in circulorespiratory endurance. To train to the point of being able to run a mile in 4 minutes and 20 seconds, you would have to run faster and faster until this point was reached. If, on the other hand, you were to run a mile in 10 minutes every day, you could do this for many, many years and still not be able to run a mile in 6 or 7 minutes. The overload principle, then, means that the readiness of the individual develops in proportion to the demand placed on it. Conversely, if the individual does less exercise than they have been accustomed to doing, they rapidly "de-conditions." Hence, people in sedentary jobs, with opportunity for only mild exercise, rapidly lose their physical readiness. The overload principle does not mean that the individual should be overloaded to the point of undue strain. It means that the physical requirements must be over his usual load. In the use of conditioning exercises, the individual can increase the intensity either by increasing the cadence or by adding to the load carried. In running, for example, the speed (cadence) can be increased. The theory of overload is one of the most important principles for physical readiness that you must understand.

Regular exercise has a tendency to increase the appetite. The body benefits if this desire for greater amounts of food is satisfied with a balanced diet. There are two main types of foods; bodybuilding foods consist of proteins, which build up and maintain body tissue. Energy-producing foods are of two types; carbohydrates and fats. Carbohydrates provide a quick source of energy, while fats act as a reserve of energy. In addition, food contains vitamins, mineral salts, and water. During hot weather and strenuous training periods, the liquid intake should be increased. Proper diet should be supplemented with proper rest to provide the digestive system with time to digest food back into the system as energy. Occasionally, violent exercise may cause vomiting. Vomiting is a natural occurrence and under normal circumstances should not be considered dangerous. Exercise during prolonged exposure to high temperature may result in heatstroke. One of the symptoms of heatstroke may be vomiting. In such case, the vomiting is a danger signal.

Continuous exercise, particularly among younger people, usually brings about certain beneficial changes to the bones. For example, regular exercise causes the cancellous plates (spongy tissue) of the bones to became strengthened and rearranged so they can stand up under greater stress and strain. Bones that are not used lose a large part of their minerals. This should be considered when you return to the readiness program after a prolonged period of inactivity. People in this category should restrain themselves from activities that might result in bone breakage before the stimulus of use has brought the bone back to normal condition.

When a muscle is exercised vigorously enough to strengthen it, it grows. Hence, the larger the muscle (other things being equal), the stronger the muscle. It is apparent that conditioned muscles function more smoothly and more efficiently than unconditioned ones. They are able to contract somewhat more vigorously and with less effort. To insure that muscles are developed to their potential, overload must be applied. Regular and strenuous exercise of the muscle also toughens it. The muscle tissue becomes firmer and can stand much more strain. This is due partly to a toughening of the sheath that protects the muscles, and also to the development of more connective tissue within the muscle bundles. Muscular endurance enables one to continue a relatively heavy load of exercises over a long period of time. For example, many people can shovel dirt for 5 minutes without experiencing undue fatigue; however, continued digging at the same rate for an hour causes then to become exhausted. We experience the muscular exhaustion brought about in local muscle groups by pushups, sit-ups, and other tests of endurance. Here the local muscle groups fatigue rapidly, but the individual is not exhausted. This type of endurance is almost entirely a combination of strength plus improved local circulation in the muscle. To improve muscular endurance, the length of workouts should be increased.

Both speed and agility are qualities related to strength and, to an extent, to muscular and circulorespiratory endurance. They are developed through specific skills that should be learned and practiced in the physical readiness-training program that you devise to suit your lifestyle. As you begin to develop your physical abilities, you increase your strength and endurance, partly because you have developed better coordination and more skill and are now using only the muscles that are relevant to the task. On the other hand, an unskilled performer may use many muscles, which are not needed, thus increasing the amount of physical work without increasing the output of mechanical work. Increase in skill is a highly desirable development, but it should be offset by an increased dosage of exercise to compensate for a possible loss in overload, which occurs when fewer muscles are used. When the rate of work is increased, the energy required is much greater than the increase in rate. For example, if you double your running speed, the amount of energy required is increased 8 times. You should be careful when you increase the speed of an exercise, to guard against making too great a demand in the length of time the exercise is performed.

When strenuous exercise is regularly pursued over a prolonged period ' the blood vessels within the muscular tissue increase in number. This increase is due partly to the number of new capillaries, which increase as much as 50% in the same volume of muscle. It is also due to the opening of the latent capillaries, which, when combined with the new capillaries, may increase the circulation as much as 400%. This gives a much greater supply of food and oxygen to the muscle, thereby increasing its endurance. It takes about 8 to 12 weeks for this increase to take place in young adult. A longer period is required as you age. To be effective, the exercise must be regular. After a period of 8 to 12 weeks of inactivity or light activity, these extra capillaries become inactive.

The heart is the chief organ of circulorespiratory endurance. The lungs transmit the oxygen from the air to the blood, but it is the heart that propels this blood through the blood vessels to the tissues If the heart fails to deliver sufficient oxygen-carrying blood to the muscles, the body quickly becomes exhausted. The heart is a muscular organ and is developed by exercise just as any other muscle. However, the heart cannot be singled out and exercised alone. In every readiness program there should be some exercises that will develop wind. Exercises of speed, carried out over a fairly long period, will rapidly develop the heart. One of the results of a speed exercise is that the heartbeat tends to become slower in rest, and each heartbeat pumps out a greater amount of blood. This is known as an increase in "stroke volume," a desirable condition because it enables the heart to pump more blood with a slower contraction rate. Whenever you get out of condition, the nerves controlling circulation relax and the legs and internal organs tend to collect excess blood in their vessels. In this state, if you engage in strenuous activity or are subject to emotional pressure, you may experience temporary brain anemia due to a lack of readily available blood to the brain. This may be to the extent that you may experience dizziness, or faint. Exercise will stimulate the movement of blood to and from the heart and counter this condition.

In tracing the circulation of the blood, the cycle begins at the point where the carbon-dioxide-laden blood is returning to the heart. A large vein, the vena cava, carries the blood to the right auricle (upper chamber) of the heart. This blood then passes through a valve into the right ventricle (lower chamber). At this point, the blood leaves the heart by way of the pulmonary artery for processing in the lungs. In the lungs, the carbon dioxide is exchanged for oxygen, and the purified blood is returned to the heart by way of the pulmonary vein. The blood then reenters the heart at the left auricle (upper chamber) and passes through a valve into the left ventricle (lower chamber). Here it is pumped into a large artery (aorta) for passage to the body. As the blood moves into the muscles, it gives off oxygen and takes on carbon dioxide. Moving through the capillaries into the veins, the blood is ready for the return trip to the heart. When there is a demand upon the heart brought about by strenuous and continued exercise, the efficiency with which the lungs transmit oxygen to the blood is increased as much as 25 Percent.

To Download FM 21-20

FM 21-20 is in US Military Academy West Point digital library.

To download as a .pdf go to:

www.usma.edu/dpe/testing/**fm21_20**.pdf

APPENDIX F

Collection of quotes associated with the art of war and leadership

(Credit for originator given where known)

The most vital quality a soldier can possess is self-confidence, utter, complete, bumptious.

Patton

Don' tell a man how to do a job. Tell him what you want accomplished and you'll be amazed at his ingenuity.

Patton

It is very easy for ignorant people to think that success in war may be gained by the use of some wonderful invention rather than by hard fighting and superior leadership.

Patton

There is only one kind of discipline; perfect discipline. If you do not enforce discipline, you are potential murders.

Patton

There is only one tactical principle, which is not subject to change. To so use the means at hand to inflict the maximum amount of wounds, death, and destruction on the enemy in the minimum amount of time..

Patton

About Russians, Patton said: "I have no desire to understand them except to ascertain how much lead or iron it takes to kill them. Someday we will have to fight them and it will take 6 years and cost us 6 million lives."

It is the cold glitter of the attacker's eye, not the point of the questing bayonet that breaks the line.

Patton

All men are afraid in battle. The coward is the one who lets his fear overcome his sense of duty.

Patton

Many soldiers are led to faulty ideas of war by knowing too much about too little

Patton

To be a successful soldier you must know history.......what you must
know is how man reacts......to win battles you do not beat weapons –
you beat the soul of man.

Patton

At the heart of all sound teaching through the centuries, whether within
military institutions or without, has dwelt the simple idea that every
vigorous man needs some kind of contest, some realization of
resistance overcome, before he can feel that his is making the best use
of his faculties.

Patton(?)

The Army is a team. It lives, eats, sleeps, trains as a team. The
pusillanimous son of a bitch that writes that individuality crap for the
Saturday Evening Post doesn't know any more about fighting than he
does about fornicating.

Patton

In battle, casualties vary directly with the time you are exposed to
effective fires. Your own fire reduces the effectiveness and volume of
the enemy's fire...Battles are won by frightening the enemy. Fear is
induced by inflicting death and wounds on him. Death and wounds are
produced by fire.

Patton

War is simple direct ruthless; it requires a simple direct ruthless man to
wage it.

Patton

If a man thinks war long enough it is bound to have a good effect on
him

Patton

It is immensely important that no soldier, whatever his rank, should wait
for war to expose him to those aspects of active service that amaze and
confuse him when he first comes across them.

Jomini

A soldier is just as proud of the hardships he has overcome as of the dangers he has faced.

Gustavous Adolphous

One could never see better illustrated, by contrast, the value of physical and moral energy, bodily endurance against stress of weather, hunger, thirst, all the hardships of war----- in a word, that stoicism which comes not suddenly but gradually, from military training, and which, after all, is simply the ingrained spirit of honor and duty.

Rousset after the battle of Katzbach (One of Napoleon's worst defeats 26 Aug 1813)

All things that count cannot be counted. All things that can be counted, don't count.

Albert Einstein

Character is habit.

Aristotle

Just because we are paranoid does not mean they are not out to screw us.

COMNAVFORLANT
CS Wes Jordan Nov 87

The first lesson of wing walking: Never let go of what you have until you have a grip on something better.

CofS Wes

Jordan 29 Dec 87

After Gettysburg, the Union Army picked up 37, 574 muskets. 24,000 were still loaded. 6000 had one charge; 12,000had two charges; 5999 had 3-10 charges; and one had 23 charges. That was one excitable soldier.

A soldier must be someone capable of holding out indefinitely with only some boiled beef and crackers for food; sleeping in the open air in his wet clothes, walking until he falls down exhausted, only to get up again and march into combat.
Montgomery

Far better it is to dare mighty things, to win glorious triumphs, even though checkered by failure, than to take rank with those poor spirits who neither enjoy much nor suffer much, because they live in the gray twilight that knows neither victory nor defeat.

Roosevelt, April 1899

Exertions must be practiced, and the mind must be made even for familiar with them than the body.
Alexander

In this inadequate training for the hardships of war, and in the lack of discipline to overcome them, lies the chief reason for the failure of improvised armies.
Maj Gen Baron von Freytag-Loringhouse

The reply of the Delphian Oracle when asked what Sparta had most to fear was one word----**Luxury.**

(Sparta fell in 371BC after the battle of Leuctra in which the Thebans beat the Spartans.)

The best form of welfare for troops is first class training.
Rommel

He who fails to read history will live to err again that which he could have known.
Von Moltke

He who moves in a element such as war must bring with him from books nothing but a trained mind
Mao

The most essential qualities for a general will always be: First, a high moral courage, capable of great resolution; Second, a physical courage which takes no account of danger. His scientific or military acquirements are secondary to these. It is not necessary that he should be a man of vast erudition; his knowledge may be limited but it should be thorough, and he should be perfectly grounded in the principles of the base of the art of war. Next in importance come the qualities of his personal character. A man who is gallant, just, firm, upright, capable of esteeming merit in others instead of being jealous of it, and skillful in making this merit add to his own glory, will always be a good general and may even pass for a great man.

Clausewitz(?)

Only willpower can substitute for the confusion caused by poor intelligence.

Clausewitz

War is the domain of physical exertion and suffering. If one is not to be overcome by them, he must possess a certain bodily and spiritual strength, native or acquired, which makes him indifferent to them.

Clausewitz

Boldness, the outstanding military quality, the genuine steel which gives to arms their luster and sharpness

Clausewitz

Boldness must imbue the force from the camp follower and private to the commander in chief.

Clausewitz

Boldness, a quality which becomes less and less common as we progress up to the higher grades.

Clauseswitz

A man who has nothing for which he is willing to fight; nothing he cares about more than his own personal safety; is a miserable creature who has no chance of being free unless made and kept so by the exertions or better men than himself.

John Stuart Mill

Silence is the only successful substitute for brains

Will Rogers (?)

The art of war is simple enough. Find out where your enemy is. Get at him as soon as you can. Strike at him as hard as you can and as often as you can, and keep moving on.

U.S.Grant

Superiority lies with he who is reared in the severest school

Thueydidies

Capabilities take a long time. Intentions can change overnight.

Gen John Galvin

War means that humble homes are laid waste with hurricanes of fire and widows are turned out roofless with their little children to wander unfriended the wastes of their desolate land.

Mark Twain

There are certain principles that make up the permanent psychology of human beings, that must be applied not only at the level of nations and armies, but also to the field of action inhabited by privates and corporals and lieutenants. Clausewitz warned us never to talk about such things outside the framework of bloodshed lest we make the world of grand strategy, strategy and tactics something it is not – antiseptic, sanitary, and salutary.

Battle is not a terrifying ordeal to be endured; It is a magnificent experience wherein all of the elements that have made man superior to the beasts are present.

Archimedes

That which immediately sets a man apart is that his intelligence be in equilibrium with his courage.

Bonaparte

I would define true courage to be a perfect sensibility of the measure of danger, and a mental willingness to incur it, rather than that insensibility to danger of which I have heard far more than I have seen

Sherman

It is a moral quality, it is not a chance gift of nature like an aptitude for games. It is a cold choice between 2 alternatives, it is the fixed resolve not to quit, an act of renunciation which must be made not once but many times by the power of will. Courage is will power.

Moran

I do not believe there is any man who would not rather be called brave than have any other virtue attributed to him

                                         Field Marshall Slim

History has shown that personal honor is the one thing valued more than life itself by the majority of men
                                         SLA Marshall

Placing the line of duty above the line of self-interest is all that distinguishes the soldier from the civilian
                                         SLA Marshall

For those who haven't fought for it, freedom has a taste the protected will never know

                              Unknown; scrawled on a c-ration
                              Carton at Khe Sahn Viet Nam

War must be carried on systematically, and to do it you must have men of character activated by principles of honor.

                                         Geo Washington

Brilliancy is not needed in war, but only accuracy, character, and simplicity.

                                         Napoleon

The Army is the most outstanding institution of every country for it alone makes possible the existence of all civic institutions.

                                         Von Moltke

A man's greatest joy in life is to break his enemies, and to take from them all things that have been theirs.

                                         Genghis Khan
Discipline is the soul of the army. It makes small numbers formidable; procures success to the weak, and esteem to all.

                                         Geo Washington

My Lord, If I attempted to answer the mass of futile correspondence that surrounds me, I should be debarred from all serious business of campaigning. I must remind your lordship, for the last time, that so long as I retain an independent position, I shall see that no officer under my

Command is debarred, by attending to the futile driveling of mere quill-driving in our lordship's office, from attending to his first duty which is, and always has been, so to train the private men under his command that they may, without question, beat any force opposed to them in the field.

Attributed to Wellington

An army is a repository of the dominant moral qualities of the parent state

Gen Sir John Hackett

No social policy has yet been devised to make an energetic people out of a community of pusillanimous and enfeebled citizens

DeTocqueville

I am tired and sick of war. It glory is all moonshine. It is only those who have never fired a shot nor heard the shrieks and screams of the wounded who cry aloud for blood, more vengeance, and more desolation. War is hell.

Sherman, 26 Nov 1914

In our times, we have permitted military thinking to become clouded by what social workers, psychiatrists, business counsel, public-relations advisers and morale experts have to say about what is proper in an army organized according to American standards, meaning the standards which are upheld in American institutions of a quite different nature. The military leader has become an unhappy worrier, confused and buffeted between rival groups of medicine men, each vending some special magic. He is told that a new order has arisen, that the rising generation is somehow different, that industrial change has revolutionized the military problem, that how he is presented to the public cuts more ice than what he really is and how he thinks, and that modern science and business methodology can rub a lamp and come up with the perfect answer to every age-old military problem. Simply to cut through part of this murk, I suggest that the pressure upon the Army in time of war (and in peace) to duplicate all of the comforts, habits and usage's of civilian living does not derive mainly from social causes or from what the rank and file demand because of what they have experienced in a different environment. Its mainspring is the commercial research for a profitable market.

LSA Marshal (I think)

When the pot boils, the scum will rise to the top

Grandfather Childers

It is not the critic who counts, nor the man who points out how the strong man stumbled or where the doer of deeds could have done them better. The credit belongs to the man who is actually in the arena; whose face is marred with sweat and dust and blood; who strives valiantly; who errs and comes up again and again; who knows the great enthusiasm; the great devotion, and spends himself in a worthy cause; who at best knows in the end the triumph of high achievement and who at worst, if he fails, at least fails while doing greatly so that his place shall never be shared with those cold and timid souls who know neither defeat or victory.

??

To predict the future is not as easy nor as sure as measuring the past
CDC

Courage cannot be instilled by contractual arrangement
CDC

Two categories of performance: Good and right.
CDC

A man becomes what he thinks about
CDC

You are what you do.
CDC

The Army should never be a laboratory for social experimentation.
CDC

Never assume that a person knows their job or that they will perform it to your satisfaction
CDC

You have an obligation to listen appropriately as opposed to an obligation not to talk too much to those who have the obligation to listen
CDC

Excuseaholics see themselves as victims of forces that prevent them from doing what they intended to do. Excuses are irrelevant. Excuses have no merit.
CDC

Good intentions are not a substitute for good performance
CDC

Three elements of war fighting: the plan, the execution, and dumb luck
CDC

In the long run, war does not solve anything, though it gratifies some and horrifies others. It relieves frustration in some; causes it in others. Casualties generate a constant stream of new players into the game who then become proponents for new rules that cause new frustrations which leads to subsequent wars in a never-ending cycle of war and peace.
CDC

Our society has become so free that pre-occupation with freedom as an end in itself has led us to neglect the responsibilities and obligations that have always been thought to accompany it.
CDC

Stereotypes of excellence are not always what you want---nor military intellectuals
CDC

Though soldiers have made an unlimited liability contract of service, Courage cannot be instilled by contractual arrangement
CDC

Integrity, is the first and last principle of every leader or he/she will be a leader without followers.
CDC

We must seek to serve the nation in the manner it has come to expect of us.
CDC

Don't confuse Progress with the ability to complicate simplicity
CDC

You are only young once; but you can be immature forever
CDC

Victory in combat is not the result of a favorable coincidence of events, but the result of the commander's intense creativity activity and the level of training of each soldier.
CDC

The climate of war is composed of 4 elements: uncertainty, exertion, danger, and luck.

CDC

Build trust and confidence by training long, hard, and good.

CDC

The commander must calm the scared, direct the lost, set the example for the inexperienced, reward the good, counsel those who fall short, and provide discharge for those on whom all of the above fails.

CDC

Training must discomfort you (the leader) as much as the troops.

CDC

Tasking and mission accomplishment drives morale and expirit; not vice-versa

CDC

Pain is a great teacher, as are errors and bad judgment. Better to learn from the mistakes of others.

CDC

No one ever became number one without trying

CDC

Commanders have three primary functions: to give guidance; to make decisions; and to be there.

CDC

If you do things right, you are efficient; if you do right things, you are effective.

CDC

Imagination impoverished is disaster in war

CDC

Skill, daring, and science overcomes superstition, fear, and BS

CDC

Education is a device by which men fool themselves into a sense of efficiency.

CDC

Execution, not the plan, wins the battle

CDC

So the plan goes to hell with the first shot; but the **planning** is still valid and remains the substance that assists in driving on to success
CDC

In the long run, war does not solve anything, though it gratifies some and horrifies others. It relieves frustration in some; causes it in others. Casualties generate a constant stream of new players into the game who then become proponents for new rules that cause new frustrations which leads to subsequent wars in a never-ending cycle of war and peace.
CDC

Leadership is the art of human response to uncertainty
CDC

Experts abound despite the fact that knowledge is scarce
CDC

The world is currently in a state of violent permanent peace
CDC

All of the following are of unknown origin to the author, but noted by a career of reading

Personality and personal preference v.s. policy and execution results in constant turbulence, lack of progress, and inefficiency of the highest order

On the battlefield the real enemy is fear and not the bayonet or bullet.

It is not the question to know a great deal but to know well; to know especially what relates to the mission appointed us.

Cohesion, discipline, confidence, morale, courage, and the will to fight are indispensable in soldiers

The end for which soldiers are recruited, clothed, armed, and trained; the whole object of his sleeping, eating, drinking, and marching is that he fights at the right place and time.

Combat is the culmination of every effort expended by the army to procure, train, discipline, and perfect fighting units.

It is in combat that the sweat of peacetime training finds its purpose

All human beings have an innate resistance to obedience. Discipline removes this resistance and by constant repetition makes obedience habitual and subconscious.

By honoring courage, punishing weakness, disgracing cowardice, we may expect to maintain high military spirit.

Perception is truth. Truth is what each person wants it to be.
The disposition to do justice to merit in others is not the most common quality; mediocre minds are always jealous and inclined to surround themselves with persons of little ability, fearing the reputation of being led and not realizing that the nominal commander of an army always receives almost all the glory for its success, even when least entitled to it.

Never put yourself in a position where you cannot retreat without loss of face nor advance without grave risk.

Analysis should never become a substitute for experience and judgment

Examine "value added" when considering reward and punishment

Awards are given for: what the soldier did for it; and what it does for the soldier who earns it.

The objective of criticism is to educate, not to punish.

To control, you must measure. Measure wisely for those things that can be measured and those things that are worth measuring are not always one.

Unless you do your best, the day will come when, tired and hungry, you will halt just short of the goal you were ordered to reach, and by halting you will make useless the efforts and deaths of thousands.

The peace dividend from the collapse of the wall, is the absence of war, and through 1999, about $800B. The peace dividend is a very uneasy peace.

To do right things is to be effective. Leaders must do this
To do things right is to be efficient. Everyone must do this, but it is the domain of the soldier

Do things right; do right things. Same words, different arrangement, different meaning, different domain.

Desperate determination to succeed is just as vital to supply as it is to the firing line.
The past is preparation; the present is glorious achievement; the future is threatening decadence

Requirements sometimes come to be regarded as intrusions on individual rights.

Imperfect metaphors and intellectual impurity

Wisdom versus timidity

The power of decision; the power of imagination

Macho mumblings of ego-infested idiots

Assertions of insufficiently competent people

Any dream of world peace is merely the product of a fertile imagination, a malady often encountered in fools who for one or another reason refuse to recognize certain things as manifestly absurd.

Where Ignorance is Bliss, tis folly to be wise

Flay the idle, rebuke the incompetent, drive the timid

Active pursuit is the key to all knowledge and skill

Everyone is a slave to his own experience.

Analysis should never become a substitute for experience and judgment

Examine "value added" when considering reward and punishment

Awards are given for: what the soldier did for it; and what it does for the soldier who earns it.

The purpose of criticism is to educate, not to punish.

To control, you must measure. Measure wisely for those things that can be measured and those things that are worth measuring are not always one.

Requirements sometimes come to be regarded as intrusions on individual rights.

Soldiers have an unlimited liability contract.

The world is currently in a state of violent permanent peace

Experts abound despite the fact that knowledge is scarce

Imperfect metaphors and intellectual impurity

Wisdom versus timidity

The power of decision; the power of imagination

Macho mumblings of ego-infested idiots

Assertions of insufficiently competent people

APPENDIX G

Sheep and Sheepdogs, by Col. David Grossman. PhD

Any dream of world peace is merely the product of a fertile imagination, a malady often encountered in fools who for one or another reason refuse to recognize certain things as manifestly absurd. Which leads me to the theory of the flock.

A PHILOSOPHY WHICH DESCRIBES THE ROLE OF RANGERS

The world is populated by three kinds of people. Their outlook on life and their willingness to step up to challenge, creates a metric with which to compare them to animals as follows. Sheep, and wolves, and sheepdogs.

Most of the people in our society are sheep. They are kind, gentle, productive creatures who can only hurt one another by accident. This is true. Remember, the murder rate is six per 100,000 per year, and the aggravated assault rate is four per 1,000 per year. What this means is that the vast majority of Americans are not inclined to hurt one another. Some estimates say that two million Americans are victims of violent crimes every year, a tragic, staggering number, perhaps an all-time record rate of violent crime. But there are almost 300 million Americans, which means that the odds of being a victim of violent crime is considerably less than one in a hundred on any given year. Furthermore, since many violent crimes are committed by repeat offenders, the actual number of violent citizens is considerably less than two million.

Thus there is a paradox, and we must grasp both ends of the situation: We may well be in the most violent times in history, but violence is still remarkably rare. This is because most citizens are kind, decent people who are not capable of hurting each other, except by accident or under extreme provocation. They are sheep.

I mean nothing negative by calling them sheep. To me it is like the pretty, blue robin's egg. Inside it is soft and gooey but someday it will grow into something wonderful. But the egg cannot survive without its hard blue shell. Police officers, soldiers, and other warriors are like that shell, and someday the civilization they protect will grow into something wonderful. For now, though, they need warriors to protect them from the predators.

Then there are the wolves and the wolves feed on the sheep without mercy. Do you believe there are wolves out there who will feed on the flock without mercy? You better believe it. There are evil men in this world and they are capable of evil deeds. The moment you forget that or pretend it is not so, you become a sheep. There is no
safety in denial.

Then there are sheepdogs and I'm a sheepdog. I live to protect the flock and confront the wolf. If you have no capacity for violence then you are a healthy productive citizen, a sheep. If you have a capacity for violence and no empathy for your fellow citizens, then you have defined an aggressive sociopath, a wolf. But what if you have a capacity for violence, and a deep love for your fellow citizens? What do you have then? A sheepdog, a warrior, someone who is walking the hero's path. Someone who can walk into the heart of darkness, into the universal human phobia, and walk out unscathed

We know that the sheep live in denial, that is what makes them sheep. They do not want to believe that there is evil in the world.

They can accept the fact that fires can happen, which is why they want fire extinguishers, fire sprinklers, fire alarms and fire exits throughout their kids' schools. But many of them are outraged at the idea of putting an armed police officer in their kid's school. Our children are thousands of times more likely to be killed or seriously injured by school violence than fire, but the sheep's only response to the possibility of violence is denial. The idea of someone coming to kill or harm their child is just too hard, and so they chose the path of denial.

The sheep generally do not like the sheepdog. He looks a lot like the wolf. He has fangs and the capacity for violence. The difference, though, is that the sheepdog must not, cannot and will not ever harm the sheep. Any sheep dog who intentionally harms the lowliest little lamb will be punished and removed. The world cannot work any other way, at least not in a representative democracy or a republic such as ours. Still, the sheepdog disturbs the sheep. He is a constant reminder that there are wolves in the land. They would prefer that he didn't tell them where to go, or give them traffic tickets, or stand at the ready in our airports in camouflage fatigues holding an M-16. The sheep would much rather have the sheepdog cash in his fangs, spray paint himself white, and go, "Baa". Until the wolf shows up. Then the entire flock tries desperately to hide behind one lonely sheepdog.

The students, the victims, at Columbine High School were big, tough high school students, and under ordinary circumstances they would not have had the time of day for a police officer. They were not bad kids; they just had nothing to say to a cop. When the school was under attack, however, and SWAT teams were clearing the rooms and hallways, the officers had to physically peel those clinging, sobbing kids off of them. This is how the little lambs feel about their sheepdog when the wolf is at the door.

Look at what happened after September 11, 2001 when the wolf pounded hard on the door. Remember how America, more than ever before, felt differently about their law enforcement officers and military personnel? Remember how many times you heard the word hero? Understand that there is nothing morally superior about being a sheepdog; it is just what you choose to be. Also understand that a sheepdog is a funny critter: He is always sniffing around out on the perimeter, checking the breeze, barking at things that go bump in the night, and yearning for a righteous battle. That is, the young sheepdogs yearn for a righteous battle. The old sheepdogs are a little older and wiser, but they move to the sound of the guns when needed right along with the young ones. Here is how the sheep and the sheepdog think differently. The sheep pretend the wolf will never come, but the sheepdog lives for that day. After the attacks on September 11, 2001, most of the sheep, that is, most citizens in America said, "Thank God I wasn't on one of those planes." The sheepdogs, the warriors, said, "Dear God, I wish I could have been on one of those planes. Maybe I could have made a difference." When you are truly transformed into a warrior and have truly invested yourself into warrior hood, you want to be there.

You want to be able to make a difference.

There is nothing morally superior about the sheepdog, the warrior, but he does have one real advantage. Only one. And that is that he is able to survive and thrive in an environment that destroys 98 percent of the population. There was research conducted a few years ago with individuals convicted of violent crimes. These cons were in prison for serious, predatory crimes of violence: assaults, murders and killing law enforcement officers. The vast majority said that they specifically targeted victims by body language: slumped walk, passive behavior and lack of awareness. They chose their victims like big cats do in Africa, when they select one out of the herd that is least able to protect itself.

Some people may be destined to be sheep and others might be genetically primed to be wolves or sheepdogs. But I believe that most people can choose which one they want to be, and I'm proud to say that more and more Americans are choosing to become sheepdogs.

Seven months after the attack on September 11, 2001, Todd Beamer was honored in his hometown of Cranbury, New Jersey. Todd, as you recall, was the man on Flight 93 over

Pennsylvania who called on his cell phone to alert an operator from United Airlines about the hijacking. When he learned of the other three passenger planes that had been used as weapons, Todd dropped his phone and uttered the words, "Let's roll," which authorities believe was a signal to the other passengers to confront the terrorist hijackers. In one hour, a transformation occurred among the passengers - athletes, business people and parents. -- from sheep to sheepdogs and together they fought the wolves, ultimately saving an unknown number of lives on the ground.

"There is no safety for honest men except by believing all possible evil of evil men." - Edmund Burke

In nature the sheep, real sheep, are born as sheep. Sheepdogs are born that way, and so are wolves. They didn't have a choice. But you are not a critter. As a human being, you can be whatever you want to be. It is a conscious, moral decision. If you want to be a sheep, then you can be a sheep and that is okay, but you must understand the price you pay. When the wolf comes, you and your loved ones are going to die if there is not a sheepdog there to protect you. If you want to be a wolf, you can be one, but the sheepdogs are going to hunt you down and you will never have rest, safety, trust or love. But if you want to be a sheepdog and walk the warrior's path, then you must make a conscious and moral decision every day to dedicate, equip and prepare yourself to thrive in that toxic, corrosive moment when the wolf comes knocking at the door.

The sheep's only response to the wolf is denial, and all too often their response to the sheepdog is scorn and disdain. But the sheepdog quietly asks himself, "Do you have and idea how hard it would be to live with yourself if your loved ones attacked and killed, and you had to stand there helplessly because you were unprepared for that day?"

It is denial that turns people into sheep. Sheep are psychologically destroyed by combat because their only defense is denial, which is counterproductive and destructive, resulting in fear, helplessness and horror when the wolf shows up. Denial kills you twice. It kills you once, at your moment of truth when you are not physically prepared: you didn't bring your gun, you didn't train. Your only defense was wishful thinking. Hope is not a strategy. Denial kills you a second time because even if you do physically survive, you are psychologically shattered by your fear helplessness and horror at your moment of truth.

Gavin de Becker puts it like this in Fear Less, his superb post-9/11 book, which should be required reading for anyone trying to come to terms with our current world situation: "...denial can be seductive, but it has an insidious side effect. For all the peace of mind deniers think they get by saying it isn't so, the fall they take when faced with new violence is all the more unsettling."

Denial is a save-now-pay-later scheme, a contract written entirely in small print, for in the long run, the denying person knows the truth on some level. And so the warrior must strive to confront denial in all aspects of his life, and prepare himself for the day when evil comes.

If you are warrior who is legally authorized to carry a weapon and you step outside without that weapon, then you become a sheep, pretending that the bad man will not come today. No one can be "on" 24/7, for a lifetime. Everyone needs down time. But if you are authorized to carry a weapon, and you walk outside without it, just take a deep breath, and say this to yourself..."Baaaaaa."

This business of being a sheep or a sheep dog is not a yes-no dichotomy. It is not an all-or-nothing, either-or choice. It is a matter of degrees, a continuum. On one end is an abject, head-in-the-sand-sheep and on the other end is the ultimate warrior. Few people exist completely on one end or the other. Most of us live somewhere in between. Since 9-11 almost everyone in America took a step up that continuum, away from denial. The sheep took a few steps toward accepting and appreciating their warriors and the warriors started taking their job more seriously. The degree to which you move up that continuum, away from sheep hood and denial, is the degree to which you and your loved ones will survive, physically and psychologically at your moment of truth.

The above credited to LTC (RET) Dave Grossman, RANGER, and Ph.D., author of "On Killing" and "On Combat," two essential reads for warriors.

No "Baaaaas" from this RANGER. Thank you RANGER Grossman for sharing that philosophy. I am a sheepdog. Childers

APPENDIX H

It was the summer of 1973, as I recall. I was then a Captain in the Army National Guard and the commander of an Armored Cavalry Troop – radically different from Light Infantry. No military assignment was ever more enjoyable. I commanded a separate Cavalry Troop, which means that I had no direct and constant supervision. The next higher level of command was a Squadron. The Squadron Headquarters was in Philadelphia, Pennsylvania. It was rare that Troop C, my Troop, got visits from either the commander or his staff. In part this was because of the geography involved, but also because Troop C was the most proficient Troop in the Squadron and we all knew it and we loved to demonstrate it to any visitor with great enthusiasm. Sometimes we got carried away but regardless of our overzealous self-confidence, oversight folks simply did not expose their depth of knowledge by attempting to find something in our actions that could be criticized. We were hot. But I digress.

The Troop was at Virginia Beach, Virginia conducting weapons training over a weekend. Sometime in the early afternoon on Saturday, my clerk came to me to say that a Navy Chief at nearby Little Creek, Virginia had called for me on the phone and asked that I return his call. The clerk handed me a phone message tab. The caller was Chief Bill Brumaster of SEAL Team II. I could not imagine what he might want. It had been a couple of years since I had contact with Bill, but in 1968 during my tour as Science Advisor to Task Force 116 in the Mekong Delta, Bill was my primary point of contact for scientific, engineering, and quick reaction events.

But I must back up a step first and explain one of the products that I delivered to the forces in Vietnam who are now know as Special Operations Forces. Back then each service had their own independent snake-eaters. There was only SEAL I and SEAL II. No Delta Force. No Special Operations Command. The standard weapon was the M-16; nothing fancy like the M-4 Carbine today. The standard magazine for the M-16 was a 20 round box magazine. Many troops had the debatable practice of only loading it to 18 rounds as there was some antidotal evidence of failure to feed with 20 rounds. The bad guys used the AK-47, which had a standard 30 round magazine. Colt Firearms had tried desperately to make a 30 round magazine for the M-16 but at that time could not. The reason was simple. The more rounds that are loaded into the magazine the more the magazine spring is compressed, thus, the greater the upward or lifting force. This lifting force manifested itself as increased drag on the moving parts of the M-16, causing it to jam or fail to feed. So I had a wonderfully simple idea to overcome this. Rather than use a standard compression spring in the magazine, I employed two constant force springs. What does that mean? It means that as more rounds are loaded in the magazine, the lifting force is not increased proportionally; rather, it is always constant. So it was a relatively straightforward engineering design to select springs that would lift the stack of ammunition at the rate required to meet the cyclic rate of the weapon. The result was a 50 round magazine. Now our side had more firepower between magazine changes than the bad guys.

I invited Cold Firearms representatives down to witness a demonstration. They laughed until they saw it work flawlessly. They could not believe it. They brought their own weapons, probably detuned, just in case the magazine worked in our M-16. They fired the magazine from their weapons; single shot fire, full auto fire, sequential bursts, a whole magazine in one burst. Whatever they tried, the magazine functioned properly.

Having passed a series of tests, an order for 85 magazines was awarded. Upon receipt and test firing of these I packed my duffle bag and took them to Vietnam and shared them with several units in the Navy, Marine Corps, and Navy. I could tell by the reaction of some units as I gave them the magazines that they were skeptical. One thing they did not like about them up front was the length that the magazine protruded from the magazine well. I couldn't argue that point. Several shooters were excited about the prospect of having that capacity but opined they would probably carry that large magazine in a handy pouch rather than have it in the weapon routinely.

The 50 round magazine was introduced to combat in the summer of 1969. The War had already began to receive large-scale protest so by now the war was beginning to spiral down to the extent that the Vietnam Laboratory Assistance Program cut back, new material introduction slowed, and feedback on such items as the 50 round magazine dried up because there was no follow up program. But the magazines were apparently being used in some quarters with great appreciation.

Fast forward from summer 1969 to summer 1973. I returned the phone call to the Chief. After the standard old-time B\S-ing he said, "Look, I have a couple of guys here at the Team that would like to meet you. Can you stop by on your way back up North?" So I said sure, I would be passing through his area somewhere about 1800 and would stop by. Arriving at the building I noted a German Shepard staked out near the walkway. I wasn't sure it was, or could possibly be, a dog that they had 4 years earlier who had a neat trick. All Shepard look more or less the same, but this one sure looked like "Rinny" to me. Rinny had developed this tactic whereby he would paw up his 20' chain in a pile near the stake and then lay on the pile thus concealing how much radius he had. The casual visitor would look at the dog, see a very short chain between the collar and the stake, and make a bad judgment. I started around to another entrance when the Chief came out laughing his @%^*^ off. "I see you remember the trick."

"Come on in. Got a few people that want to see you. Member that 50 round mag you gave us? Well there are a couple guys in town right now from deployment that put it to good use and they want to tell you about it."

He led me on into a small conference room, poured coffee, asked the standard how ya bin what ya doin stuff; then three men joined us, introductions all around, shook my hand vigorously, smiling like I was a long lost uncle, and obviously very glad to meet me. Course I was honored; in the presence of 4 Vietnam heroes and members of SEAL Team II. Most people didn't know what a SEAL Team was at that time.

The story was simple. They found themselves in a tremendous firefight for their lives. It was obvious that the NVA soldiers knew who they were dealing with and were intent on capturing one or more of these SEALs alive. The engagement eventually got down to one combat effective SEAL left pulling a trigger. He said, "It was clear to me that they were in the round counting mode so when I changed mags for the last time, and it was the last mag I had on me, I put in the 50 rounder. They figured that at about my 17th or 18th round, if they all rushed, they could take me with only a couple more of them lost. I can still see the look on some of their faces as I continued to take em out. And that was it. I went to my nearest teammate and grabbed a couple of his mags just in case and changed out the 50 rounder. It had two rounds left in it; three counting the chambered round. That mag saved our @%^*^. These two (pointing at the other two SEALs) were *taking a nap*[6] at the time."

I never felt better in my life to that point.

RANGERS LEAD THE WAY

---

[6] Of course it wasn't a nap they were taking; they were wounded out of action

APPENDIX I

ILLUSTRATIONS

Follows are sketches of the various obstacle courses at RANGER School as I remember them. Childers.

THE RANGER PUSH-UP
ONCE ADMINISTERED, NEVER FORGOTTEN

RANGER   PUSH-UP

CAT WALK

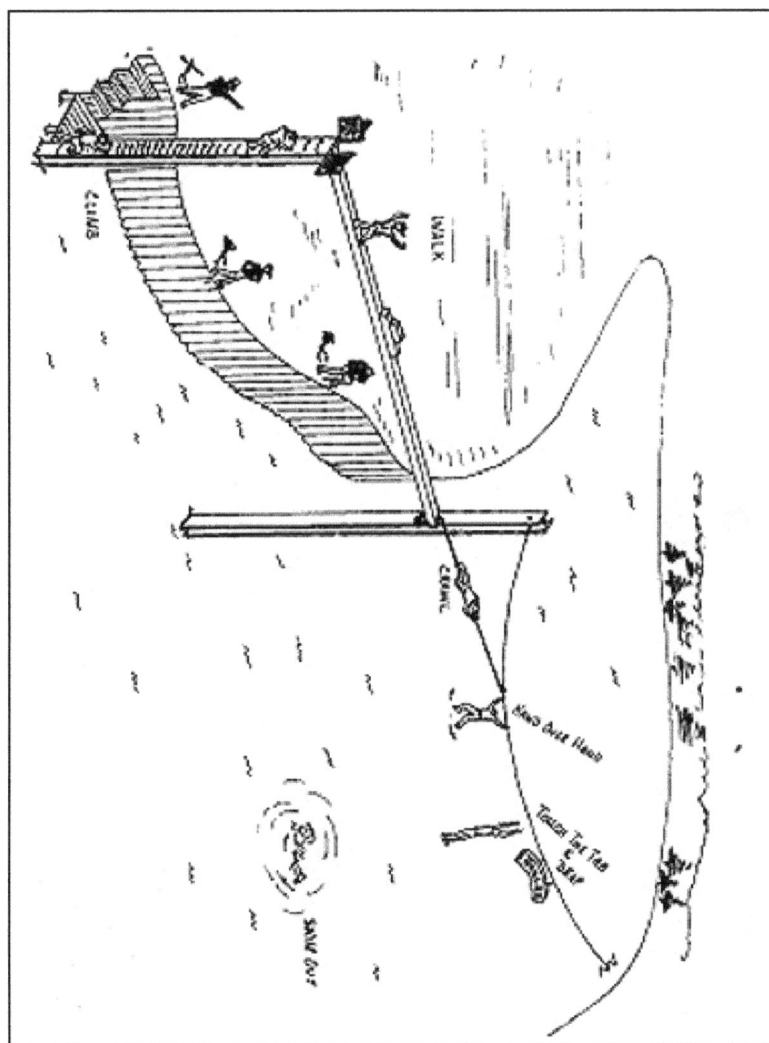

SHORT CONFIDENCE COURSE

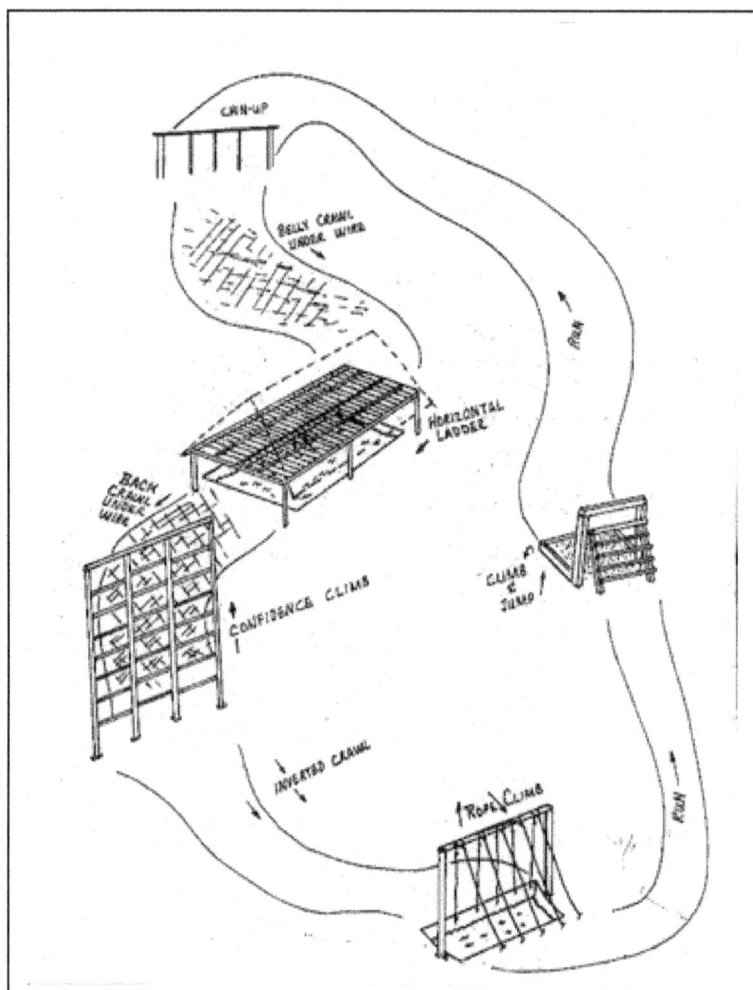

DARBY QUEEN

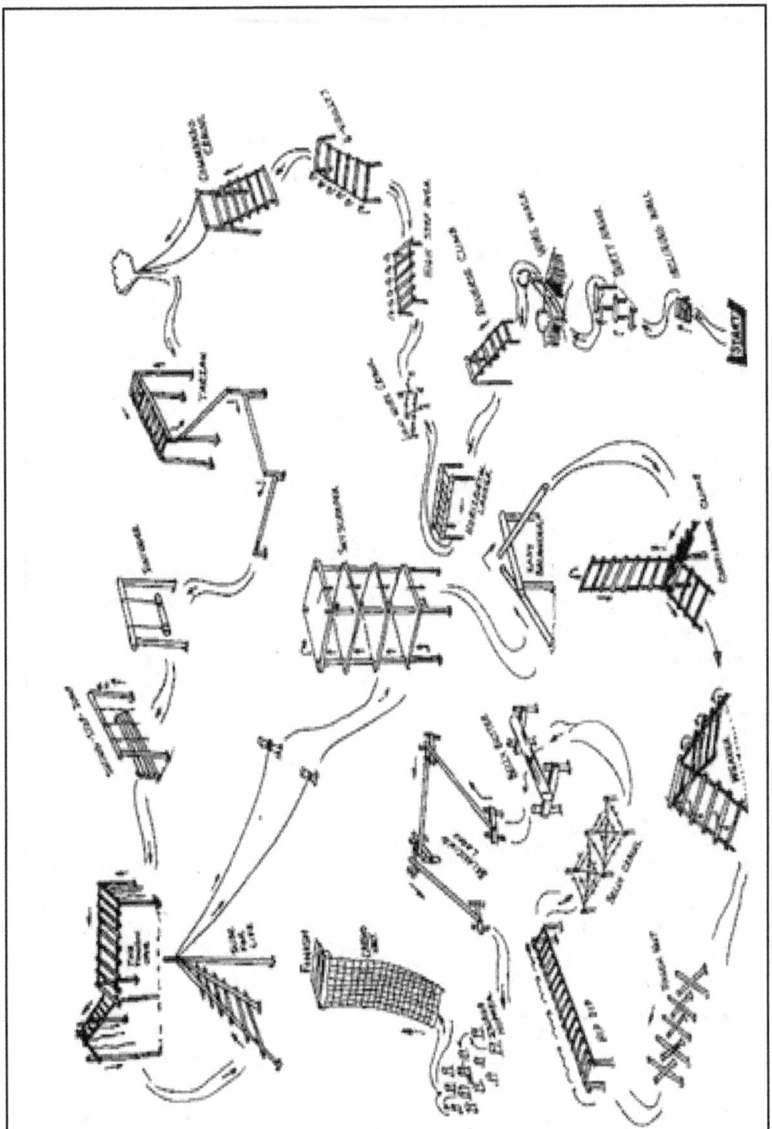

FIGURE 5

RAPPELLING TOWER

SLIDE FOR LIFE

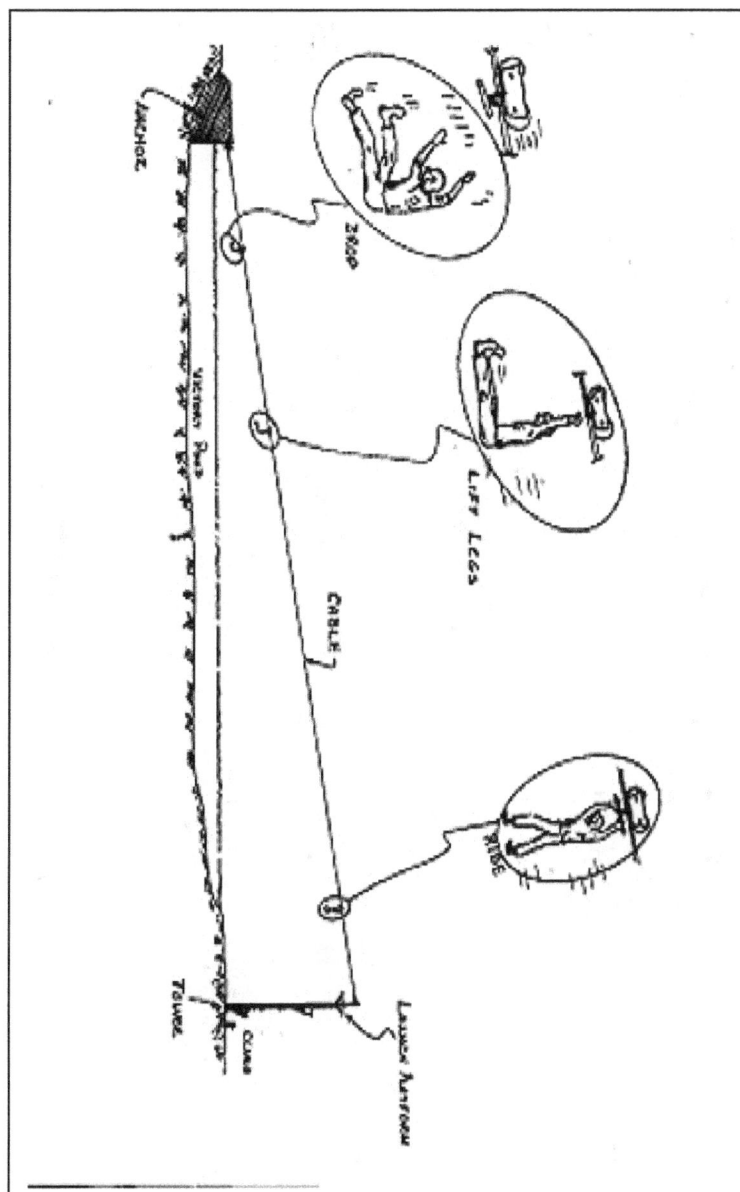

PLANNING BAY

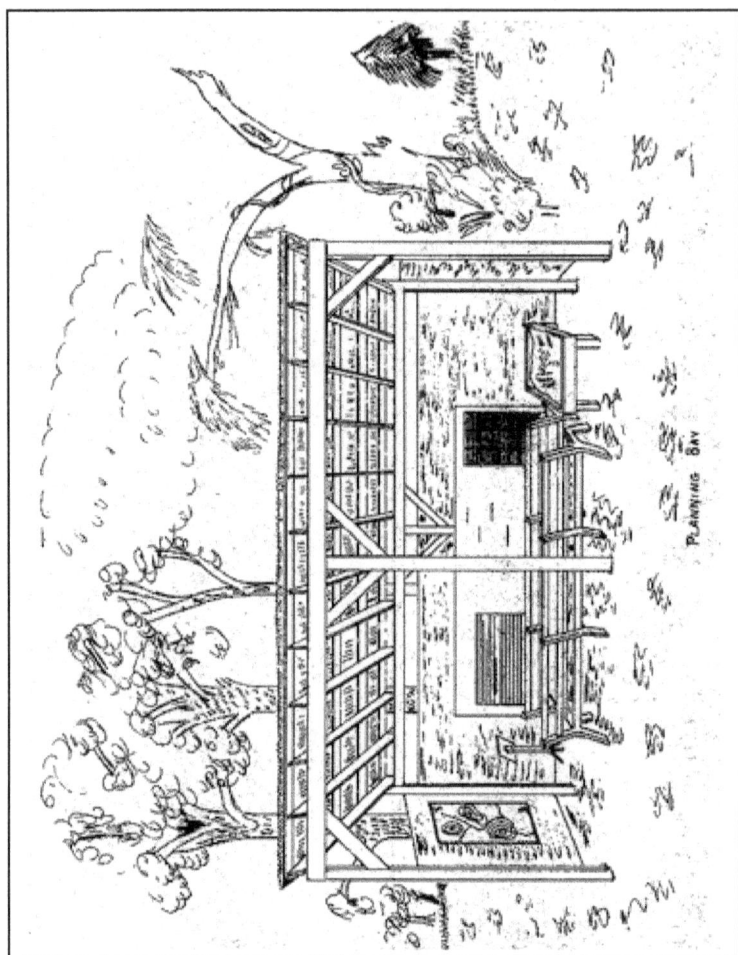

NOTES

NOTES